NINJA FOODI
XL PRO AIR FRYER OVEN
Cookbook for Beginners

1500-Day Easy & Affordable Ninja Foodi XL Pro Air Oven
Recipes for Your Ninja Foodi Smart XL Pro Air Oven

Susan Castagna

© Copyright 2022 – All rights reserved

This document is geared towards providing exact and reliable information with regards to the topic and issue covered. The publication is sold with the idea that the publisher is not required to render accounting, officially permitted, or otherwise, qualified services. If advice is necessary, legal, or professional, a practiced individual in the profession should be ordered. - From a Declaration of Principles which was accepted and approved equally by a Committee of the American Bar Association and a Committee of Publishers and Associations. In no way is it legal to reproduce, duplicate, or transmit any part of this document in either electronic means or in printed format. Recording of this publication is strictly prohibited and any storage of this document is not allowed unless with written permission from the publisher.

All rights reserved. The information provided herein is stated to be truthful and consistent, in that any liability, in terms of inattention or otherwise, by any usage or abuse of any policies, processes, or directions contained within is the solitary and utter responsibility of the recipient reader.

Under no circumstances will any legal responsibility or blame be held against the publisher for any reparation, damages, or monetary loss due to the information herein, either directly or indirectly. Respective authors own all copyrights not held by the publisher.

The information herein is offered for informational purposes solely, and is universal as so. The presentation of the information is without contract or any type of guarantee assurance. The trademarks that are used are without any consent, and the publication of the trademark is without permission or backing by the trademark owner.

All trademarks and brands within this book are for clarifying purposes only and are the owned by the owners themselves, not affiliated with this document.

TABLE OF CONTENTS

Introduction 1

Fundamentals of Ninja Foodi Smart XL Pro Air Fry Oven 2

Chapter 1 Breakfast Recipes 11

Chapter 2 Snacks and Appetizer Recipes 25

Chapter 3 Poultry Mains Recipes 40

Chapter 4 Beef, Pork, and Lamb Recipes 60

Chapter 5 Fish and Seafood Recipes 80

Chapter 6 Vegetables and Sides Recipes 98

Chapter 7 Dessert Recipes... 114

Conclusion.. 128

Appendix 1 Measurement Conversion Chart 129

Appendix 2 Recipes Index 130

Introduction

You have a lot of cooking options with the Ninja Foodi 10-in-1 Smart XL Pro Air Fry Oven which is a sizable countertop device. These possibilities include air frying and multiple rack roasting. It provides great toast and functions just like a regular oven.

One of the best-designed toasters we've examined, it features a distinctive and user-friendly digital control panel on the door handle.

A very flexible air fryer/oven that may be used for air frying, searing crisp baking, rapid baking, fresh pizza, frozen pizza, griddling, air roasting, baking, broiling, toasting, bagels, dehydrating, and reheating. sufficient in size to roast a turkey.

It can be challenging to keep spotless, much like with all oven-style air fryers. It could be more user-friendly, but a few design peculiarities prevent that.

With measurements of 17 x 20 x 13, the Ninja Foodi 10-in-1 XL Pro Air Fry Oven is big and boxy. The glass door has a black plastic handle that houses all of the electronic controls, and the housing is made of stainless steel. This indicates that the product's size is identical to the size of the oven cavity. Additionally, it places the controls at eye level, making them simple to see and use.

Fundamentals of Ninja Foodi Smart XL Pro Air Fry Oven

When air frying Brussels sprouts, chicken wings, breaded chicken, and handmade French fries, the Ninja Foodi 10-in-1 XL Pro Air Oven performed admirably, however it struggled with frozen French fries. It delivered a pleasing outcome when broiling hamburgers and roasting a whole chicken. It performed admirably when it came to making cookies and a cake, and it perfectly reheated frozen pizza. Bagels didn't brown as good as bagels, but white bread was evenly toasted.

Features of the item
- True Surround Convection offers consistent 2-level cooking without the need for rotation.
- Compared to a full-size convection oven, there is an increase in convection power of up to 10 times.
- Among the 10 features are Toast, Air Fry, Bake, Roast, and more
- Quick family meals can be prepared in under 35 minutes.
- Large countertop oven with a 12-lb turkey capacity, 1800 watts of power, and a 90-second preheating time
- Rack positioning is made more certain thanks to digital displays.
- Healthful family meals prepared in an air fryer
- Dehydration function on an oven for wholesome snacks

What is Ninja Foodi Smart XL Pro Air Fry Oven?

Ninja Foodi Smart XL Pro Air Fry Oven: an incredibly versatile air fryer/oven that may be used for air frying, searing crisp baking, quick baking, fresh pizza, frozen pizza, griddling, air roasting, baking, broiling, toasting, bagels, dehydrating, and reheating. large enough to cook a turkey.

Similar to all oven-style air fryers, it can be difficult to maintain clean. There are several design quirks that could make it more user-friendly, but they prohibit that.

REAL SURFACE CONVECTION: For quicker, crispier, and juicier results, use an oven with up to 10X the convection power of a conventional full-size convection oven.

10-IN-1 VERSATILITY: One robust, 1800-watt appliance can air fry, air roast, bake, whole roast, broil, toast, bagel, dehydrate, reheat, and make pizza.

FASTER COOKING: Up to 30% faster cooking than a conventional full-size convection oven with a 90-second preheat period for the oven.

Family-sized capacity for XL: Fit a 12-lb turkey, two 12-inch pizzas, a 5-lb chicken, and a sheet pan of vegetables; two levels of uniform cooking; no turning required.

LESS FAT: When using the Air Fry function as opposed to conventional deep frying, you may indulge in all of your favourite air-fried foods guilt-free with up to 75% less fat. compared to hand-cut, deep-fried French fries in a test.

DIGITAL DISPLAY HANDLE: Depending on the chosen function, the ideal oven rack placements will be illuminated. Display settings freeze while the door is open to avoid accidental changes to the cook cycle. Results are up to 30% crispier compared to a conventional convection oven.

BAKING PERFECT: Up to 50% more evenly baked outcomes compared to a top countertop oven. Cooking for large groups is simple. For entertaining or weekly meal preparation, prepare two sheet pan dinners at once.

Ninja Foodi Smart XL Pro Air Fry Oven Function

WHOLE ROAST: The Ninja Foodi Smart XL Pro Oven has a 12-lbs capacity, which allows you to fit an entire chicken or even a medium-sized turkey inside. And the embedded thermometer will be useful if you want to cook your prime rib to perfection. Your steak will be perfectly cooked because the

oven will shut off at the precise temperature you've chosen.

You can cook your sides in the air fryer basket on Rack #4 while roasting your protein on Rack #1.

AIR ROAST: The Air Roast feature is designed for roasting small amounts of meat or possibly vegetables. Your roast tray and sheet pan should be placed on rack #3 for single rack cooking.

Move your roast tray and sheet pan to Rack #1 if you need to roast two batches of vegetables or meat. The air fry basket can then be placed on Rack #3.

AIR FRY: The ideal location for single-level air frying would be Rack #3. The air fry basket works perfectly for crisping French fries or other starchy vegetables.

To avoid the grease spilling onto the crumb tray, use the roast tray and sheet pan combination when cooking fatty foods like chicken wings or any other protein.

Racks #2 and #4 are suitable for air frying if you need to use two rack levels.

Use high smoke point oils for air frying, such as canola, avocado, vegetable, or grapeseed.

BAKE: Evenly prepare all of your favourite baked goods, including cakes.

On Racks #2 and #3, you can bake two trays of cookies, bacon, brownies, or muffins.

DEHYDRATE: One of the best capabilities of the Ninja is dehydrating fruits and vegetables. Fruits can take two to three hours to dehydrate. Depending on how thick your beef is, this

could take four to six hours if you adore jerkies.

For large amounts of dehydration, racks #2 and #3 can be used, or only rack #3.

BROIL: You must master the skill of broiling if you want to improve as a home cook. This feature can be useful for cooking steak or possibly adding a golden brown finish to your casserole dish to make it a little more interesting. Use rack #3 for this purpose, by the way.

TOAST: I suppose the toasting feature is pretty self-explanatory. You must, however, keep in mind that Rack #3 is where you should toast your bread.

BAGEL: The Ninja Foodi Smart Oven's bagel setting is no different. Make advantage of Rack #3. To guarantee a proper toast, the bagel must be cut-side up.

PIZZA: The Ninja Smart XL Air Fry Oven can bake two 12-inch pizzas on Racks #1 and #3. This convection oven will give it right whether you enjoy making it from scratch or you have a frozen pizza in your refrigerator.

REHEAT: The sogginess that results from microwave reheating of leftover food is something I detest. It holds true whether the food is day-old chicken, fries, or pizza. Therefore, I frequently use my large oven to preserve the dish's crispiness. Having a small convection oven will unquestionably fix that issue.

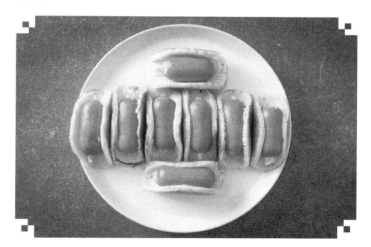

Benefits of Using It

- **Modern design:** a very flexible air fryer/oven that can air fry, sear crisp, rapid bake, cook a frozen pizza, fresh pizza, griddle, air roast, bake, broil, toast, and make toasted bagels, as well as dehydrate food and reheat it. sufficient in size to roast a turkey. It can be challenging to keep spotless, much like with all oven-style air fryers. It could be more user-friendly, but a few design peculiarities prevent that.

- **Has a smart thermometer included:** The embedded thermometer is the single feature that distinguishes the Ninja as smart. When the predetermined temperature is attained, the oven will shut off. Only a medium-rare prime rib can be prepared using it. I suppose naming this device "smart" rather than "XL Pro Oven with a Thermometer" makes it

more appealing. Anyway, choosing the Ninja Foodi Air Oven model will save you some money if you already have a meat thermometer at home. It does the same function without the thermometer.

- **An oven's 90-second preheating time is quicker than usual:** A preheating mode that the Ninja automatically enters lasts always just one minute and 30 seconds. You must have your food prepared prior to starting the preheating process since once the preheating is complete, it immediately begins to countdown the cooking time.
- **Easy to use:** The Ninja Foodi features a very small number of buttons, which makes it very simple to use. You just need to get accustomed to where the racks should be placed for each function, and once you do, you'll be cooking like a pro. You can always refer to the quick start instructions if you ever become perplexed. It works as a cheat sheet for all the features and ideal rack positioning.

It's also very straightforward in terms of the integrated thermometer. Simply set your target temperature and place the thermometer into the area of your protein that is the thickest. It will automatically stop once it reaches the temperature you want.

You won't need to open the oven door to check the temperature of your meat as frequently as you would with a conventional thermometer. The surround convection function of the Ninja Foodi Smart XL Pro Air Oven eliminates the need for turning as well. The point is that it's more user-friendly and practical than a conventional full-sized oven.

- **Cooking time is 30% faster than in regular ovens.**
- **Large capacity: Can roast a full chicken and a 12-pound turkey; 10-in-1 features include air frying, entire roasting, baking, dehydrating, broiling, toasting, and reheating.**
- **1-year BPA-free warranty**
- **Convection with full surround for best heat dispersion**
- **Simple on the wallet**

Step-By-Step Using It

Ahead of first use

- Take off and throw away all tape, labels, and packaging from the device.
- Take out all the accessories from the box and carefully read this handbook. To prevent any injuries or property damage, please pay close attention to operational directions, warnings, and crucial protections.
- The air fry basket, sheet pan, wire rack, roast tray, and removable crumb tray should all be washed in warm, soapy water before being properly rinsed and dried. Sheet pans, roast trays, and removable crumb trays should not be placed in the dishwasher. Finishes could deteriorate. never immerse the primary device in water.
- We advise putting all of the oven's attachments inside and using the Air Roast setting at 450°F for 20 minutes without adding any food. This gets rid of any leftovers. This is entirely secure and won't affect the oven's functionality.

NOTE: Hand washing is advised for the accessories. The wire racks and air fryer basket can be cleaned in the dishwasher, however over time, wear may occur more quickly.

Control Panel Display & Operating Buttons

Press the **(Power) button** to turn the device on and off.
Cooking time is displayed on the timer.
When cooking is taking place, the time will begin to run out.
PREHEAT: The unit flashes during preheating. The appliance will skip preheating if the oven is already heated up after utilising a prior cooking mode.
SLICES: When the Toast or Bagel function is used to specify the amount of slices, the SLICES indicator lights up.
Cook temperature is displayed on the temperature display.
NOTE: The oven will always revert to the time and temperature settings used the last time it was used.
RACK LEVEL: Depending on the function you select; the lighted rack level or levels will show you where to put your attachment in the device.
2 LEVEL: Press the button to select 2-level cooking when a function allows you to cook on two levels, and the rack levels will update.
Pressing the **FUNCTION** +/- buttons will allow you to choose

a cooking function.

NOTE: The recommended rack level changes when you switch between functions for best results.

TIME/SLICES +/- buttons: Use the TIME +/- buttons to choose a cook time.

These buttons alter the number of slices or bagel halves, not the time when using the toast or bagel function.

Under one hour, the passage of time will advance by one minute; over one hour, it will advance by five minutes. If you press and hold the +/- buttons for 2 seconds, you can speed up the scrolling by 5 minutes.

TEMP/SHADE +/- buttons: Use the TEMP +/- buttons to change the temperature. These buttons will change the shade level (1, lightest - 7, darkest) rather than the temperature while the Toast or Bagel function is in use. There will be 5-degree jumps in temperature. When the +/- buttons are held down for two seconds, faster 10-degree scrolling is enabled.

NOTE: During the cooking cycle, the cooking time and temperature can be changed at any moment.

Press the **START/STOP button** to initiate or terminate cooking.

SHADE: When the Toast or Bagel feature is used to select the desired shade, it illuminates.

Button (Light) Press to switch the inner oven light on and off.

NOTE: The light will automatically turn on if the door is open and when there is just one minute left to cook.

WHEN TO USE THE ROAST TRAY WHEN USING YOUR FOODITM XL PRO AIR OVEN

Use a roasting tray on a sheet pan for cooking with convection (such as whole roasting, air roasting, and air frying), or when cooking oily items like entire chickens, chicken wings, bacon, marinated meats, or oiled vegetables.

Accessing the Cooking Features

Plug the power wire into an outlet and push the button to turn the device on. After ten minutes of inactivity, the device will turn itself off automatically.

Whole Roast:

Press the function +/- buttons until the WHOLE ROAST shines brightly to pick the function. The time and temperature will be displayed by default. Select the 2 LEVEL button so that "2 LEVEL" displays on the display when cooking two layers.

To choose a cook time up to 4 hours, press the TIME/SLICES +/- buttons.

NOTE: The clock will count down by minutes and seconds if cooking for one hour or less. The clock will count down in hours and minutes if cooking takes more than an hour.

To choose a temperature between 250°F and 450°F, use the TEMP/SHADE +/- buttons.

To start preheating, press START/STOP.

Place the ingredients either directly on the sheet pan or the roasting pan. Place the roast tray on the sheet pan on the wire rack on Level 1 as soon as the machine beeps to indicate that it has finished preheating. Shut the oven door. Place the sheet pan on Level 1 and use the air fry basket as the second layer on Level 4 when cooking on two layers.

NOTE: Once the unit has preheated, the timer will begin to count down. Simply press the TIME +/- buttons to extend the cooking time if the items aren't ready to go into the oven.

The appliance will beep and "END" will show up on the display when cook time is over.

Air Roast:

Press the function +/- buttons until AIR ROAST becomes clearly visible to pick the function. The time and temperature will be displayed by default. Select the 2 LEVEL button so that "2 LEVEL" displays on the display when cooking two layers.

To choose a cook time up to 4 hours, press the TIME/SLICES

+/- buttons.

NOTE: The clock will count down by minutes and seconds if cooking for one hour or less. The clock will count down in hours and minutes if cooking takes more than an hour.

To choose a temperature between 250°F and 450°F, use the TEMP/SHADE +/- buttons.

To start preheating, press START/STOP.

Put the ingredients on the baking sheet.

Place the roast tray on the sheet pan on the wire rack on Level 1 as soon as the appliance beeps to indicate that it has finished preheating.

Shut the oven door. Use the sheet pan as the first layer when cooking on two levels, and the air fry basket as the second layer when cooking on level three.

NOTE: Once the unit has preheated, the timer will begin to count down. Simply press the TIME +/- buttons to add more time if the ingredients are not ready to go into the oven.

The appliance will beep and "END" will show up on the display when cook time is over.

Air Fry:

Press the function +/- buttons until AIR FRY becomes clearly visible to pick the function. The time and temperature will be displayed by default.

When cooking two layers, press the LEVEL button until the display reads "2 LEVEL."

To choose a cook time of up to 4 hours, press the TIME/SLICES +/- buttons.

Select a temperature between 250°F and 450°F by using the TEMP/SHADE +/- buttons.

To start preheating, press START/STOP.

Place the contents in the roast tray with a sheet pan and the air fry basket. Put the basket on the sheet pan if the ingredients are fatty, greasy, or marinated. For dry ingredients, use an air frying basket.

Slide the basket into the rack level(s) indicated on the control panel as soon as the appliance beeps to indicate that it has warmed. If using a sheet pan as well, slide both into the oven at the same time, the pan on the wire rack below the basket in the upper rack. Shut the oven door.

The appliance will beep and "END" will show up on the display when cook time is over.

NOTE: Once the unit has preheated, the timer will begin to count down. Simply press the TIME +/- buttons to extend the cooking time if the items aren't ready to go into the oven.

Reheat

Press the function +/- buttons until REHEAT brightly glows to pick the function.

To choose a reheat time of up to four hours, use the TIME/SLICES +/- buttons.

To choose a temperature between 100°F and 450°F, use the TEMP/SHADE +/- buttons.

Food should be placed on a sheet pan or in a container suitable for the oven, which should then be placed on a wire rack. To start warming, close the oven door and hit START/STOP.

The appliance will beep and "END" will show up on the display when cook time is over.

Pizza

Press the function +/- buttons until PIZZA shines brightly to select the function. The default slice count and amount of darkness will be shown.

To choose a cook time up to 4 hours, press the TIME/SLICES +/- buttons.

In order to choose a temperature between 180°F and 450°F, press the TEMP +/- buttons.

Pizza can be placed directly on the wire rack or on a sheet pan.

To start cooking, close the oven door and select START/STOP.

The appliance will beep and "END" will show up on the display when cook time is over.

Bagel

Press the function +/- buttons until BAGEL starts to glow brightly to select the function. The default slice count and amount of darkness will be shown.

The number of slices can be chosen by using the TIME/SLICES +/- buttons. Up to nine bagel pieces can be toasted at once.

Choose the level of darkness by pressing the TEMP +/- buttons.

NOTE: The bagel function does not allow for temperature modification, and the appliance does not preheat when in bagel mode. To prevent over- or under-toasting, it is crucial to choose the precise amount of slices.

Put the cut-side-up side of the bagels in the center of the wire rack. To start cooking, close the oven door and select START/STOP.

The appliance will beep and "END" will show up on the display when cook time is over.

Toast

Press the function +/- buttons until TOAST brightly glows to pick the function. Slice count and level of darkness will automatically default.

To choose the amount of slices of bread, use the TIME/SLICES +/- buttons. 9 slices can be toasted at once.

To choose a level of darkness, press the TEMP/SHADE +/- buttons.

NOTE: The Toast feature does not allow for temperature modification, and the appliance does not preheat while in Toast mode. To prevent over- or under-toasting, it is crucial to choose the precise amount of slices.

Place the wire rack with the bread pieces on it. To start cooking, close the oven door and select START/STOP.

The appliance will beep and "END" will show up on the display when cook time is over.

Dehydrate

Press the function +/- buttons until DEHYDRATE shines brightly to pick the function. The time and temperature will be displayed by default.

Select the 2 LEVEL button so that "2 LEVEL" displays on the display when dehydrating two layers.

To choose a dehydration time between one and twenty-four hours, press the TIME/SLICES +/- buttons.

To choose a temperature between 85°F and 200°F, press the TEMP/SHADE +/- buttons.

Put the air fryer basket in the oven with the items inside. To

start cooking, close the oven door and select START/STOP.

NOTE: Don't stack food; instead, place ingredients flat on each layer for optimal results.

The appliance will beep and "END" will show up on the display when cook time is over.

NOTE: Additional dehydration accessories can be purchased to dehydrate up to four levels simultaneously.

Bake

Press the function +/- buttons until BAKE becomes clearly visible to pick the function. The time and temperature will be displayed by default. When cooking two layers, press the LEVEL button until the display reads "2 LEVEL."

To choose a cook time up to 4 hours, press the TIME/SLICES +/- buttons.

To choose a temperature between 180°F and 450°F, use the TEMP/SHADE +/- buttons.

To start preheating, press START/STOP.

Put the ingredients in the cake pan, casserole dish, air fryer basket, or sheet pan. Place the sheet pan on the wire rack as soon as the appliance beeps to indicate that it has reached preheating. Shut the oven door.

NOTE: Once the unit has preheated, the timer will begin to count down. Simply press the TIME +/- buttons to extend the cooking time if the items aren't ready to go into the oven.

You can switch on the light during cooking to monitor the process.

The appliance will beep and "END" will show up on the display when cook time is over.

Accessories for Ninja Foodi Smart XL Pro Air Fry Oven

Accessories for the Ninja Foodi Smart XL Pro Air Oven include an air fry basket, two wire racks, two sheet pans, a roast tray, and a thermometer.

You also possess a smart thermometer that is housed in a magnetic container. Like wired headphones, it functions. At the bottom right corner of the handle, there is a jack.

A crumb tray is also present beneath the heating element. Along with removing food debris, it keeps greases from sinking to the bottom of your oven.

The Ninja can use such accessories with all 10 of his or her talents. For processing a sizable amount of fruits and beef jerky, the firm also sells a dehydrating kit, a 2-inch casserole plate, and a muffin pan.

Cleaning and Caring for Your Air Fry Oven

On the handle, which is at eye level and is simple to read and reach, are all the settings and the digital readout. The oven's buttons are extremely touch-responsive, and programming the oven is incredibly simple. The display tells you which oven rack position to use when you choose one of the 10 functions. You also receive a roast tray, two sheet pans, an air fryer basket, two oven racks, and a removable crumb tray in addition to the oven.

DAILY CLEANING

After each usage, the appliance needs to be completely cleaned. Before cleaning, unplug the appliance from the outlet and give it time to cool.

Remove the crumb tray from the oven and empty it.

NOTE: Frequently empty the crumb tray. When required, wash your hands.

Use a gentle, moist sponge to remove any food spatter from the internal walls and glass door of the appliance after each use.

Use a moist cloth to clean the exterior of the main unit and the control panel. You could use a gentle spray solution or non-abrasive liquid cleaner. Before cleaning, apply the cleaner on the sponge rather than on the oven's surface.

Before placing food on top of accessories, we advise smearing them with butter or oil or covering them with parchment paper or aluminium foil. Avoid covering roast tray openings with foil or parchment paper.

MASSIVE CLEANING

Before cleaning, unplug the appliance from the outlet and give it time to cool.

Remove all of the unit's attachments, including the crumb tray, and wash each one separately. To wash the air fry basket more completely, use a non-abrasive cleaning brush. It is advised to

hand wash accessories. The wire racks and air fryer basket can be cleaned in the dishwasher, however over time, wear may occur more quickly.

DO NOT put a sheet pan, a crumb tray, or a roast tray in the dishwasher.

To clean the interior and glass door of the oven, use warm, soapy water and a soft cloth. DO NOT use abrasive cleaners, scrubbing brushes, or chemical cleaners as they will harm the oven.

WARNING: DO NOT submerge the main unit in water or any other liquid or put it in the dishwasher.

Sheet pans and roasting trays should be soaked in warm, soapy water overnight to remove stubborn grease before being washed with a nonabrasive sponge or brush.

Dry each component completely before re-entering the oven. Place the crumb tray beneath the lower heating elements. Slide into no rack positions at all.

Frequently Asked Questions & Notes

The oven won't turn on, why?
- Ascertain that the power cord is firmly inserted into the outlet.
- Change the outlet where the power cord is plugged in.
- If necessary, reset the circuit breaker.
- Activate the power switch.

Is it possible to use a sheet pan rather than an air fry basket with the air fry function?
Yes, however the results may vary in crispiness.

Do the cook times and temperatures for conventional oven recipes need to be changed?
Keep an eye on your meal while it's cooking for the greatest outcomes. For more information on cook times and temperatures, consult the cook charts in the Inspiration Guide.

Can I reset the device to its factory defaults?
Even if you disconnect the oven, it will remember the last setting you used for each function.
Press the Light and 2 LEVEL buttons at the same time for 5 seconds to return the oven's settings to default for each function.

Why do the heating elements seem to be on and off repeatedly?
That is typical. The power levels of the heating components can be changed to precisely manage the temperature for each function in the oven.

Why does steam emanate from the oven door?
That is standard. Foods with a high moisture content could produce steam at the door.

Why is water dripping over the counter from underneath the door?
That is standard. High moisture content foods, such frozen bread, can cause condensation to form on the surface and drip down the inside of the door.

Why is the equipment emitting smoke?
- Make sure the roast tray on the sheet pan is being utilised when using the Air Fry, Air Roast, or Whole Roast functions or while cooking any fatty things.
- Try running a Toast cycle on shade 7 with the accessories off to see whether the problem persists. Any further grease on the smoking heating components will be burned off as a result.

How can I clean the sheet pan?
Soak the sheet pan with the food that has stuck to it before washing it.
Line the sheet pan with parchment paper or aluminium foil to make clean-up after cooking easier.

When the device was in use, why did a circuit breaker trip?
The appliance uses 1800 watts of power, thus it needs to be hooked into an outlet with a 15-amp circuit breaker. Additionally, while it is running, the device must be the only appliance plugged into an outlet. To avoid tripping the 15-amp breaker, make sure the device is the only one plugged into the socket.

Why does the device sound like it's still running if the power is off?
Even after the device has been turned off, the cooling fan may continue to operate. This is a regular practise, so there is no need for concern. The cooling fan will stop operating whenever the device reaches a temperature of less than 95°F (35°C).

The Ninja Foodi XL Pro air oven is compatible with parchment paper, right?
Absolutely! If the fryer is safe for the oven, it is also safe to use. Most parchment papers can withstand temperatures of up to 400°F.

Is aluminium foil acceptable in a Ninja Foodi XL Pro air oven?
Yes, you can use aluminium foil with the Max Health Grill and the nine-in-one Ninja Foodi machines in the same way that you would on an outdoor grill.

4-Week Diet Plan

Week 1

Day 1:
Breakfast: Breakfast Bake
Lunch: Roasted Vegetables
Snack: Carrot Chips
Dinner: Lamb Kebabs
Dessert: Blueberry Cobbler

Day 2:
Breakfast: Savory French Toast
Lunch: Spicy Potato
Snack: Pasta Chips
Dinner: Simple Turkey Wings
Dessert: Walnut Brownies

Day 3:
Breakfast: Zucchini Fritters
Lunch: Vegetable Casserole
Snack: Tortilla Chips
Dinner: Rum-Glazed Shrimp
Dessert: Brownie Bars

Day 4:
Breakfast: Carrot & Raisin Bread
Lunch: Pita Bread Pizza
Snack: Tofu Nuggets
Dinner: Za'atar Chops
Dessert: Cherry Clafoutis

Day 5:
Breakfast: Banana Bread
Lunch: Blue Cheese Soufflés
Snack: Mini Hot Dogs
Dinner: Crispy Sirloin Steaks
Dessert: Apple Pastries

Day 6:
Breakfast: Date Bread
Lunch: Cauliflower in Buffalo Sauce
Snack: Fried Pickles
Dinner: Herbed Chicken Thighs
Dessert: Carrot Mug Cake

Day 7:
Breakfast: French Toast
Lunch: Tofu with Broccoli
Snack: Cod Nuggets
Dinner: Tangy Sea Bass
Dessert: Cannoli

Week 2

Day 1:
Breakfast: Banana & Walnut Bread
Lunch: Stuffed Peppers
Snack: Risotto Bites
Dinner: American Roast Beef
Dessert: Brownie Muffins

Day 2:
Breakfast: Cloud Eggs
Lunch: Roasted Green Beans
Snack: Zucchini Fries
Dinner: Spiced Turkey Breast
Dessert: Cookie Cake

Day 3:
Breakfast: Ham and Cheese Scones
Lunch: Veggie Rice
Snack: Potato Bread Rolls
Dinner: Seafood Medley Mix
Dessert: Fried Oreo

Day 4:
Breakfast: Simple Bread
Lunch: Herbed Bell Peppers
Snack: Corn on the Cob
Dinner: Baked Pork Chops
Dessert: Cherry Jam tarts

Day 5:
Breakfast: Ricotta Toasts with Salmon
Lunch: Baked Potato
Snack: Spicy Carrot Fries
Dinner: Herbed Turkey Legs
Dessert: Cranberry-Apple Pie

Day 6:
Breakfast: Bacon, Spinach & Egg Cups
Lunch: Broccoli Cheese Casserole
Snack: Glazed Chicken Wings
Dinner: Buttered Trout
Dessert: Air Fried Doughnuts

Day 7:
Breakfast: Mushrooms Frittata
Lunch: Stuffed Zucchini
Snack: Potato Chips
Dinner: Salmon Burgers
Dessert: Nutella Banana Muffins

Week 3

Day 1:
Breakfast: Breakfast Casserole
Lunch: Vegan Cakes
Snack: Pumpkin Fries
Dinner: Zucchini Beef Meatloaf
Dessert: Honeyed Banana

Day 2:
Breakfast: Cinnamon Donut Muffins
Lunch: Fried Tortellini
Snack: Crispy Avocado Fries
Dinner: Roasted Duck
Dessert: Banana Pancakes Dippers

Day 3:
Breakfast: Pancetta & Spinach Frittata
Lunch: Broccoli with Cauliflower
Snack: Baked Potatoes
Dinner: Cod Burgers
Dessert: Air Fryer Churros

Day 4:
Breakfast: Puff Pastry Danishes
Lunch: Broccoli Casserole
Snack: French Toast Bites
Dinner: Herbed Chuck Roast
Dessert: Caramel Apple Pie

Day 5:
Breakfast: Mushroom Frittata
Lunch: Beans & Veggie Burgers
Snack: Eggplant Fries
Dinner: Crispy Chicken Cutlets
Dessert: Blueberry Hand Pies

Day 6:
Breakfast: Sausage Patties
Lunch: Cheesy Green Bean Casserole
Snack: Roasted Cashews
Dinner: Shrimp Fajitas
Dessert: Vanilla Soufflé

Day 7:
Breakfast: Cinnamon Sugar Donuts
Lunch: Parmesan Carrot
Snack: Potato Croquettes
Dinner: Citrus Pork Chops
Dessert: Strawberry Cupcakes

Week 4

Day 1:
Breakfast: Sweet Potato Rosti
Lunch: Wine Braised Mushrooms
Snack: Bacon-Wrapped Filled Jalapeno
Dinner: BBQ Pork Chops
Dessert: Fudge Brownies

Day 2:
Breakfast: Sweet & Spiced Toasts
Lunch: Roast Cauliflower and Broccoli
Snack: Buttermilk Biscuits
Dinner: Primavera Chicken
Dessert: Nutella Banana Pastries

Day 3:
Breakfast: Breakfast Pizzas with Muffins
Lunch: Soy Sauce Green Beans
Snack: Air Fryer Pop-Tarts
Dinner: Cajun Salmon
Dessert: Shortbread Fingers

Day 4:
Breakfast: Parmesan Eggs in Avocado Cups
Lunch: Sweet Potato Casserole
Snack: Persimmon Chips
Dinner: Chicken Kebabs
Dessert: Raisin Bread Pudding

Day 5:
Breakfast: Hash Browns
Lunch: Stuffed Eggplants
Snack: Cauliflower Poppers
Dinner: Mustard Lamb Loin Chops
Dessert: Chocolate Chip Cookies

Day 6:
Breakfast: Hard Boiled Eggs
Lunch: Vinegar Green Beans
Snack: Baked Mozzarella Sticks
Dinner: Lobster Tail Casserole
Dessert: Cinnamon Rolls

Day 7:
Breakfast: Savory Sausage & Beans Muffins
Lunch: Broiled Broccoli
Snack: Avocado Fries
Dinner: Chicken Potato Bake
Dessert: Mini Crumb Cake Bites

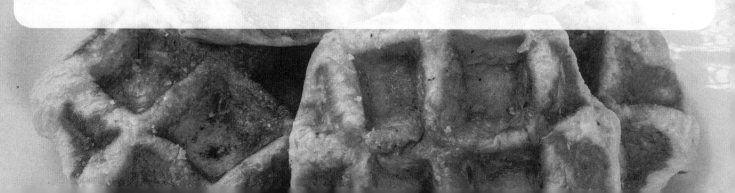

Chapter 1 Breakfast Recipes

12	Eggs, Tofu & Mushroom Omelet	18	Zucchini Fritters
12	Cheddar & Cream Omelet	18	Ricotta Toasts with Salmon
12	Cloud Eggs	19	Sweet Potato Rosti
13	Pumpkin Muffins	19	Bacon, Spinach & Egg Cups
13	Sheet Pan Breakfast Pizza with Sausage & Potatoes	19	Pancetta & Spinach Frittata
13	Ham and Cheese Scones	20	Breakfast Casserole
14	Savory Parsley Soufflé	20	Parmesan Eggs in Avocado Cups
14	Breakfast Bake	20	Banana Bread
14	Puffed Egg Tarts	21	Cinnamon Sugar Donuts
15	Simple Bread	21	Mushroom Frittata
15	Savory Sausage & Beans Muffins	21	Potato & Corned Beef Casserole
15	Mushrooms Frittata	22	Sausage Patties
16	Carrot & Raisin Bread	22	Hash Browns
16	Savory French Toast	22	French Toast
16	Sweet & Spiced Toasts	23	Hard Boiled Eggs
17	Date Bread	23	Breakfast Pizzas with Muffins
17	Banana & Walnut Bread	23	Peanut Butter Banana Baked Oatmeal
17	Puff Pastry Danishes	24	Cinnamon Donut Muffins
18	Ham & Egg Cups	24	German Pancake

Eggs, Tofu & Mushroom Omelet

Prep Time: 15 minutes | **Cook Time:** 35 minutes | **Serves:** 2

Ingredients:

- 2 teaspoons canola oil
- ¼ of onion, chopped
- 1 garlic clove, minced
- 3½ ounces fresh mushrooms, sliced
- 8 ounces silken tofu, pressed, drained and crumbled
- Salt and ground black pepper, as needed
- 3 eggs, beaten

Preparation:

1. In a skillet, heat the oil over medium heat and sauté the onion, and garlic for about 4-5 minutes. 2. Add the mushrooms and cook for about 4-5 minutes. 3. Remove from the heat and stir in the tofu, salt, and black pepper. 4. Place the tofu mixture into sheet pan and top with the beaten eggs. 5. Press "Power" button of Ninja Foodi XL Pro Air Oven and select "Air Fry" function. 6. Press TEMP/SHADE +/- buttons to set the temperature at 355°F/180°C. 7. Now press TIME/SLICES +/- buttons to set the cooking time to 25 minutes. 8. Press "Start/Stop" button to start. 9. When the unit beeps to show that it is preheated, open the oven door. 10. Arrange pan over the wire rack on the Level 3. 11. When cooking time is completed, open the oven door, and remove the pan. 12. Cut into equal-sized wedges and serve hot.

Serving Suggestions: Serve alongside the greens.
Variation Tip: Make sure to drain the tofu completely.
Nutritional Information per Serving: Calories: 224 | Fat: 14.5g | Sat Fat: 2.9g | Carbohydrates: 6.6g | Fiber: 0.9g | Sugar: 3.4g | Protein: 17.9g

Cheddar & Cream Omelet

Prep Time: 10 minutes | **Cook Time:** 8 minutes | **Serves:** 2

Ingredients:

- 4 eggs
- ¼ cup cream
- 1 teaspoon fresh parsley, minced
- Salt and ground black pepper, as required
- ¼ cup Cheddar cheese, grated

Preparation:

1. In a bowl, add the eggs, cream, parsley, salt, and black pepper and beat well. 2. Place the egg mixture into Ninja sheet pan. 3. Press "Power" button of Ninja Foodi XL Pro Air Oven and select "Air Fry" function. 4. Press TEMP/SHADE +/- buttons to set the temperature at 350°F/175°C. 5. Now press TIME/SLICES +/- buttons to set the cooking time to 8 minutes. 6. Press "Start/Stop" button to start. 7. When the unit beeps to show that it is preheated, open the oven door. 8. Arrange pan over the wire rack into the rails of Level 4. 9. After 4 minutes, sprinkle the omelet with cheese evenly. 10. When cooking time is completed, open the oven door, and remove the baking pan. 11. Cut the omelet into 2 portions and serve hot.

Serving Suggestions: Serve alongside the toasted bread slices.
Variation Tip: You can add the seasoning of your choice.
Nutritional Information per Serving: Calories: 202 | Fat: 15.1g | Sat Fat: 6.8g | Carbohydrates: 1.8g | Fiber: 0g | Sugar: 1.4g | Protein: 14.8g

Cloud Eggs

Prep Time: 10 minutes | **Cook Time:** 7 minutes | **Serves:** 2

Ingredients:

- 2 eggs, whites and yolks separated
- Pinch of salt
- Pinch of freshly ground black pepper

Preparation:

1. In a bowl, add the egg white, salt and black pepper and beat until stiff peaks form. 2. Line a baking pan with parchment paper. 3. Carefully, make a pocket in the center of each egg white circle. 4. Now press TIME/SLICES +/- buttons to set the cooking time to 7 minutes. 5. Press "Power" button of Ninja Foodi XL Pro Air Oven and select "Broil" function. 6. Press the TEMP/SHADE +/- buttons to select LO. 7. Press "START/STOP" button to start. 8. When the unit beeps to show that it is preheated, open the lid and insert the baking pan in the oven. 9. Place 1 egg yolk into each egg white pocket after 5 minutes of cooking. 10. When cooking time is completed, open the lid and serve.

Serving Suggestions: Serve alongside toasted bread slices.
Variation Tip: Add some seasoning of your choice.
Nutritional Information per Serving: Calories: 63 | Fat: 4.4g | Sat Fat: 1.4g | Carbohydrates: 0.3g | Fiber: 0g | Sugar: 0.3g | Protein: 5.5g

Pumpkin Muffins

Prep Time: 15 minutes | Cook Time: 15 minutes | Serves: 6

Ingredients:

- 1 cup pumpkin puree
- 2 cups oats
- ½ cup honey
- 2 medium eggs beaten
- 1 teaspoon coconut butter
- 1 tablespoon cocoa nibs
- 1 tablespoon vanilla essence
- 1 teaspoon nutmeg

Preparation:

1. Whisk pumpkin puree with remaining ingredients in a mixer until smooth. 2. Divide this pumpkin oat batter into 12 muffin cups of a muffin tray. 3. Transfer the tray to the 2nd rack position of Ninja Foodi XL Pro Air Oven and close the door. 4. Select the "Air Fry" Mode using FUNCTION +/- buttons and select Rack Level 2. 5. Set its cooking time to 15 minutes and temperature to 360°F/180°C, then press "START/STOP" to initiate cooking. 6. Serve fresh.

Serving Suggestion: Serve the pumpkin muffins with morning pudding.
Variation Tip: Add shredded pumpkin flesh for good texture.
Nutritional Information Per Serving: Calories 234 | Fat 5.1g | Sodium 231mg | Carbs 46g | Fiber 5g | Sugar 2.1g | Protein 7g

Sheet Pan Breakfast Pizza with Sausage & Potatoes

Prep Time: 10 minutes | Cook Time: 25 minutes | Serves: 8

Ingredients:

- 6 egg whites
- 6 eggs
- ½ cup unsweetened almond milk
- ½ cup baby spinach
- 16 ounces turkey breakfast sausage
- 5 cups shredded potato
- 2 tablespoons light cheddar cheese
- Salt and pepper, to taste
- Avocado cooking spray

Preparation:

1. Insert a wire rack on Level 3 in your oven. Select the BAKE function, 375°F/190°C, for 25 minutes. While the oven is preheating, grease the sheet pan with avocado cooking spray and prepare the ingredients. 2. Add the turkey sausage to a greased skillet over medium heat. Use a spatula to break up the sausage as it cooks. When it's cooked, drain it, and keep it aside. 3. Take a medium bowl and mix the milk, salt, eggs, pepper, and spinach. 4. Lay the shredded potatoes on the prepared sheet pan. Sprinkle the sausage over the potatoes and pour over the egg mixture, spreading it evenly. 5. Top it with the cheese. 6. When the unit beeps to signify it ha preheated, open the oven and insert the sheet pan on the wire rack. Bake for about 25 to 30 minutes. 7. Take out the sheet pan and slice it into squares before serving.

Serving Suggestion: Serve it alongside some greens.
Variation Tip: You can use any milk of your choice. You can omit cheddar cheese to make it dairy-free.
Nutritional Information Per Serving: Calories: 179 | Fat: 1.7g | Sodium: 379.8mg | Carbs: 9.8g | Fiber: 1.3g | Sugar: 0.2g | Protein: 14.7g

Ham and Cheese Scones

Prep Time: 15 minutes | Cook Time: 25 minutes | Serves: 6

Ingredients:

- 2 cups all-purpose flour
- 1 tablespoon baking powder
- 2 teaspoons sugar
- 1 teaspoon kosher salt
- 2 tablespoons butter, cubed
- 1 cup ham, diced, cooked
- ¼ cup scallion, chopped
- 4 ounces cheddar cheese, shredded
- ¼ cup milk
- ¾ cup heavy cream

Preparation:

1. Whisk baking powder with flour, sugar, salt, and butter in a mixing bowl. 2. Beat milk, cream, and all other ingredients in another bowl. 3. Stir in the flour-butter mixture and mix well until it forms a smooth dough. 4. Place this scones dough on a floured surface and spread it into a 7-inch round sheet. 5. Cut this dough sheet into 6 wedges of equal size. 6. Place these wedges in the cooking pan, lined with parchment paper. 7. Transfer the pan to the 2nd rack position of Ninja Foodi XL Pro Air Oven and close the door. 8. Select the "Bake" Mode using FUNCTION +/- buttons and select Rack Level 2. 9. Set its cooking time to 25 minutes and temperature to 400°F/200°C, then press "START/STOP" to initiate cooking. 10. When baked, serve the scones with morning eggs.

Serving Suggestion: Serve the scones with the cream cheese dip.
Variation Tip: Add chopped parsley to the scones.
Nutritional Information Per Serving: Calories 387 | Fat 6g | Sodium 154mg | Carbs 37.4g | Fiber 2.9g | Sugar 15g | Protein 15g

Savory Parsley Soufflé

Prep Time: 10 minutes | Cook Time: 8 minutes | Serves: 2

Ingredients:

2 tablespoons light cream
2 eggs
1 tablespoon fresh parsley, chopped
1 fresh red chili pepper, chopped
Salt, as required

Preparation:

1. Grease 2 soufflé dishes. 2. In a bowl, add all the ingredients and beat until well combined. 3. Divide the mixture into prepared soufflé dishes. 4. Press "Power" button of Ninja Foodi XL Pro Air Oven and select "Air Fry" function. 5. Now press TIME/SLICES +/- buttons to set the cooking time to 8 minutes. 6. Press TEMP/SHADE +/- buttons to set the temperature at 390°F/200°C. 7. Press "START/STOP" button to start. 8. When the unit beeps to show that it is preheated, open the lid and grease the air fry basket. 9. Arrange the soufflé dishes into the air fry basket and insert in the oven. 10. When cooking time is completed, open the lid and serve hot.

Serving Suggestions: Serve alongside a piece of crusty bread.
Variation Tip: You can replace chives with parsley.
Nutritional Information per Serving: Calories: 108 | Fat: 9g | Sat Fat: 4.3g | Carbohydrates: 1.1g | Fiber: 0.22g | Sugar: 0.5g | Protein: 6g

Breakfast Bake

Prep Time: 15 minutes | Cook Time: 50 minutes | Serves: 6

Ingredients:

24 ounces bulk pork sausage
1 medium bell pepper, chopped
1 medium onion, chopped
3 cups frozen hash brown potatoes
2 cups shredded Cheddar cheese
1 cup Bisquick mix
2 cups milk
¼ teaspoon pepper
4 eggs

Preparation:

1. Whisk Bisquick with milk, eggs, and pepper in a mixer. 2. Sauté pork sausage, onion, and bell pepper in a 10-inch skillet over medium heat. 3. Stir cook until the sausage turns brown in color, then transfer to a casserole dish. 4. Toss in potatoes, 1½ cups of cheese, and the Bisquick mixture. 5. Transfer the casserole dish to the 2nd rack position of Ninja Foodi XL Pro Air Oven and close the door. 6. Select the "Bake" Mode using FUNCTION +/- buttons and select Rack Level 2. 7. Set its cooking time to 45 minutes and temperature to 350°F/175°C, then press "START/STOP" to initiate cooking. 8. Drizzle the remaining cheese over the casserole and bake for 5 minutes. 9. Serve.

Serving Suggestion: Serve the bake with crispy bacon and bread.
Variation Tip: Top egg with fresh herbs or chopped bell pepper.
Nutritional Information Per Serving: Calories 297 | Fat 15g | Sodium 202mg | Carbs 58.5g | Fiber 4g | Sugar 1g | Protein 33g

Puffed Egg Tarts

Prep Time: 15 minutes | Cook Time: 21 minutes | Serves: 4

Ingredients:

½ (17.3-ounce package) frozen puff pastry, thawed
¾ cup Cheddar cheese, shredded
4 large eggs
1 tablespoon fresh parsley, minced

Preparation:

1. Spread the pastry sheet on a floured surface and cut it into 4 squares of equal size. 2. Place the four squares in the air fry basket and roast tray with sheet pan. 3. Transfer the sheet to the 3rd rack position of Ninja Foodi XL Pro Air Oven and close the door. 4. Select the "Air Fry" Mode using FUNCTION +/- buttons and select Rack Level 3. 5. Set its cooking time to 10 minutes and temperature to 300°F/150°C, then press "START/STOP" to initiate cooking. 6. Press the center of each pastry square using the back of a metal spoon, 7. Divide cheese into these indentations and crack one egg into each pastry. 8. Return to Ninja Foodi XL Pro Air Oven and close its lid. 9. Select the "Air Fry" mode and cook for 11 minutes at 350°F/175°C. 10. Garnish the squares with parsley. 11. Serve warm.

Serving Suggestion: Serve these tarts with crispy bacon on the side.
Variation Tip: Add crumbled bacon on top before baking.
Nutritional Information Per Serving: Calories 305 | Fat 15g | Sodium 548mg | Carbs 26g | Fiber 2g | Sugar 1g | Protein 19g

Simple Bread

Prep Time: 15 minutes | Cook Time: 18 minutes | Serves: 4

Ingredients:

⅞ cup whole-wheat flour
⅞ cup plain flour
1¾ ounces pumpkin seeds
1 teaspoon salt
½ of sachet instant yeast
½-1 cup lukewarm water

Preparation:

1. In a bowl, mix the flours, pumpkin seeds, salt and yeast and mix well together. 2. Slowly, add the desired amount of water and mix until a soft dough ball forms. 3. With your hands, knead the dough until smooth and elastic. 4. Place the dough ball into a bowl. 5. With a plastic wrap, cover the bowl and set aside in a warm place for 30 minutes or until doubled in size. 6. Press "Power" button of Ninja Foodi XL Pro Air Oven and select "Air Fry" function. 7. Press TEMP/SHADE +/- buttons to set the temperature at 350°F/175°C. 8. Now press TIME/SLICES +/- buttons to set the cooking time to 18 minutes. 9. Press "START/STOP" button to start. 10. Place the dough ball in a greased cake pan and brush the top of the dough with water. 11. When the unit beeps to show that it is preheated, open the lid. 12. Place the cake pan into the air fry basket and insert in the oven. 13. When cooking time is completed, open the lid and place the pan onto a wire rack for about 10-15 minutes. 14. Carefully, invert the bread onto the wire rack to cool completely before slicing. 15. Cut the bread into desired sized slices and serve.

Serving Suggestions: Serve with your favorite jam.
Variation Tip: Add some nuts for a crispy taste.
Nutritional Information per Serving: Calories: 268 | Fat: 6g | Sat Fat: 1.1g | Carbohydrates: 43.9g | Fiber: 2.5g | Sugar: 1.1g | Protein: 9.2g

Savory Sausage & Beans Muffins

Prep Time: 15 minutes | Cook Time: 20 minutes | Serves: 6

Ingredients:

4 eggs
½ cup cheddar cheese, shredded
3 tablespoons heavy cream
1 tablespoon tomato paste
¼ teaspoon salt
Pinch of freshly ground black pepper
Cooking spray
4 cooked breakfast sausage links, chopped
3 tablespoons baked beans

Preparation:

1. Grease a 6 cups muffin pan. 2. In a bowl, add the eggs, cheddar cheese, heavy cream, tomato paste, salt and black pepper and beat until well combined. 3. Stir in the sausage pieces and beans. 4. Divide the mixture into prepared muffin cups evenly. 5. Press "Power" button of Ninja Foodi XL Pro Air Oven and select "Bake" function. 6. Press TEMP/SHADE +/- buttons to set the temperature at 350°F/175°C. 7. Now press TIME/SLICES +/- buttons to set the cooking time to 20 minutes. 8. Press "START/STOP" button to start. 9. When the unit beeps to show that it is preheated, open the lid. 10. Arrange the muffin pan over the wire rack and insert in the oven. 11. When cooking time is completed, open the lid and place the muffin pan onto a wire rack to cool for 5 minutes before serving.

Serving Suggestions: Serve with drizzling of melted butter.
Variation Tip: You can use cooked beans of your choice.
Nutritional Information per Serving: Calories: 258 | Fat: 20.4g | Sat Fat: 9.3g | Carbohydrates: 4.2g | Fiber: 0.8g | Sugar: 0.9g | Protein: 14.6g

Mushrooms Frittata

Prep Time: 15 minutes | Cook Time: 15 minutes | Serves: 2

Ingredients:

1 cup egg whites
2 tablespoons skim milk
¼ cup tomato, sliced
Black pepper, to taste
¼ cup mushrooms, sliced
2 tablespoons fresh chives, chopped

Preparation:

1. Beat egg whites with mushrooms and the rest of the ingredients in a bowl. 2. Spread this egg white mixture in a suitable casserole dish. 3. Transfer the dish to the 2nd rack position of Ninja Foodi XL Pro Air Oven and close the door. 4. Select the "Air Fry" Mode using FUNCTION +/- buttons and select Rack Level 2. 5. Set its cooking time to 15 minutes and temperature to 320°F/160°C, then press "START/STOP" to initiate cooking. 6. Slice and serve warm.

Serving Suggestion: Serve the mushrooms frittata with crispy bacon on the side.
Variation Tip: Add chopped bell pepper to the frittata.
Nutritional Information Per Serving: Calories 354 | Fat 7.9g | Sodium 704mg | Carbs 6g | Fiber 3.6g | Sugar 6g | Protein 18g

Carrot & Raisin Bread

Prep Time: 15 minutes | Cook Time: 35 minutes | Serves: 8

Ingredients:

- 2 cups all-purpose flour
- 1½ teaspoons ground cinnamon
- 2 teaspoons baking soda
- ½ teaspoon salt
- 3 eggs
- ½ cup sunflower oil
- ½ cup applesauce
- ¼ cup honey
- ¼ cup plain yogurt
- 2 teaspoons vanilla essence
- 2½ cups carrots, peeled and shredded
- ½ cup raisins
- ½ cup walnuts

Preparation:

1. Line the bottom of a greased sheet pan with parchment paper. 2. In a medium bowl, sift together the flour, baking soda, cinnamon, and salt. 3. In a large bowl, add the eggs, oil, applesauce, honey, and yogurt and with a hand-held mixer, mix on medium speed until well combined. 4. Add the eggs, one at a time and whisk well. 5. Add the vanilla and mix well. 6. Add the flour mixture and mix until just combined. 7. Fold in the carrots, raisins, and walnuts. 8. Place the mixture into the greased sheet pan. 9. With a piece of foil, cover the pan loosely. 10. Press "Power" button of Ninja Foodi XL Pro Air Oven and press FUNCTION +/- buttons to select "Air Fry" function. 11. Press TEMP/SHADE +/- buttons to set the temperature at 350°F/175°C. 12. Now press TIME/SLICES +/- buttons to set the cooking time to 30 minutes. 13. Press "Start/Stop" button to start. 14. When the unit beeps to show that it is preheated, open the oven door. 15. Arrange the pan over wire rack on Level 3. 16. After 25 minutes of cooking, remove the foil. 17. When cooking time is completed, open the oven door and place the pan onto a wire rack to cool for about 10 minutes. 18. Carefully invert the bread onto the wire rack to cool completely before slicing. 19. Cut the bread into desired-sized slices and serve.

Serving Suggestions: Serve with butter.
Variation Tip: Dried cranberries can also be used instead of raisins.
Nutritional Information per Serving: Calories: 441 | Fat: 20.3g | Sat Fat: 2.2g | Carbohydrates: 57.6g | Fiber: 5.7g | Sugar: 23.7g | Protein: 9.2g

Savory French Toast

Prep Time: 10 minutes | Cook Time: 5 minutes | Serves: 2

Ingredients:

- ¼ cup chickpea flour
- 3 tablespoons onion, finely chopped
- 2 teaspoons green chili, seeded and finely chopped
- ½ teaspoon red chili powder
- ¼ teaspoon ground turmeric
- ¼ teaspoon ground cumin
- Salt, to taste
- Water, as needed
- 4 bread slices

Preparation:

1. Add all the ingredients except bread slices in a large bowl and mix until a thick mixture forms. 2. With a spoon, spread the mixture over both sides of each bread slice. 3. Arrange the bread slices into the lightly greased air fry basket. 4. Press "Power" button of Ninja Foodi XL Pro Air Oven and select "Air Fry" function. 5. Now press TIME/SLICES +/- buttons to set the cooking time to 5 minutes. 6. Press TEMP/SHADE +/- buttons to set the temperature at 390°F/200°C. 7. Press "Start/Stop" button to start. 8. When the unit beeps to show that it is preheated, open the oven door and insert the air fry basket on the rails of Level 3 in oven. 9. Flip the bread slices once halfway through. 10. When cooking time is completed, open the oven door and serve warm.

Serving Suggestions: Serve with the topping of butter.
Variation Tip: You can add herbs of your choice in flour batter.
Nutritional Information per Serving: Calories: 151 | Fat: 2.3g | Sat Fat: 0.3g | Carbohydrates: 26.7g | Fiber: 5.4g | Sugar: 4.3g | Protein: 6.5g

Sweet & Spiced Toasts

Prep Time: 10 minutes | Cook Time: 4 minutes | Serves: 3

Ingredients:

- ¼ cup sugar
- ½ teaspoon ground cinnamon
- ⅛ teaspoon ground cloves
- ⅛ teaspoon ground ginger
- ½ teaspoons vanilla extract
- ¼ cup salted butter, softened
- 6 bread slices

Preparation:

1. In a bowl, add the sugar, vanilla, cinnamon, pepper, and butter. Mix until smooth. 2. Spread the butter mixture evenly over each bread slice. 3. Press "Power" button of Ninja Foodi XL Pro Air Oven and select "Air Fry" function. 4. Press TEMP/SHADE +/- buttons to set the temperature at 400°F/200°C. 5. Now press TIME/SLICES +/- buttons to set the cooking time to 4 minutes. 6. Press "START/STOP" button to start. 7. When the unit beeps to show that it is preheated, open the lid and grease the air fry basket. 8. Place the bread slices into the prepared air fry basket, buttered-side up and insert in the oven. 9. Flip the slices once halfway through. 10. When cooking time is completed, open the lid and transfer the French toasts onto a platter. 11. Serve warm.

Serving Suggestions: Serve with the drizzling of maple syrup.
Variation Tip: Adjust the ratio of spices according to your taste.
Nutritional Information per Serving: Calories: 261 | Fat: 12g | Sat Fat: 3.6g | Carbohydrates: 30.6g | Fiber: 0.3g | Sugar: 22.3g | Protein: 9.1g

Date Bread

Prep Time: 15 minutes | Cook Time: 22 minutes | Serves: 10

Ingredients:

- 2½ cups dates, pitted and chopped
- ¼ cup butter
- 1 cup hot water
- 1½ cups flour
- ½ cup brown sugar
- 1 teaspoon baking powder
- 1 teaspoon baking soda
- ½ teaspoon salt
- 1 egg

Preparation:

1. In a large bowl, add the dates, butter and top with the hot water. Set aside for about 5 minutes. 2. In a separate bowl, mix together the flour, brown sugar, baking powder, baking soda, and salt. 3. In the same bowl of dates, add the flour mixture and egg and mix well. 4. Grease a non-stick loaf pan. 5. Place the mixture into the prepared pan. 6. Press "Power" button of Ninja Foodi XL Pro Air Oven and select "Air Fry" function. 7. Press TEMP/SHADE +/- buttons to set the temperature at 340°F/170°C. 8. Now press TIME/SLICES +/- buttons to set the cooking time to 22 minutes. 9. Press "START/STOP" button to start. 10. When the unit beeps to show that it is preheated, open the lid. 11. Place the pan into the air fry basket and insert in the oven. 12. When cooking time is completed, open the lid and place the pan onto a wire rack for about 10-15 minutes. 13. Carefully, invert the bread onto the wire rack to cool completely cool before slicing. 14. Cut the bread into desired sized slices and serve.

Serving Suggestions: Serve these bread slices with butter.
Variation Tip: Use soft dates.
Nutritional Information per Serving: Calories: 129 | Fat: 5.4g | Sat Fat: 3.1g | Carbohydrates: 55.1g | Fiber: 4.1g | Sugar: 35.3g | Protein: 3.6g

Banana & Walnut Bread

Prep Time: 15 minutes | Cook Time: 25 minutes | Serves: 10

Ingredients:

- 1½ cups self-rising flour
- ¼ teaspoon bicarbonate of soda
- 5 tablespoons plus 1 teaspoon butter
- ⅔ cup plus ½ tablespoon caster sugar
- 2 medium eggs
- 3½ ounces walnuts, chopped
- 2 cups bananas, peeled and mashed

Preparation:

1. In a bowl, mix together the flour and bicarbonate of soda. 2. In another bowl, add the butter and sugar and beat until pale and fluffy. 3. Add the eggs, one at a time, along with a little flour and mix well. 4. Stir in the remaining flour and walnuts. 5. Add the bananas and mix until well combined. 6. Grease sheet pan. 7. Place the mixture into the prepared pan. 8. Press "Power" button of Ninja Foodi XL Pro Air Oven and select "Air Fry" function. 9. Press TEMP/SHADE +/- buttons to set the temperature at 355°F/180°C. 10. Now press TIME/SLICES +/- buttons to set the cooking time to 10 minutes. 11. Press "Start/Stop" button to start. 12. When the unit beeps to show that it is preheated, open the oven door. 13. Arrange the pan over wire rack on Level 3. 14. After 10 minutes of cooking, set the temperature at 340°F/170°C for 15 minutes. 15. When cooking time is completed, open the oven door and place the pan onto a wire rack to cool for about 10 minutes. 16. Carefully invert the bread onto the wire rack to cool completely before slicing. 17. Cut the bread into desired sized slices and serve.

Serving Suggestions: Serve with strawberry jam.
Variation Tip: Walnuts can be replaced with pecans.
Nutritional Information per Serving: Calories: 270 | Fat: 12.8g | Sat Fat: 4.3g | Carbohydrates: 35.5g | Fiber: 2g | Sugar: 17.2g | Protein: 5.8g

Puff Pastry Danishes

Prep Time: 30 minutes | Cook Time: 15 minutes | Serves: 4 to 5

Ingredients:

- 8 ounces cream cheese
- ¼ cup sugar
- 2 tablespoons all-purpose flour
- ½ teaspoon vanilla extract
- 2 large egg yolks
- 1 tablespoon water
- 17.3 ounces frozen puff pastry (thawed)
- ⅔ cup seedless raspberry jam

Preparation:

1. Insert a wire rack in your oven on Level 3. Select the Bake function, 425°F/220°C, for 16 minutes. 2. While the unit is preheating, line the sheet pan with parchment paper and prepare the ingredients. 3. Beat the sugar, cream cheese, flour, and 1 egg yolk in a bowl. 4. In a separate bowl, mix the remaining egg yolk with water. 5. Lightly flour a surface and lay out the puff pastry sheets. Roll them into 12-inch squares. Cut each into 4-inch squares, and transfer to the sheet pan. 6. Top all the squares with 1 tablespoon of the cream cheese mixture and 1 rounded tablespoon of jam. 7. Bring the two opposite corners of pastry over the filling and seal with the yolk mixture. Use the remaining mixture to brush the tops. 8. When the unit beeps to show that it has preheated, open the oven and insert the sheet pan on wire rack into the rail of Level 3 in oven. 9. Bake the pastries for about 14 to 16 minutes.

Serving Suggestion: Sprinkle with powdered sugar and serve warm.
Variation Tip: You can use the jam of your choice.
Nutritional Information Per Serving: Calories: 197 | Fat: 12g | Sodium: 130mg | Carbs: 20g | Fiber: 2g | Protein: 3g

Ham & Egg Cups

Prep Time: 10 minutes | Cook Time: 18 minutes | Serves: 6

Ingredients:

- 6 ham slices
- 6 eggs
- 6 tablespoons cream
- 3 tablespoon mozzarella cheese, shredded
- ¼ teaspoon dried basil, crushed

Preparation:

1. Lightly grease 6 cups of a silicone muffin tin. 2. Line each prepared muffin cup with 1 ham slice. 3. Crack 1 egg into each muffin cup and top with cream. 4. Sprinkle with cheese and basil. 5. Press "Power" button of Ninja Foodi XL Pro Air Oven and select "Air Fry" function. 6. Press TEMP/SHADE +/- buttons to set the temperature at 350°F/175°C. 7. Now press TIME/SLICES +/- buttons to set the cooking time to 18 minutes. 8. Press "Start/Stop" button to start. 9. When the unit beeps to show that it is preheated, open the oven door. 10. Arrange the muffin tin over the wire rack and insert on Level 3. 11. When cooking time is completed, open the oven door, and place the muffin tin onto another wire rack to cool for about 5 minutes. 12. Carefully invert the muffins onto the platter and serve warm.

Serving Suggestions: Serve alongside the buttered bread slices.

Variation Tip: Use room temperature eggs.

Nutritional Information per Serving: Calories: 156 | Fat: 10g | Sat Fat: 4.1g | Carbohydrates: 2.3g | Fiber: 0.4g | Sugar: 0.6g | Protein: 14.3g

Zucchini Fritters

Prep Time: 15 minutes | Cook Time: 7 minutes | Serves: 4

Ingredients:

- 10½ ounces zucchini, grated and squeezed
- 7 ounces Halloumi cheese
- ¼ cup all-purpose flour
- 2 eggs
- 1 teaspoon fresh dill, minced
- Salt and ground black pepper, as required

Preparation:

1. In a large bowl and mix all the ingredients together. 2. Make small-sized fritters from the mixture. 3. Press "Power" button of Ninja Foodi XL Pro Air Oven and select "Air Fry" function. 4. Press TEMP/SHADE +/- buttons to set the temperature at 355°F/180°C. 5. Now press TIME/SLICES +/- buttons to set the cooking time to 7 minutes. 6. Press "Start/Stop" button to start. 7. When the unit beeps to show that it is preheated, open the oven door. 8. Arrange fritters into the air fry basket and insert into the rails of Level 3. 9. When cooking time is completed, open the oven door and serve warm.

Serving Suggestions: Serve with the topping of sour cream.

Variation Tip: Make sure to squeeze the zucchini completely.

Nutritional Information per Serving: Calories: 253 | Fat: 17.2g | Sat Fat: 1.4g | Carbohydrates: 10g | Fiber: 1.1g | Sugar: 2.7g | Protein: 15.2g

Ricotta Toasts with Salmon

Prep Time: 10 minutes | Cook Time: 4 minutes | Serves: 2

Ingredients:

- 4 bread slices
- 1 garlic clove, minced
- 8 ounces ricotta cheese
- 1 teaspoon lemon zest
- Freshly ground black pepper, to taste
- 4 ounces smoked salmon

Preparation:

1. In a food processor, add the garlic, ricotta, lemon zest and black pepper and pulse until smooth. 2. Spread ricotta mixture over each bread slices evenly. Evenly arrange the bread slices in the air fry basket. 3. Press "Power" button of Ninja Foodi XL Pro Air Oven and select "Air Fry" function. 4. Press TEMP/SHADE +/- buttons to set the temperature at 355°F/180°C. 5. Now press TIME/SLICES +/- buttons to set the cooking time to 4 minutes. 6. Press "Start/Stop" button to start. 7. When the unit beeps to show that it is preheated, open the oven door and slide basket into rails of Level 3. 8. When cooking time is completed, open the oven door and transfer the slices onto serving plates. 9. Top with salmon and serve.

Serving Suggestions: Serve with the garnishing of fresh herbs.

Variation Tip: Ricotta cheese can be replaced with feta.

Nutritional Information per Serving: Calories: 274 | Fat: 12g | Sat Fat: 6.3g | Carbohydrates: 15.7g | Fiber: 0.5g | Sugar: 1.2g | Protein: 24.8g

Sweet Potato Rosti

Prep Time: 15 minutes | Cook Time: 15 minutes | Serves: 2

Ingredients:

½ pound sweet potatoes, peeled, grated and squeezed
1 tablespoon fresh parsley, chopped finely
Salt and ground black pepper, as required

Preparation:

1. In a large bowl, mix the grated sweet potato, parsley, salt, and black pepper together. 2. Arrange the sweet potato mixture into the lightly greased the sheet pan and shape it into an even circle. 3. Press "Power" button of Ninja Foodi XL Pro Air Oven and select "Air Fry" function. 4. Press TEMP/SHADE +/- buttons to set the temperature at 355°F/180°C. 5. Now press TIME/SLICES +/- buttons to set the cooking time to 15 minutes. 6. Press "Start/Stop" button to start. 7. When the unit beeps to show that it is preheated, open the oven door and insert the pan on wire rack on Level 3. 8. When cooking time is completed, open the oven door. 9. Cut the potato rosti into wedges and serve immediately.

Serving Suggestions: Serve alongside the yogurt dip.
Variation Tip: Potato can also be used instead of sweet potato.
Nutritional Information per Serving: Calories: 160 | Fat: 2.1g | Sat Fat: 1.4g | Carbohydrates: 30.3g | Fiber: 4.7g | Sugar: 0.6g | Protein: 2.2g

Bacon, Spinach & Egg Cups

Prep Time: 15 minutes | Cook Time: 16 minutes | Serves: 3

Ingredients:

3 eggs
6 cooked bacon slices, chopped
2 cups fresh baby spinach
⅓ cup heavy cream
3 tablespoons Parmesan cheese, grated
Salt and ground black pepper, as required

Preparation:

1. Heat a nonstick skillet over medium-high heat and cook the bacon for about 5 minutes. 2. Add the spinach and cook for about 2-3 minutes. 3. Stir in the heavy cream and Parmesan cheese and cook for about 2-3 minutes. 4. Remove from the heat and set aside to cool slightly. 5. Grease 3 (3-inch) ramekins. 6. Crack 1 egg in each prepared ramekin and top with bacon mixture. 7. Press "Power" button of Ninja Foodi XL Pro Air Oven and select "Air Fry" function. 8. Press TEMP/SHADE +/- buttons to set the temperature at 350°F/175°C. 9. Now press TIME/SLICES +/- buttons to set the cooking time to 5 minutes. 10. Press "START/STOP" button to start. 11. When the unit beeps to show that it is preheated, open the lid and grease the air fry basket. 12. Arrange the ramekins into the air fry basket and insert in the oven. 13. When cooking time is completed, open the lid and sprinkle each ramekin with salt and black pepper. 14. Serve hot.

Serving Suggestions: Serve alongside the English muffins.
Variation Tip: Use freshly grated cheese.
Nutritional Information per Serving: Calories: 442 | Fat: 34.5g | Sat Fat: 12.9g | Carbohydrates: 2.3g | Fiber: 0.5g | Sugar: 0.4g | Protein: 29.6g

Pancetta & Spinach Frittata

Prep Time: 15 minutes | Cook Time: 16 minutes | Serves: 2

Ingredients:

¼ cup pancetta
½ of tomato, cubed
¼ cup fresh baby spinach
3 eggs
Salt and ground black pepper, as required
¼ cup Parmesan cheese, grated

Preparation:

1. Heat a nonstick skillet over medium heat and cook the pancetta for about 5 minutes. 2. Add the tomato and spinach cook for about 2-3 minutes. 3. Remove from the heat and drain the grease from skillet. 4. Set aside to cool slightly. 5. Meanwhile, in a small bowl, add the eggs, salt and black pepper and beat well. 6. In the bottom of a greased sheet pan, place the pancetta mixture and top with the eggs, followed by the cheese. 7. Press "Power" button of Ninja Foodi XL Pro Air Oven and select "Air Fry" function. 8. Press TEMP/SHADE +/- buttons to set the temperature at 355°F/180°C. 9. Now press TIME/SLICES +/- buttons to set the cooking time to 8 minutes. 10. Press "Start/Stop" button to start. 11. When the unit beeps to show that it is preheated, open the oven door. 12. Arrange pan over the wire rack on Level 3. 13. When cooking time is completed, open the oven door, and remove the pan. 14. Cut into equal-sized wedges and serve.

Serving Suggestions: Serve alongside the green salad.
Variation Tip: You can use bacon instead of pancetta.
Nutritional Information per Serving: Calories: 287 | Fat: 20.8g | Sat Fat: 7.2g | Carbohydrates: 1.7g | Fiber: 0.3g | Sugar: 0.9g | Protein: 23.1g

Breakfast Casserole

Prep Time: 15 minutes | Cook Time: 30 minutes | Serves: 8

Ingredients:

- 8 eggs
- 1 pound pork sausage
- 1½ cups whole milk
- 850g frozen hash browns, shredded
- 2 cups cheddar cheese
- 1½ teaspoons salt
- ¼ teaspoon garlic powder

Preparation:

1. Toss the uncooked ground sausage into the pan. 2. Sauté and cook for 6-8 minutes, or until sausage is browned. 3. Mix in the frozen hash browns thoroughly. 4. Mix in 1 cup of cheese. 5. Whisk together the eggs, Cheddar cheese, and spices in a separate basin. Fill the pot with the egg mixture. 6. Place the mixture into the roast tray. 7. Install a sheet pan on Level 3 in oven. Turn on your Ninja Foodi XL Pro Air Oven and select "Air Fry". 8. Select the timer for 30 minutes and the temperature for 350°F/175°C. 9. When the unit beeps to show that it has preheated, open the oven and insert the roast tray on the sheet pan in oven. 10. Serve while hot.

Serving Suggestions: You can also add olives.
Variation Tip: You can use cream cheese instead of milk.
Nutritional Information per Serving: Calories: 350 | Fat: 29g | Sat Fat: 12g | Carbohydrates: 1g | Fiber: 1g | Sugar: 1g | Protein: 21g

Parmesan Eggs in Avocado Cups

Prep Time: 10 minutes | Cook Time: 22 minutes | Serves: 2

Ingredients:

- 1 large ripe but firm avocado, halved and pitted
- 2 eggs
- Salt and ground black pepper, as required
- 2 tablespoons Parmesan cheese, grated
- Pinch of cayenne pepper
- 1 teaspoon fresh chives, minced

Preparation:

1. With a spoon, scoop out some of the flesh from the avocado halves to make a hole. 2. Arrange the avocado halves onto a baking pan. 3. Crack 1 egg into each avocado half and sprinkle with salt and black pepper. 4. Press "Power" button of Ninja Foodi XL Pro Air Oven and select "Air Fry" function. 5. Press TEMP/SHADE +/- buttons to set the temperature at 350°F/175°C. 6. Now press TIME/SLICES +/- buttons to set the cooking time to 22 minutes. 7. Press "START/STOP" button to start. 8. When the unit beeps to show that it is preheated, open the lid and grease the air fry basket. 9. Arrange the avocado halves into the air fry basket and insert in the oven. 10. After 12 minutes of cooking, sprinkle the top of avocado halves with Parmesan cheese. 11. When cooking time is completed, open the lid and transfer the avocado halves onto a platter. 12. Sprinkle with cayenne pepper and serve hot with the garnishing of chives.

Serving Suggestions: Serve alongside baby greens.
Variation Tip: Add some seasoning as you like.
Nutritional Information per Serving: Calories: 286 | Fat: 25.2g | Sat Fat: 6.1g | Carbohydrates: 9g | Fiber: 0.9g | Sugar: 0.9g | Protein: 9.5g

Banana Bread

Prep Time: 15 minutes | Cook Time: 25 minutes | Serves: 6

Ingredients:

- 4 medium bananas, peeled and sliced
- ¼ cup plain Greek yogurt
- 2 large eggs
- ½-ounce vanilla extract
- 10 ounces all-purpose flour
- ¾ cup sugar
- 3 ounces oat flour
- 1 teaspoon baking powder
- 1 teaspoon baking soda
- ¾ teaspoon kosher salt
- ¾ teaspoon ground cinnamon
- ½ teaspoon ground cloves
- ¼ teaspoon ground nutmeg
- ¾ cup coconut oil
- 1 cup toasted pecan

Preparation:

1. Layer a 10.5-by-5.5-inch loaf pan with a parchment sheet and keep it aside. 2. Mash the banana in a suitable bowl and add eggs, vanilla, and Greek yogurt, then mix well. 3. Cover this banana yogurt mixture and leave it for 30 minutes. 4. Meanwhile, mix cinnamon, flour, sugar, baking powder, oat flour, salt, baking soda, coconut oil, cloves, and nutmeg in a mixer. 5. Now slowly add banana mash mixture to the flour and continue mixing until smooth. 6. Fold in nuts and mix gently until evenly incorporated. 7. Spread this banana-nut batter in the prepared loaf pan. 8. Transfer the loaf pan to the 2nd rack position of Ninja Foodi XL Pro Air Oven and close the door. 9. Select the "Bake" Mode using FUNCTION +/- buttons and select Rack Level 2. 10. Set its cooking time to 25 minutes and temperature to 350°F/175°C, then press "START/STOP" to initiate cooking. 11. Slice and serve.

Serving Suggestion: Serve the bread with fried eggs and crispy bacon.
Variation Tip: Add some crushed oats for a different texture.
Nutritional Information Per Serving: Calories 331 | Fat 2.5g | Sodium 595mg | Carbs 69g | Fiber 12g | Sugar 12g | Protein 7g

Cinnamon Sugar Donuts

Prep Time: 10 minutes | Cook Time: 5 minutes | Serves: 8

Ingredients:

- 450g refrigerated flaky jumbo biscuits
- ½ cup granulated white sugar
- 2 teaspoons ground cinnamon
- 4 tablespoons butter, melted
- Olive oil spray

Preparation:

1. Combine the sugar and cinnamon in a bowl; leave aside. 2. Take the biscuits out of the can, divide them, and lay them out on a flat surface. Make holes in each biscuit with a 1-inch-round biscuit cutter. 3. Using an olive or coconut oil spray, lightly coat the roast tray. 4. In the roast tray, arrange 4 doughnuts in a single layer. Make certain they aren't in contact. 5. Turn on your Ninja Foodi XL Pro Air Oven and select "Bake". 6. Select the timer for 5 minutes and the temperature for 360°F/180°C. 7. When the unit beeps to show that it has preheated, open the oven and insert the roast tray on sheet pan into the rail of Level 3 in oven. 8. Serve and enjoy!

Serving Suggestions: Serve with chocolate sauce.
Variation Tip: Sprinkle sugar on top.
Nutritional Information per Serving: Calories: 316 | Fat: 15g | Sat Fat: 5g | Carbohydrates: 42g | Fiber: 1g | Sugar: 16g | Protein: 3g

Mushroom Frittata

Prep Time: 15 minutes | Cook Time: 36 minutes | Serves: 4

Ingredients:

- 2 tablespoons olive oil
- 1 shallot, sliced thinly
- 2 garlic cloves, minced
- 4 cups white mushrooms, chopped
- 6 large eggs
- ¼ teaspoon red pepper flakes, crushed
- Salt and ground black pepper, as required
- ½ teaspoon fresh dill, minced
- ½ cup cream cheese, softened

Preparation:

1. In a skillet, heat the oil over medium heat and cook the shallot, mushrooms and garlic for about 5-6 minutes, stirring frequently. 2. Remove from the heat and transfer the mushroom mixture into a bowl. 3. In another bowl, add the eggs, red pepper flakes, salt and black peppers and beat well. 4. Add the mushroom mixture and stir to combine. 5. Place the egg mixture into a greased baking pan and sprinkle with the dill. 6. Spread cream cheese over egg mixture evenly. 7. Press "Power" button of Ninja Foodi XL Pro Air Oven and select "Air Fry" function. 8. Press TEMP/SHADE +/- buttons to set the temperature at 330°F/165°C. 9. Now press TIME/SLICES +/- buttons to set the cooking time to 30 minutes. 10. Press "START/STOP" button to start. 11. When the unit beeps to show that it is preheated, open the lid. 12. Arrange pan over the wire rack and insert in the oven. 13. When cooking time is completed, open the lid and place the baking pan onto a wire rack for about 5 minutes. 14. For better taste, let the frittata sit at room temperature for a few minutes to set before cutting. 15. Cut into equal-sized wedges and serve.

Serving Suggestions: Serve with green salad.
Variation Tip: Feel free to add some seasoning as you like.
Nutritional Information per Serving: Calories: 290 | Fat: 24.8g | Sat Fat: 9.7g | Carbohydrates: 5g | Fiber: 0.8g | Sugar: 1.9g | Protein: 14.1g

Potato & Corned Beef Casserole

Prep Time: 15 minutes | Cook Time: 1 hour 20 minutes | Serves: 3

Ingredients:

- 3 Yukon Gold potatoes
- 2 tablespoons unsalted butter
- ½ of onion, chopped
- 2 garlic cloves, minced
- 2 tablespoons vegetable oil
- ½ teaspoon salt
- 12 ounces corned beef
- 3 eggs

Preparation:

1. Press "Power" button of Ninja Foodi XL Pro Air Oven and select "Bake" function. 2. Press TEMP/SHADE +/- buttons to set the temperature at 350°F/175°C. 3. Now press TIME/SLICES +/- buttons to set the cooking time to 30 minutes. 4. Press "START/STOP" button to start. 5. When the unit beeps to show that it is preheated, open the lid and grease the air fry basket. 6. Place the potatoes into the prepared air fry basket and insert in the oven. 7. When cooking time is completed, open the lid and transfer the potatoes onto a tray. 8. Set aside to cool for about 15 minutes. 9. After cooling, cut the potatoes into ½-inch-thick slices. 10. In a skillet, melt the butter over medium heat and cook the onion and garlic for about 10 minutes. 11. Remove from the heat and place the onion mixture into a casserole dish. 12. Add the potato slices, oil salt and corned beef and mix well. 13. Press "Power" button of Ninja Foodi XL Pro Air Oven and select "Bake" function. 14. Now press TIME/SLICES +/- buttons to set the cooking time to 40 minutes. 15. Press TEMP/SHADE +/- buttons to set the temperature at 350°F/175°C. 16. Press "START/STOP" button to start. 17. When the unit beeps to show that it is preheated, open the lid. 18. Arrange the casserole dish over the wire rack and insert in the oven. 19. After 30 minutes of cooking, remove the casserole dish and crack 3 eggs on top. 20. When cooking time is completed, open the lid and serve immediately.

Serving Suggestions: Serve with fresh baby kale.
Variation Tip: Cut the potatoes in equal-sized slices.
Nutritional Information per Serving: Calories: 542 | Fat: 35.6g | Sat Fat: 14.1g | Carbohydrates: 33.1g | Fiber: 2.8g | Sugar: 2.3g | Protein: 24.7g

Sausage Patties

Prep Time: 5 minutes | Cook Time: 6 minutes | Serves: 6

Ingredients:
- 1 pound pork sausage patties
- Fennel seeds

Preparation:
1. Prepare the sausage by slicing it into patties or using new patties, then flavor it with fennel seed or your favorite seasoning. 2. Insert a wire rack on Level 3. 3. Turn on your Ninja Foodi XL Pro Air Oven and select "Broil". 4. Select the timer for 8 minutes and temperature to LO. 5. When the unit beeps to show that it has preheated, open the oven and insert the air fry basket on the wire rack. 6. Cook for another 4 minutes after carefully flipping the patties. 7. Serve.

Serving Suggestions: Serve with garlic sauce.
Variation Tip: You can use any seasoning.
Nutritional Information per Serving: Calories: 123 | Fat: 10g | Sat Fat: 3g | Carbohydrates: 1g | Fiber: 0g | Sugar: 0g | Protein: 7g

Hash Browns

Prep Time: 5 minutes | Cook Time: 5 minutes | Serves: 2

Ingredients:
- 4 hash brown patties
- Cooking oil spray

Preparation:
1. Coat the air fry basket with your preferred cooking oil spray. 2. Place the hash brown patties in the oven in an even layer on Level 3. 3. Spray them with your favorite cooking oil spray. 4. Turn on your Ninja Foodi XL Pro Air Oven and select "Air Fry". 5. Select the timer for 5 minutes and the temperature for 390°F/200°C. 6. Dish out and serve immediately.

Serving Suggestions: Serve with maple syrup.
Variation Tip: Sprinkle sugar on top.
Nutritional Information per Serving: Calories: 64 | Fat: 19.1g | Sat Fat: 2.9g | Carbohydrates: 8g | Fiber: 1g | Sugar: 0g | Protein: 1g

French Toast

Prep Time: 5 minutes | Cook Time: 6 minutes | Serves: 4

Ingredients:
- 1 cup heavy cream
- 1 egg, beaten
- ¼ powdered sugar
- 1 teaspoon cinnamon
- 8 slices of bread

Preparation:
1. Place your bread on the wire rack. 2. Turn on your Ninja Foodi XL Pro Air Oven and select "Air Roast". 3. Select the timer for 4 minutes and the temperature for 390°F/200°C. 4. While the bread is toasting, combine the remaining ingredients in a mixing bowl. 5. Dip bread in batches into the mixture, making sure both sides are covered. 6. Separate them on the air fry basket and wire rack evenly. 7. Now again, turn on your Ninja Foodi XL Pro Air Oven and select "Air Fry". 8. Select the timer for 4 minutes and the temperature for 390°F/200°C. 9. When the unit beeps to show that it has preheated, open the oven. Insert the air fry basket on the rail of Level 3 in oven and the wire rack on Level 1. 10. Serve with butter.

Serving Suggestions: Top with maple syrup.
Variation Tip: You can also use low-carb bread.
Nutritional Information per Serving: Calories: 342 | Fat: 29g | Sat Fat: 15g | Carbohydrates: 16g | Fiber: 8g | Sugar: 2g | Protein: 13g

Hard Boiled Eggs

Prep Time: 5 minutes | Cook Time: 12 minutes | Serves: 6

Ingredients:
6 eggs

Preparation:
1. Add the eggs in the air fry basket. 2. Turn on your Ninja Foodi XL Pro Air Oven and select "Air Fry". 3. Select the timer for 12 minutes and the temperature for 300°F/150°C. 4. When the unit beeps to show that it has preheated, open the oven and insert the air fry basket on the rail of Level 3 in oven. Close the oven door and let it cook. 5. After the cooking time has been completed, immerse for 5 minutes in a bowl of icy water. 6. After that, peel and serve.

Serving Suggestions: Serve with bread.
Variation Tip: Sprinkle salt and pepper on top.
Nutritional Information per Serving: Calories: 72 | Fat: 5g | Sat Fat: 2g | Carbohydrates: 80 | Fiber: 0g | Sugar: 0g | Protein: 6g

Breakfast Pizzas with Muffins

Prep Time: 5 minutes | Cook Time: 6 minutes | Serves: 3

Ingredients:
- 6 eggs, cooked and scrambled
- 1 pound ground sausage
- ½ cup Colby jack cheese, shredded
- 3 egg muffins, sliced in half
- Olive oil spray

Preparation:
1. Using olive oil cooking spray, spray the air fry basket. 2. Place each half in the basket. 3. Using a light layer of olive oil spray, lightly coat the English muffins and top with scrambled eggs and fried sausages. 4. Add cheese on top of each one. 5. Insert a wire rack on Level 3. Turn on your Ninja Foodi XL Pro Air Oven and select "Bake". 6. Select the timer for 5 minutes and the temperature for 355°F/180°C. 7. When the unit beeps to show that it has preheated, open the oven and insert the air fry basket on the wire rack of Level 3 in oven. 8. Serve hot.

Serving Suggestions: Top with fresh parsley.
Variation Tip: You can also add fennel seeds.
Nutritional Information per Serving: Calories: 429 | Fat: 32g | Sat Fat: 11g | Carbohydrates: 15g | Fiber: 1g | Sugar: 1g | Protein: 20g

Peanut Butter Banana Baked Oatmeal

Prep Time: 5 minutes | Cook Time: 30 minutes | Serves: 9

Ingredients:
- 1½ cups quick-cooking oats
- 1 teaspoon baking powder
- ½ teaspoon sea salt
- 1 teaspoon ground cinnamon
- 2 overripe bananas, mashed
- ¼ cup creamy peanut butter
- 1 teaspoon vanilla extract
- ¼ cup pure maple syrup
- 1 large egg lightly beaten
- ¾ cup almond milk unsweetened
- ¼ cup melted creamy peanut butter

Preparation:
1. Insert the wire rack on Level 3. Select the BAKE function, 350°F/175°C, for 25 minutes. While the oven is preheating, prepare a baking pan and the ingredients. 2. Take a small bowl, and mix the baking powder, quick-cooking oats, cinnamon, and sea salt. Set it aside. 3. Take a large bowl and mix the peanut butter with the mashed banana. Add the vanilla extract, egg, and maple syrup. Mix evenly. 4. Next, add in the almond milk and stir to combine. 5. Add the dry ingredients to the wet ingredients and mix well. 6. Empty the combined mixture into the prepared baking pan. 7. When the unit beeps to signify it has preheated, open the oven and insert the baking pan on wire rack in the oven. 8. Bake it for about 25 minutes. Once done, cut into squares and serve.

Serving Suggestion: Melt peanut butter and drizzle it on top before serving.
Variation Tip: If you want to give it a vegan spin, use chia seeds instead of eggs.
Nutritional Information Per Serving: Calories: 125 | Fat: 5g | Sodium: 118mg | Carbs: 16.7g | Fiber: 3g | Sugar: 4g | Protein: 5g

Cinnamon Donut Muffins

Prep Time: 15 minutes | Cook Time: 20 minutes | Serves: 10

Ingredients:

1¾ cups all-purpose flour
1½ teaspoon baking powder
½ teaspoon salt
½ teaspoon ground nutmeg
¾ cup sugar
Topping:
¼ cup melted butter
⅓ cup sugar

⅓ cup canola oil
1 large egg, lightly beaten
¾ cup 2% milk
10 teaspoons seedless strawberry jam

1 teaspoon ground cinnamon

Preparation:

1. Insert a wire rack on Level 3 in the oven. Select the BAKE function, 350°F/175°C, for 20 minutes. While the oven is preheating, prepare the ingredients. 2. Mix the baking powder, nutmeg, salt, flour, and cinnamon in a large bowl. 3. In a small bowl, combine the oil, sugar, egg, and milk. Then stir the mixture into the dry ingredients. 4. Grease 10 muffin cups, fill them halfway with the mixture and then top each with 1 teaspoon of jam. 5. Cover with the rest of the batter. 6. When the unit beeps to signify it has preheated, open the oven and insert the muffin cups on the wire rack. 7. Then bake the muffins for about 20 to 25 minutes. 8. For the topping: put the melted butter in a small bowl and combine the sugar with cinnamon in another bowl. 9. Right after taking the muffins out of the oven, dip the tops in butter and cinnamon sugar. Then serve warm.
Serving Suggestion: You can drizzle some honey over the muffins before serving.
Variation Tip: You can use some other jam of your choice.
Nutritional Information Per Serving: Calories: 288 | Fat: 13g | Sodium: 240mg | Carbs: 40g | Fiber: 1g | Sugar: 22g | Protein: 4g

German Pancake

Prep Time: 5 minutes | Cook Time: 30 minutes | Serves: 8

Ingredients:

6 large eggs
1 cup 2% milk
1 cup all-purpose flour
Buttermilk Syrup:
½ cup butter
1½ cups sugar
¾ cup buttermilk

½ teaspoon salt
2 tablespoons butter, melted
Powdered sugar, for serving

2 tablespoons corn syrup
1 teaspoon baking soda
2 teaspoons vanilla extract

Preparation:

1. Insert a wire rack on level 3 in your oven. Select the BAKE function, 400°F/200°C, for 30 minutes. While the oven is preheating, prepare the ingredients. 2. Put the eggs, 2% milk, flour, and salt in a blender and blend until smooth. 3. Pour the melted butter into an oven-safe baking dish and coat the surface. Then add the batter. 4. When the unit beeps to signify it has preheated, open the oven. Insert the baking dish on wire rack and bake for about 20 minutes, uncovered. 5. Meanwhile, take a small saucepan, put in the sugar, butter, corn syrup, buttermilk, and baking soda, and bring to a boil. 6. Cook for about 7 minutes, then remove from the heat and stir in the vanilla extract. 7. Take out the pancake and sprinkle it with confectioners' sugar.
Serving Suggestion: Serve with syrup and fresh blueberries or strawberries.
Variation Tip: You can fill the pancake with sautéed fruit for a healthy spin.
Nutritional Information Per Serving: Calories: 428 | Fat: 19g | Sodium: 543mg | Carbs: 56g | Fiber: 0g | Sugar: 42g | Protein: 8g

Chapter 2 Snacks and Appetizer Recipes

26	Beet Chips	33	Mini Hot Dogs
26	Crispy Prawns	33	Roasted Peanuts
26	Onion Rings	33	Glazed Chicken Wings
27	Cod Nuggets	34	Zucchini Fries
27	Crispy Avocado Fries	34	Baked Mozzarella Sticks
27	Fiesta Chicken Fingers	34	Tortilla Chips
28	Carrot Chips	35	Persimmon Chips
28	Pumpkin Fries	35	Spicy Carrot Fries
28	Cheesy Broccoli Bites	35	Potato Bread Rolls
29	Pasta Chips	36	Spicy Spinach Chips
29	Beef Taquitos	36	Bacon-Wrapped Filled Jalapeno
29	Risotto Bites	36	Tofu Nuggets
30	Roasted Cashews	37	Air Fryer Ravioli
30	Potato Chips	37	French Toast Bites
30	Potato Croquettes	37	Air Fryer Blueberry Bread
31	Fried Pickles	38	Corn on the Cob
31	Ranch Kale Chips	38	Air Fryer Sweet Potato Tots
31	Avocado Fries	38	Air Fryer Pop-Tarts
32	Baked Potatoes	39	Cauliflower Poppers
32	Buttermilk Biscuits	39	Vegan Dehydrated Cookies
32	Eggplant Fries	39	Salt and Vinegar Cucumber Chips

Beet Chips

Prep Time: 10 minutes | Cook Time: 15 minutes | Serves: 6

Ingredients:

4 medium beetroots, peeled and thinly sliced
2 tablespoons olive oil
¼ teaspoon smoked paprika
Salt, to taste

Preparation:

1. In a large bowl and mix together all the ingredients. 2. Press "Power" button of Ninja Foodi XL Pro Air Oven and select "Air Fry" function. Select 2 LEVEL. 3. Press TEMP/SHADE +/- buttons to set the temperature at 325°F/160°C. 4. Now press TIME/SLICES +/- buttons to set the cooking time to 15 minutes. 5. Press "Start/Stop" button to start. 6. When the unit beeps to show that it is preheated, open the oven door. 7. Separate the beetroot chips into the air fry basket on Level 4 and sheet pan on Level 2. 8. Toss the beet chips once halfway through. 9. When cooking time is completed, open the oven door and transfer the beet chips onto a platter. 10. Serve at room temperature.

Serving Suggestions: Serve with a sprinkling of cinnamon.
Variation Tip: For a beautiful presentation, use colorful beets.
Nutritional Information per Serving: Calories: 70 | Fat: 4.8g | Sat Fat: 0.7g | Carbohydrates: 6.7g | Fiber: 1.4g | Sugar: 5.3g | Protein: 1.1g

Crispy Prawns

Prep Time: 15 minutes | Cook Time: 8 minutes | Serves: 4

Ingredients:

1 egg
½ pound nacho chips, crushed
12 prawns, peeled and deveined

Preparation:

1. In a shallow dish, beat the egg. 2. In another shallow dish, place the crushed nacho chips. 3. Coat the prawn into egg and then roll into nacho chips. 4. Press "Power" button of Ninja Foodi XL Pro Air Oven and select "Air Fry" function. 5. Press TEMP/SHADE +/- buttons to set the temperature at 355°F/180°C. 6. Now press TIME/SLICES +/- buttons to set the cooking time to 8 minutes. 7. Press "Start/Stop" button to start. 8. When the unit beeps to show that it is preheated, open the oven door. 9. Arrange the prawns into the air fry basket on Level 3. 10. When cooking time is completed, open the oven door and serve immediately.

Serving Suggestions: Serve alongside your favorite dip.
Variation Tip: Make sure to pat dry the shrimp thoroughly before applying the coating.
Nutritional Information per Serving: Calories: 386 | Fat: 17g | Sat Fat: 2.9g | Carbohydrates: 36.1g | Fiber: 2.6g | Sugar: 2.2g | Protein: 21g

Onion Rings

Prep Time: 15 minutes | Cook Time: 15 minutes | Serves: 4

Ingredients:

½ cup all-purpose flour
1 teaspoon paprika
1 teaspoon salt, divided
½ cup buttermilk
1 egg
1 cup panko breadcrumbs
2 tablespoons olive oil
1 sweet onion, sliced into rings

Preparation:

1. Mix flour with paprika and salt on a plate. 2. Coat the onion rings with the flour mixture. 3. Beat egg with buttermilk in a bowl and dip all the onion rings. 4. Spread the breadcrumbs in a bowl. 5. Coat the onion rings with breadcrumbs. 6. Place the onion rings in the air fry basket and spray them with cooking oil. 7. Transfer the basket to the 3rd rack position of Ninja Foodi XL Pro Air Oven and close the door. 8. Select the "Air Fry" Mode using FUNCTION +/- buttons and select Rack Level 3. 9. Set its cooking time to 15 minutes and temperature to 400°F/200°C, then press "START/STOP" to initiate cooking. 10. Serve warm.

Serving Suggestion: Serve the onion rings with chili sauce or mayo dip.
Variation Tip: Coat the onion rings with parmesan cheese.
Nutritional Information Per Serving: Calories 106 | Fat 5g | Sodium 244mg | Carbs 16g | Fiber 1g | Sugar 1g | Protein 7g

Cod Nuggets

Prep Time: 15 minutes | Cook Time: 18 minutes | Serves: 5

Ingredients:
- 1 cup all-purpose flour
- 2 eggs
- ¾ cup breadcrumbs
- Pinch of salt
- 2 tablespoons olive oil
- 1 pound cod, cut into 1x2½-inch strips

Preparation:
1. In a shallow dish, place the flour. 2. Crack the eggs in a second dish and beat well. 3. In a third dish, mix together the breadcrumbs, salt and oil. 4. Coat the nuggets with flour, then dip into beaten eggs and finally, coat with the breadcrumbs. 5. Press "Power" button of Ninja Foodi XL Pro Air Oven and select "Air Fry" function. 6. Press TEMP/SHADE +/- buttons to set the temperature at 390°F/200°C. 7. Now press TIME/SLICES +/- buttons to set the cooking time to 8 minutes. 8. Press "START/STOP" button to start. 9. When the unit beeps to show that it is preheated, open the lid. 10. Arrange the nuggets in air fry basket and insert in the oven. 11. When cooking time is completed, open the lid and transfer the nuggets onto a platter. 12. Serve warm.

Serving Suggestions: Enjoy with tartar sauce.
Variation Tip: Use fresh fish.
Nutritional Information per Serving: Calories: 323 | Fat: 9.2g | Sat Fat: 1.7g | Carbohydrates: 30.9g | Fiber: 1.4g | Sugar: 1.2g | Protein: 27.7g

Crispy Avocado Fries

Prep Time: 15 minutes | Cook Time: 7 minutes | Serves: 2

Ingredients:
- ¼ cup all-purpose flour
- Salt and ground black pepper, as required
- 1 egg
- 1 teaspoon water
- ½ cup panko breadcrumbs
- 1 avocado, peeled, pitted, and sliced into 8 pieces
- Non-stick cooking spray

Preparation:
1. In a shallow bowl, mix together the flour, salt, and black pepper. 2. In a second bowl, mix well egg and water. 3. In a third bowl, put the breadcrumbs. 4. Coat the avocado slices with flour mixture, then dip into egg mixture and finally, coat evenly with the breadcrumbs. 5. Now, spray the avocado slices evenly with cooking spray. 6. Press "Power" button of Ninja Foodi XL Pro Air Oven and select "Air Fry" function. 7. Press TEMP/SHADE +/- buttons to set the temperature at 400°F/200°C. 8. Now press TIME/SLICES +/- buttons to set the cooking time to 7 minutes. 9. Press "Start/Stop" button to start. 10. When the unit beeps to show that it is preheated, open the oven door. 11. Arrange the avocado fries into the air fry basket on Ninja sheet pan on Level 3. 12. When cooking time is completed, open the oven door, and transfer the avocado fries onto a platter. 13. Serve warm.

Serving Suggestions: Serve with ketchup.
Variation Tip: Make sure to use firm avocados that are not too ripe.
Nutritional Information per Serving:
Calories: 391 | Fat: 23.8g | Sat Fat: 5.6g | Carbohydrates: 24.8g | Fiber: 7.3g | Sugar: 0.8g | Protein: 7g

Fiesta Chicken Fingers

Prep Time: 15 minutes | Cook Time: 12 minutes | Serves: 4

Ingredients:
- ¾-pound boneless chicken breasts, cut into strips
- ½ cup buttermilk
- ¼ teaspoon pepper
- 1 cup all-purpose flour
- 3 cups corn chips, crushed
- 1 envelope taco seasoning
- Sour cream ranch dip or salsa

Preparation:
1. Coat the chicken with pepper and flour. 2. Mix corn chips with taco seasoning. 3. Dip the chicken fingers in the buttermilk, then coat with the corn chips. 4. Place the chicken fingers in the air fry basket and spray with cooking oil. 5. Transfer the basket to the 4th rack position of Ninja Foodi XL Pro Air Oven and close the door. 6. Select the "Air Fry" Mode using FUNCTION +/- buttons and select Rack Level 4. 7. Set its cooking time to 12 minutes and temperature to 325°F/160°C, then press "START/STOP" to initiate cooking. 8. Flip the chicken fingers once cooked halfway through, then resume cooking. 9. Serve warm with sour cream ranch dip or fresh salsa.

Serving Suggestion: Serve the chicken fingers with chili garlic sauce.
Variation Tip: Use mayonnaise to coat the fingers for a rich taste.
Nutritional Information Per Serving: Calories 218 | Fat 12g | Sodium 710mg | Carbs 44g | Fiber 5g | Sugar 3g | Protein 24g

Carrot Chips

Prep Time: 15 minutes | Cook Time: 15 minutes | Serves: 8

Ingredients:

- 2 pounds carrots, sliced
- ¼ cup olive oil
- 1 tablespoon of sea salt
- 1 teaspoon ground cumin
- 1 teaspoon ground cinnamon

Preparation:

1. Toss the carrot slices with oil, cumin, and cinnamon in a large bowl. 2. Grease the sheet pan and spread the carrot slices in it. 3. Transfer the sheet pan to the 2nd rack position of Ninja Foodi XL Pro Air Oven and close the door. 4. Select the "Bake" Mode using FUNCTION +/- buttons and select Rack Level 2. 5. Set its cooking time to 15 minutes and temperature to 450°F/230°C, then press "START/STOP" to initiate cooking. 6. Flip the chips after 7-8 minutes of cooking and resume baking. 7. Serve fresh.

Serving Suggestion: Serve the chips with tomato ketchup or cheese dip.
Variation Tip: Toss the carrot chips with maple-honey syrup to coat.
Nutritional Information Per Serving: Calories 182 | Fat 2g | Sodium 350mg | Carbs 12.2g | Fiber 0.7g | Sugar 1g | Protein 4.3g

Pumpkin Fries

Prep Time: 15 minutes | Cook Time: 12 minutes | Serves: 6

Ingredients:

- ½ cup plain Greek yogurt
- 2 tablespoons maple syrup
- 3 teaspoons chipotle peppers in adobo sauce
- ⅛ teaspoon salt
- 1 medium pie pumpkin
- ¼ teaspoon garlic powder
- ¼ teaspoon ground cumin
- ¼ teaspoon chili powder
- ¼ teaspoon pepper

Preparation:

1. Peel and cut the pumpkin into sticks. 2. Mix garlic powder, cumin, chili powder, salt, and black pepper. 3. Coat the pumpkin sticks with the spice mixture. 4. Spread the pumpkin fries in the air fry basket and spray them with cooking spray. 5. Transfer the basket to the 3rd rack position of Ninja Foodi XL Pro Air Oven and close the door. 6. Select the "Air Fry" Mode using FUNCTION +/- buttons and select Rack Level 3. 7. Set its cooking time to 12 minutes and temperature to 400°F/200°C, then press "START/STOP" to initiate cooking. 8. Toss the fries once cooked halfway through, then resume cooking. 9. Mix yogurt with maple syrup and adobo sauce in a bowl. 10. Serve fries with its sauce.

Serving Suggestion: Serve the pumpkin chips with tomato ketchup.
Variation Tip: Coat the pumpkin fries with breadcrumbs before cooking.
Nutritional Information Per Serving: Calories 215 | Fat 16g | Sodium 255mg | Carbs 31g | Fiber 1.2g | Sugar 5g | Protein 4.1g

Cheesy Broccoli Bites

Prep Time: 15 minutes | Cook Time: 12 minutes | Serves: 5

Ingredients:

- 1 cup broccoli florets
- 1 egg, beaten
- ¾ cup cheddar cheese, grated
- 2 tablespoons Parmesan cheese, grated
- ¾ cup panko breadcrumbs
- Salt and freshly ground black pepper, as needed

Preparation:

1. In a food processor, add the broccoli and pulse until finely crumbled. 2. In a large bowl, mix together the broccoli and remaining ingredients. 3. Make small equal-sized balls from the mixture. 4. Press "Power" button of Ninja Foodi XL Pro Air Oven and select "Air Fry" function. 5. Press TEMP/SHADE +/- buttons to set the temperature at 350°F/175°C. 6. Now press TIME/SLICES +/- buttons to set the cooking time to 12 minutes. 7. Press "Start/Stop" button to start. 8. When the unit beeps to show that it is preheated, open the oven door. 9. Arrange the broccoli balls into the air fry basket on Level 3. 10. When cooking time is completed, open the oven door and transfer the broccoli bites onto a platter. 11. Serve warm.

Serving Suggestions: Serve with your favorite dipping sauce.
Variation Tip: You can use cheese of your choice.
Nutritional Information per Serving: Calories: 153 | Fat: .2g | Sat Fat: 4.5g | Carbohydrates: 4g | Fiber: 0.5g | Sugar: 0.5g | Protein: 7.1g

Pasta Chips

Prep Time: 15 minutes | Cook Time: 10 minutes | Serves: 4

Ingredients:

½ tablespoon olive oil
½ tablespoon nutritional yeast
1 cup bow tie pasta
⅔ teaspoon Italian Seasoning Blend
¼ teaspoon salt

Preparation:

1. Cook and boil the pasta in salted water half of the time as stated on the box, then drain it. 2. Toss the boiled pasta with salt, Italian seasoning, nutritional yeast, and olive oil in a bowl. 3. Spread this pasta in the air fry basket. 4. Transfer the basket to the 3rd rack position of Ninja Foodi XL Pro Air Oven and close the door. 5. Select the "Air Fry" Mode using FUNCTION +/- buttons and select Rack Level 3. 6. Set its cooking time to 5 minutes and temperature to 390°F/200°C, then press "START/STOP" to initiate cooking. 7. Toss the pasta and continue air frying for another 5 minutes. 8. Enjoy.
Serving Suggestion: Serve the chips with white cheese dip.
Variation Tip: Drizzle white peppers ground on top before baking.
Nutritional Information Per Serving: Calories 167 | Fat 2g | Sodium 48mg | Carbs 26g | Fiber 2g | Sugar 0g | Protein 1g

Beef Taquitos

Prep Time: 15 minutes | Cook Time: 8 minutes | Serves: 6

Ingredients:

6 corn tortillas
2 cups cooked beef, shredded
½ cup onion, chopped
1 cup pepper jack cheese, shredded
Olive oil cooking spray

Preparation:

1. Arrange the tortillas onto a smooth surface. 2. Place the shredded meat over one corner of each tortilla, followed by onion and cheese. 3. Roll each tortilla to secure the filling and secure with toothpicks. 4. Spray each taquito with cooking spray evenly. 5. Arrange the taquitos onto the greased sheet pan. 6. Place the tofu mixture in the greased sheet pan. 7. Press "Power" button of Ninja Foodi XL Pro Air Oven and select "Air Fry" function. 8. Press TEMP/SHADE +/- buttons to set the temperature at 400°F/200°C. 9. Now press TIME/SLICES +/- buttons to set the cooking time to 8 minutes. 10. Press "START/STOP" button to start. 11. When the unit beeps to show that it is preheated, open the lid and insert the sheet pan in oven. 12. When cooking time is completed, open the lid and transfer the taquitos onto a platter. 13. Serve warm.
Serving Suggestions: Serve with yogurt dip.
Variation Tip: You can use any kind of cooked meat in this recipe.
Nutritional Information per Serving: Calories: 228 | Fat: 9.6g | Sat Fat: 4.8g | Carbohydrates: 12.3g | Fiber: 1.7g | Sugar: 0.6g | Protein: 22.7g

Risotto Bites

Prep Time: 15 minutes | Cook Time: 10 minutes | Serves: 4

Ingredients:

1½ cups cooked risotto
3 tablespoons Parmesan cheese, grated
½ egg, beaten
1½ ounces mozzarella cheese, cubed
⅓ cup breadcrumbs

Preparation:

1. In a bowl, add the risotto, Parmesan and egg and mix until well combined. 2. Make 20 equal-sized balls from the mixture. 3. Insert a mozzarella cube in the center of each ball. 4. With your fingers smooth the risotto mixture to cover the ball. 5. In a shallow dish, place the breadcrumbs. 6. Coat the balls with the breadcrumbs evenly. 7. Press "Power" button of Ninja Foodi XL Pro Air Oven and select "Air Fry" function. Select 2 LEVEL. 8. Press TEMP/SHADE +/- buttons to set the temperature at 390°F/200°C. 9. Now press TIME/SLICES +/- buttons to set the cooking time to 10 minutes. 10. Press "Start/Stop" button to start. 11. When the unit beeps to show that it is preheated, open the oven door. 12. Separate 10 balls into the air fry basket on Level 3 and 10 into Ninja sheet pan on Level 1. 13. When cooking time is completed, open the oven door, and transfer the risotto bites onto a platter. 14. Serve warm.
Serving Suggestions: Serve with blue cheese dip.
Variation Tip: Make sure to use dry breadcrumbs.
Nutritional Information per Serving: Calories: 340 | Fat: 4.3g | Sat Fat: 2g | Carbohydrates: 62.4g | Fiber: 1.3g | Sugar: 0.7g | Protein: 11.3g

Roasted Cashews

Prep Time: 5 minutes | Cook Time: 5 minutes | Serves: 6

Ingredients:

1½ cups raw cashew nuts
1 teaspoon butter, melted

Salt and freshly ground black pepper, as required

Preparation:

1. In a bowl, mix all the ingredients together. 2. Press "Power" button of Ninja Foodi XL Pro Air Oven and select "Air Fry" function. 3. Press TEMP/SHADE +/- buttons to set the temperature at 355°F/180°C. 4. Now press TIME/SLICES +/- buttons to set the cooking time to 5 minutes. 5. Press "Start/Stop" button to start. 6. When the unit beeps to show that it is preheated, open the oven door. 7. Arrange the cashews into the air fry basket on sheet pan on Level 3. 8. Shake the cashews once halfway through. 9. When cooking time is completed, open the oven door, and transfer the cashews into a heatproof bowl. 10. Serve warm.

Serving Suggestions: Serve with a sprinkling of little salt.
Variation Tip: Make sure to use raw walnuts.
Nutritional Information per Serving: Calories: 202 | Fat: 16.5g | Sat Fat: 3.5g | Carbohydrates: 11.2g | Fiber: 1g | Sugar: 1.7g | Protein: 5.3g

Potato Chips

Prep Time: 15 minutes | Cook Time: 25 minutes | Serves: 2

Ingredients:

1 medium Russet potato, sliced
1 tablespoon canola oil
¼ teaspoon sea salt

¼ teaspoon black pepper
1 teaspoon chopped fresh rosemary

Preparation:

1. Fill a suitable glass bowl with cold water and add sliced potatoes. 2. Leave the potatoes for 20 minutes, then drain them. Pat dry the chips with a paper towel. 3. Toss the potatoes with salt, black pepper, and oil to coat well. 4. Spread the potato slices in the air fry basket evenly. 5. Transfer the basket to the 3rd rack position of Ninja Foodi XL Pro Air Oven and close the door. 6. Select the "Air Fry" Mode using FUNCTION +/- buttons and select Rack Level 3. 7. Set its cooking time to 25 minutes and temperature to 375°F/190°C, then press "START/STOP" to initiate cooking. 8. Garnish with rosemary. 9. Serve warm.

Serving Suggestion: Serve the chips with tomato sauce.
Variation Tip: Toss the potato chips with paprika.
Nutritional Information Per Serving: Calories 134 | Fat 3g | Sodium 216mg | Carbs 27g | Fiber 3g | Sugar 4g | Protein 1g

Potato Croquettes

Prep Time: 15 minutes | Cook Time: 8 minutes | Serves: 4

Ingredients:

2 medium Russet potatoes, peeled and cubed
2 tablespoons all-purpose flour
½ cup Parmesan cheese, grated
1 egg yolk
2 tablespoons fresh chives, minced

Pinch of ground nutmeg
Salt and freshly ground black pepper, as needed
2 eggs
½ cup breadcrumbs
2 tablespoons vegetable oil

Preparation:

1. In a pan of a boiling water, add the potatoes and cook for about 15 minutes. 2. Drain the potatoes well and transfer into a large bowl. 3. With a potato masher, mash the potatoes and set aside to cool completely. 4. In the bowl of mashed potatoes, add the flour, Parmesan cheese, egg yolk, chives, nutmeg, salt, and black pepper and mix until well combined. 5. Make small equal-sized balls from the mixture. 6. Now, roll each ball into a cylinder shape. 7. In a shallow dish, crack the eggs and beat well. 8. In another dish, mix the breadcrumbs and oil together. 9. Dip the croquettes in egg mixture and then coat with the breadcrumb mixture. 10. Press "Power" button of Ninja Foodi XL Pro Air Oven and select "Air Fry" function. 11. Press TEMP/SHADE +/- buttons to set the temperature at 390°F/200°C. 12. Now press TIME/SLICES +/- buttons to set the cooking time to 8 minutes. 13. Press "START/STOP" button to start. 14. When the unit beeps to show that it is preheated, open the lid. 15. Arrange the croquettes in air fry basket and insert in the oven. 16. When cooking time is completed, open the lid and transfer the croquettes onto a platter. 17. Serve warm.

Serving Suggestions: Serve with mustard sauce.
Variation Tip: Make sure to use dried breadcrumbs.
Nutritional Information per Serving: Calories: 283 | Fat: 13.4g | Sat Fat: 3.8g | Carbohydrates: 29.9g | Fiber: 3.3g | Sugar: 2.3g | Protein: 11.5g

Fried Pickles

Prep Time: 10 minutes | Cook Time: 15 minutes | Serves: 4

Ingredients:

- ½ cup Italian style bread crumbs
- ½ cup panko bread crumbs
- ¼ cup parmesan cheese
- 1 tablespoon garlic powder
- 1 teaspoon Cajun seasoning
- 2 eggs
- 1½ cups dill pickles, sliced and drained
- Cooking spray

Preparation:

1. In a mixing bowl, combine Italian-style bread crumbs, Panko bread crumbs, Parmesan cheese, garlic powder, and Cajun spice. 2. Whisk together the eggs in a separate bowl. 3. Cover the slightly dry pickle slices completely with egg using a fork. 4. Dip the pickle slices in the breadcrumb mixture and completely coat them. 5. Using nonstick cooking spray, lightly coat the air fry basket. Place the pickle slices in the air fry basket gently. 6. Turn on Ninja Foodi XL Pro Air Oven and select "Air Fry". 7. Select the timer for 10 minutes and the temperature for 360°F/180°C. 8. When the unit beeps to signify it has preheated, open the oven and slide the air fry basket into the rail of Level 3 in oven. 9. When the fried pickles are done, carefully remove them with tongs from the Ninja Foodi and serve.

Serving Suggestions: Serve with your favorite ranch dressing.
Variation Tip: You can use any pickle.
Nutritional Information per Serving: Calories: 150 | Fat: 5g | Sat Fat: 2g | Carbohydrates: 17g | Fiber: 2g | Sugar: 2g | Protein: 8g

Ranch Kale Chips

Prep Time: 15 minutes | Cook Time: 5 minutes | Serves: 6

Ingredients:

- 2 tablespoons olive oil
- 4 cups kale leaves
- 2 teaspoons vegan ranch seasoning
- 1 tablespoon nutritional yeast flakes
- ¼ teaspoon salt

Preparation:

1. Toss the kale leaves with oil, salt, yeast, and ranch seasoning in a large bowl. 2. Spread the seasoned kale leaves in the oven. 3. Transfer the air fry basket to the 3rd rack position of Ninja Foodi XL Pro Air Oven and close the door. 4. Select the "Air Fry" Mode using FUNCTION +/- buttons and select Rack Level 3. 5. Set its cooking time to 5 minutes and temperature to 370°F/185°C, then press "START/STOP" to initiate cooking. 6. Serve warm.

Serving Suggestion: Serve the chips with a cream cheese dip on the side.
Variation Tip: Drizzle shredded parmesan on top before cooking.
Nutritional Information Per Serving: Calories 123 | Fat 8g | Sodium 146mg | Carbs 8g | Fiber 5g | Sugar 1g | Protein 7g

Avocado Fries

Prep Time: 15 minutes | Cook Time: 20 minutes | Serves: 4

Ingredients:

- ½ cup panko breadcrumbs
- ½ teaspoon salt
- 1 avocado, peeled, pitted, and sliced
- 1 cup egg, whisked

Preparation:

1. Toss breadcrumbs with salt in a shallow bowl. 2. First, dip the avocado strips in the egg, then coat them with panko. 3. Spread these slices in the air fry basket. 4. Transfer the sandwich to the 2nd rack position of Ninja Foodi XL Pro Air Oven and close the door. 5. Select the "Bake" Mode using FUNCTION +/- buttons and select Rack Level 2. 6. Set its cooking time to 20 minutes and temperature to 400°F/200°C, then press "START/STOP" to initiate cooking. 7. Serve fresh.

Serving Suggestion: Serve the fries with chili sauce or mayonnaise dip.
Variation Tip: Coat the fries with crushed cornflakes for crisper.
Nutritional Information Per Serving: Calories 110 | Fat 9g | Sodium 318mg | Carbs 19g | Fiber 5g | Sugar 3g | Protein 7g

Baked Potatoes

Prep Time: 15 minutes | Cook Time: 45 minutes | Serves: 3

Ingredients:

3 russet potatoes, scrubbed and rinsed
Cooking spray
½ teaspoon sea salt
½ teaspoon garlic powder

Preparation:

1. Rub the potatoes with salt and garlic powder. 2. Place the potatoes in the air fry basket and spray with cooking spray. 3. Transfer the basket to the 2nd rack position of Ninja Foodi XL Pro Air Oven and close the door. 4. Select the "Bake" Mode using FUNCTION +/- buttons and select Rack Level 2. 5. Set its cooking time to 45 minutes and temperature to 350°F/175°C, then press "START/STOP" to initiate cooking. 6. Make a slit on top of the potatoes and score the flesh inside. 7. Serve warm.

Serving Suggestion: Serve the baked potatoes with butter sauce or mayo dip.
Variation Tip: Add shredded cheese and crumbled bacon to the toppings.
Nutritional Information Per Serving: Calories 269 | Fat 5g | Sodium 510mg | Carbs 37g | Fiber 5g | Sugar 4g | Protein 1g

Buttermilk Biscuits

Prep Time: 15 minutes | Cook Time: 8 minutes | Serves: 8

Ingredients:

½ cup cake flour
1¼ cups all-purpose flour
¼ teaspoon baking soda
½ teaspoon baking powder
1 teaspoon granulated sugar
Salt, to taste
¼ cup cold unsalted butter, cut into cubes
¾ cup buttermilk
2 tablespoons butter, melted

Preparation:

1. In a large bowl, sift together flours, baking soda, baking powder, sugar and salt. 2. With a pastry cutter, cut cold butter and mix until coarse crumb forms. 3. Slowly, add buttermilk and mix until a smooth dough forms. 4. Place the dough onto a floured surface and with your hands, press it into ½ inch thickness. 5. With a 1¾-inch round cookie cutter, cut the biscuits. 6. Arrange the biscuits into sheet pan and coat with the butter. 7. Press "Power" button of Ninja Foodi XL Pro Air Oven and select "Air Fry" function. 8. Press TEMP/SHADE +/- buttons to set the temperature at 400°F/200°C. 9. Now press TIME/SLICES +/- buttons to set the cooking time to 8 minutes. 10. Press "Start/Stop" button to start. 11. When the unit beeps to show that it is preheated, open the oven door. 12. Arrange pan over the wire rack on Level 3. 13. When cooking time is completed, open the oven door and place the sheet pan onto a wire rack for about 5 minutes. 14. Carefully invert the biscuits onto the wire rack to cool completely before serving.

Serving Suggestions: Serve with the drizzling of melted butter.
Variation Tip: Shortening can also be used instead of butter.
Nutritional Information per Serving: Calories: 187 | Fat: 9.1g | Sat Fat: 5.6g | Carbohydrates: 22.6g | Fiber: 0.8g | Sugar: 1.7g | Protein: 3.7g

Eggplant Fries

Prep Time: 15 minutes | Cook Time: 10 minutes | Serves: 4

Ingredients:

2 large eggs
½ cup grated Parmesan cheese
½ cup toasted wheat germ
1 teaspoon Italian seasoning
¾ teaspoon garlic salt
1 (1 ¼ pounds) eggplant, peeled
Cooking spray
1 cup marinara sauce, warmed

Preparation:

1. Cut the eggplant into sticks. 2. In a bowl, whisk the eggs. Mix parmesan cheese, wheat germ, seasoning, and garlic salt in another bowl. 3. Coat the eggplant sticks first with the eggs then into the parmesan mixture. 4. Place the eggplant fries in the air fry basket and spray them with cooking spray. 5. Transfer the basket to the 3rd rack position of Ninja Foodi XL Pro Air Oven and close the door. 6. Select the "Air Fry" Mode using FUNCTION +/- buttons and select Rack Level 3. 7. Set its cooking time to 10 minutes and temperature to 375°F/190°C, then press "START/STOP" to initiate cooking. 8. Serve warm with marinara sauce.

Serving Suggestion: Serve the eggplant fries with tomato sauce.
Variation Tip: Drizzle paprika on top for more spice.
Nutritional Information Per Serving: Calories 201 | Fat 7g | Sodium 269mg | Carbs 35g | Fiber 4g | Sugar 12g | Protein 6g

Mini Hot Dogs

Prep Time: 15 minutes | Cook Time: 4 minutes | Serves: 8

Ingredients:

- 8 ounces refrigerated crescent rolls
- 24 cocktail hot dogs

Preparation:

1. Spread the crescent rolls into 8 triangles and cut each into 3 triangles. 2. Place one mini hot dog at the center of each crescent roll. 3. Wrap the rolls around the hot dog and place them in the air fry basket. 4. Transfer the basket to the 3rd rack position of Ninja Foodi XL Pro Air Oven and close the door. 5. Select the "Air Fry" Mode using FUNCTION +/- buttons and select Rack Level 3. 6. Set its cooking time to 4 minutes and temperature to 325°F/160°C, then press "START/STOP" to initiate cooking. 7. Serve warm.

Serving Suggestion: Serve the hot dogs with tomato ketchup or cream cheese dip.
Variation Tip: Drizzle butter on top of the wrapped hot dogs.
Nutritional Information Per Serving: Calories 152 | Fat 4g | Sodium 232mg | Carbs 17g | Fiber 1g | Sugar 0g | Protein 24g

Roasted Peanuts

Prep Time: 5 minutes | Cook Time: 14 minutes | Serves: 6

Ingredients:

- 1½ cups raw peanuts
- Nonstick cooking spray

Preparation:

1. Press "Power" button of Ninja Foodi XL Pro Air Oven and select "Air Fry" function. 2. Press TEMP/SHADE +/- buttons to set the temperature at 320°F/160°C. 3. Now press TIME/SLICES +/- buttons to set the cooking time to 14 minutes. 4. Press "START/STOP" button to start. 5. When the unit beeps to show that it is preheated, open the lid. 6. Arrange the peanuts in air fry basket and insert in the oven. 7. While cooking, toss the peanuts twice. 8. After 9 minutes of cooking, spray the peanuts with cooking spray. 9. When cooking time is completed, open the lid and transfer the peanuts into a heatproof bowl. 10. Serve warm.

Serving Suggestions: Serve with a sprinkling of little cinnamon.
Variation Tip: Choose raw peanuts.
Nutritional Information per Serving: Calories: 207 | Fat: 18g | Sat Fat: 2.5g | Carbohydrates: 5.9g | Fiber: 3.1g | Sugar: 1.5g | Protein: 9.4g

Glazed Chicken Wings

Prep Time: 15 minutes | Cook Time: 25 minutes | Serves: 4

Ingredients:

- 1½ pounds chicken wingettes and drumettes
- ⅓ cup tomato sauce
- 2 tablespoons balsamic vinegar
- 2 tablespoons maple syrup
- ½ teaspoon liquid smoke
- ¼ teaspoon red pepper flakes, crushed
- Salt, as required

Preparation:

1. Arrange the wings onto the greased sheet pan. 2. Press "Power" button of Ninja Foodi XL Pro Air Oven and select "Air Fry" function. 3. Press TEMP/SHADE +/- buttons to set the temperature at 380°F/195°C. 4. Now press TIME/SLICES +/- buttons to set the cooking time to 25 minutes. 5. Press "START/STOP" button to start. 6. When the unit beeps to show that it is preheated, open the lid and insert the sheet pan in oven. 7. Meanwhile, in a small pan, add the remaining ingredients over medium heat and cook for about 10 minutes, stirring occasionally. 8. When cooking time is completed, open the lid and place the chicken wings into a bowl. 9. Add the sauce and toss to coat well. 10. Serve immediately.

Serving Suggestions: Serve with your favorite dip.
Variation Tip: Honey can replace the maple syrup.
Nutritional Information per Serving: Calories: 356 | Fat: 12.7g | Sat Fat: 3.5g | Carbohydrates: 7.9g | Fiber: 0.3g | Sugar: 6.9g | Protein: 49.5g

Zucchini Fries

Prep Time: 10 minutes | Cook Time: 12 minutes | Serves: 4

Ingredients:

1 pound zucchini, sliced into 2½-inch sticks
Salt, as required
2 tablespoons olive oil
¾ cup panko breadcrumbs

Preparation:

1. In a colander, add the zucchini and sprinkle with salt. Set aside for about 10 minutes. 2. Gently pat dry the zucchini sticks with the paper towels and coat with oil. 3. In a shallow dish, add the breadcrumbs. 4. Coat the zucchini sticks with breadcrumbs evenly. 5. Press "Power" button of Ninja Foodi XL Pro Air Oven and select "Air Fry" function. 6. Press TEMP/SHADE +/- buttons to set the temperature at 400°F/200°C. 7. Now press TIME/SLICES +/- buttons to set the cooking time to 12 minutes. 8. Press "START/STOP" button to start. 9. When the unit beeps to show that it is preheated, open the lid. 10. Arrange the zucchini fries in air fry basket and insert in the oven. 11. When cooking time is completed, open the lid and transfer the zucchini fries onto a platter. 12. Serve warm.

Serving Suggestions: Serve with ketchup.
Variation Tip: You can use breadcrumbs of your choice.
Nutritional Information per Serving: Calories: 151 | Fat: 8.6g | Sat Fat: 1.6g | Carbohydrates: 6.9g | Fiber: 1.3g | Sugar: 2g | Protein: 1.9g

Baked Mozzarella Sticks

Prep Time: 5 minutes | Cook Time: 8 minutes | Serves: 6

Ingredients:

½ cup Italian Style bread crumbs
¾ cup panko break crumbs
¼ cup parmesan cheese
1 tablespoon garlic powder
12 mozzarella cheese sticks
Cooking spray

Preparation:

1. Make mozzarella sticks by freezing them for an hour or two. Take the mozzarella sticks out of the fridge and cut them in half so that each one is 2-3 inches long. 2. Combine the Panko, Italian Style bread crumbs, parmesan cheese, and garlic powder on a dish and stir well. 3. Whisk together the eggs in a separate bowl. 4. Cover the mozzarella stick completely with egg with a fork, then dip and totally cover the mozzarella stick in the breadcrumb mixture. 5. On a nonstick pan, arrange mozzarella sticks in a single layer. 6. Freeze for an hour and take the mozzarella sticks out of the freezer and dip them in the egg and breadcrumb mixture once more. 7. Using cooking spray, lightly coat the roast tray. Place the cheese sticks. 8. Insert the wire rack on Level 3. Turn on Ninja Foodi XL Pro Air Oven and select "Bake". 9. Select the timer for 10 minutes and the temperature for 360°F/180°C. 10. When the unit beeps to signify it has preheated, slide the roast tray onto the wire rack in the oven. 11. Remove and serve.

Serving Suggestions: Serve with marinara sauce.
Variation Tip: You can use any cheese sticks.
Nutritional Information per Serving: Calories: 130 | Fat: 8g | Sat Fat: 4g | Carbohydrates: 7g | Fiber: 1g | Sugar: 1g | Protein: 9g

Tortilla Chips

Prep Time: 10 minutes | Cook Time: 3 minutes | Serves: 3

Ingredients:

4 corn tortillas, cut into triangles
1 tablespoon olive oil
Salt, to taste

Preparation:

1. Coat the tortilla chips with oil and then sprinkle each side of the tortillas with salt. 2. Press "Power" button of Ninja Foodi XL Pro Air Oven and select "Air Fry" function. 3. Press TEMP/SHADE +/- buttons to set the temperature at 390°F/200°C. 4. Now press TIME/SLICES +/- buttons to set the cooking time to 3 minutes. 5. Press "START/STOP" button to start. 6. When the unit beeps to show that it is preheated, open the lid. 7. Arrange the tortilla chips in air fry basket and insert in the oven. 8. When cooking time is completed, open the lid and transfer the tortilla chips onto a platter. 9. Serve warm.

Serving Suggestions: Serve with guacamole.
Variation Tip: Use whole grain tortillas.
Nutritional Information per Serving: Calories: 110 | Fat: 5.6g | Sat Fat: 0.8g | Carbohydrates: 14.3g | Fiber: 2g | Sugar: 0.3g | Protein: 1.8g

Persimmon Chips

Prep Time: 10 minutes | Cook Time: 10 minutes | Serves: 2

Ingredients:

- 2 ripe persimmons, cut into slices horizontally
- Salt and ground black pepper, as required

Preparation:

1. Arrange the persimmons slices onto the greased sheet pan. 2. Press "Power" button of Ninja Foodi XL Pro Air Oven and select "Air Fry" function. 3. Press TEMP/SHADE +/- buttons to set the temperature at 400°F/200°C. 4. Now press TIME/SLICES +/- buttons to set the cooking time to 10 minutes. 5. Press "START/STOP" button to start. 6. When the unit beeps to show that it is preheated, open the lid. 7. Insert the sheet pan in oven. 8. Flip the chips once halfway through. 9. When cooking time is completed, open the lid and transfer the chips onto a platter. 10. Serve warm.

Serving Suggestions: Serve with a sprinkling of ground cinnamon.
Variation Tip: You can use these chips in a homemade trail mix.
Nutritional Information per Serving: Calories: 32 | Fat: 0.1g | Sat Fat: 0g | Carbohydrates: 8.4g | Fiber: 0g | Sugar: 0g | Protein: 0.2g

Spicy Carrot Fries

Prep Time: 10 minutes | Cook Time: 12 minutes | Serves: 2

Ingredients:

- 1 large carrot, peeled and cut into sticks
- 1 tablespoon fresh rosemary, chopped finely
- 1 tablespoon olive oil
- ¼ teaspoon cayenne pepper
- Salt and ground black pepper, as required

Preparation:

1. In a bowl, add all the ingredients and mix well. 2. Press "Power" button of Ninja Foodi XL Pro Air Oven and select "Air Fry" function. 3. Press TEMP/SHADE +/- buttons to set the temperature at 390°F/200°C. 4. Now press TIME/SLICES +/- buttons to set the cooking time to 12 minutes. 5. Press "Start/Stop" button to start. 6. When the unit beeps to show that it is preheated, open the oven door. 7. Arrange the carrot fries into the air fry basket on Level 3. 8. When cooking time is completed, open the oven door and transfer the carrot fries onto a platter. 9. Serve warm.

Serving Suggestions: Serve with mustard sauce.
Variation Tip: You can add the spices of your choice.
Nutritional Information per Serving: Calories: 81 | Fat: 8.3g | Sat Fat: 1.1g | Carbohydrates: 4.7g | Fiber: 1.7g | Sugar: 1.8g | Protein: 0.4g

Potato Bread Rolls

Prep Time: 20 minutes | Cook Time: 33 minutes | Serves: 8

Ingredients:

- 5 large potatoes, peeled
- 2 tablespoons vegetable oil, divided
- 2 small onions, finely chopped
- 2 green chilies, seeded and chopped
- 2 curry leaves
- ½ teaspoon ground turmeric
- Salt, as required
- 8 bread slices, trimmed

Preparation:

1. In a pan of boiling water, add the potatoes and cook for about 15-20 minutes. 2. Drain the potatoes well and with a potato masher, mash the potatoes. 3. In a skillet, heat 1 teaspoon of oil over medium heat and sauté the onion for about 4-5 minutes. 4. Add the green chilies, curry leaves, and turmeric and sauté for about 1 minute. 5. Add the mashed potatoes and salt and mix well. 6. Remove from the heat and set aside to cool completely. 7. Make 8 equal-sized oval-shaped patties from the mixture. 8. Wet the bread slices completely with water. 9. Press each bread slice between your hands to remove the excess water. 10. Place 1 bread slice in your palm and place 1 patty in the center of the bread. 11. Roll the bread slice in a spindle shape and seal the edges to secure the filling. 12. Coat the roll with some oil. 13. Repeat with the remaining slices, filling and oil. 14. Press "Power" button of Ninja Foodi XL Pro Air Oven and select "Air Fry" function. Select 2 LEVEL. 15. Press TEMP/SHADE +/- buttons to set the temperature at 390°F/200°C. 16. Now press TIME/SLICES +/- buttons to set the cooking time to 13 minutes. 17. Press "Start/Stop" button to start. 18. When the unit beeps to show that it is preheated, open the oven door. 19. Separate the bread rolls into the air fry basket on Level 4 and sheet pan on wire rack on Level 2. 20. When cooking time is completed, open the oven door and transfer the rolls onto a platter. 21. Serve warm.

Serving Suggestions: Serve alongside the ketchup.
Variation Tip: Remove the moisture from bread slices completely.
Nutritional Information per Serving: Calories: 222 | Fat: 4g | Sat Fat: 0.8g | Carbohydrates: 42.5g | Fiber: 6.2g | Sugar: 3.8g | Protein: 4.8g

Spicy Spinach Chips

Prep Time: 10 minutes | Cook Time: 10 minutes | Serves: 4

Ingredients:

- 2 cups fresh spinach leaves, torn into bite-sized pieces
- ½ tablespoon coconut oil, melted
- ⅛ teaspoon garlic powder
- Salt, as required

Preparation:

1. In a large bowl, mix all the ingredients together. 2. Arrange the spinach pieces onto the greased sheet pan. 3. Press "Power" button of Ninja Foodi XL Pro Air Oven and select "Air Fry" function. 4. Press TEMP/SHADE +/- buttons to set the temperature at 300°F/150°C. 5. Now press TIME/SLICES +/- buttons to set the cooking time to 10 minutes. 6. Press "START/STOP" button to start. 7. When the unit beeps to show that it is preheated, open the lid. 8. Insert the sheet pan in oven. 9. Toss the spinach chips once halfway through. 10. When cooking time is completed, open the lid and transfer the spinach chips onto a platter. 11. Serve warm.

Serving Suggestions: Serve with a sprinkling of cayenne pepper.
Variation Tip: Make sure to pat dry the spinach leaves before using.
Nutritional Information per Serving: Calories: 18 | Fat: 1.5g | Sat Fat: 0g | Carbohydrates: 0.5g | Fiber: 0.3g | Sugar: 0.1g | Protein: 0.5g

Bacon-Wrapped Filled Jalapeno

Prep Time: 10 minutes | Cook Time: 15 minutes | Serves: 6

Ingredients:

- 12 jalapenos
- 226g cream cheese
- ½ cup cheddar cheese, shredded
- ¼ teaspoon garlic powder
- ⅛ teaspoon onion powder
- 12 slices bacon, thinly cut
- Salt and pepper, to taste

Preparation:

1. Discard the seeds from the jalapenos by cutting them in half and removing the stems. 2. Combine cream cheese, shredded cheddar cheese, garlic powder, onion powder, salt, and pepper. To blend, stir everything together. 3. Fill each jalapeno just to the top with the cream mixture using a tiny spoon. 4. Turn on Ninja Foodi XL Pro Air Oven and select "Bake". 5. Insert a wire rack on Level 3. Select the timer for 15 minute and temperature for 350°F/175°C. Press START/STOP to begin. 6. Cut each slice of bacon in half. 7. Wrap one piece of bacon around each half of a jalapeño. 8. In the sheet pan, arrange the bacon-wrapped filled jalapenos in an even layer. 9. When the unit beep to signify it has preheated, slide the sheet pan on wire rack in the oven. 10. Serve and enjoy!

Serving Suggestions: Serve with ketchup.
Variation Tip: You can also sprinkle black pepper on top.
Nutritional Information per Serving: Calories: 188 | Fat: 17g | Sat Fat: 10g | Carbohydrates: 4g | Fiber: 1g | Sugar: 3g | Protein: 5g

Tofu Nuggets

Prep Time: 10 minutes | Cook Time: 15 minutes | Serves: 4

Ingredients:

- 400g extra firm tofu
- ⅓ cup nutritional yeast
- ¼ cup water
- 1 tablespoon garlic powder
- 1 teaspoon onion powder
- 1 teaspoon sweet paprika
- 1 teaspoon poultry spice

Preparation:

1. Press the tofu for 10 minutes. 2. Add all ingredients to a bowl and stir to combine. 3. Over the bowl, break the tofu into bite-sized chunks. Use your thumb to create rough, rounded edges as you go. 4. Fold the chunks into the paste gently, taking care not to break the tofu. 5. Place the tofu in air fry basket in a single layer. 6. Turn on Ninja Foodi XL Pro Air Oven and select "Air Fry". 7. Select the timer for 15 minutes and the temperature for 350°F/175°C. 8. When the unit beeps to signified it has preheated, quickly open the oven and slide the air fry basket into the rail of Level 3. Close the oven door and let it cook. 9. Halfway through, pause and shake the basket. Serve immediately or save for later.

Serving Suggestions: Serve with any sauce.
Variation Tip: You can use black pepper instead of paprika.
Nutritional Information per Serving: Calories: 83 | Fat: 2g | Sat Fat: 1g | Carbohydrates: 6g | Fiber: 2g | Sugar: 1g | Protein: 11g

Air Fryer Ravioli

Prep Time: 5 minutes | Cook Time: 10 minutes | Serves: 2

Ingredients:
- 12 frozen ravioli
- ½ cup buttermilk
- ½ cup Italian breadcrumbs
- Cooking oil

Preparation:
1. Place two bowls next to each other. In one bowl, put the buttermilk, and in the other, put the breadcrumbs. 2. Dip Each ravioli piece in buttermilk and then breadcrumbs, making sure it is well coated. 3. Place each breaded ravioli in a single layer in the air fry basket and spritz the tops halfway through with oil. 4. Turn on Ninja Foodi XL Pro Air Oven and select "Air Fry". 5. Select the timer for 7 minutes and the temperature for 400°F/200°C. 6. When the unit beeps to signify it has preheated, open the oven and slide the air fry basket into the rail of Level 3. Close the oven and let it cook. 7. Remove from Ninja Foodi XL Pro Air Oven to serve hot.

Serving Suggestions: Top with fresh parsley.
Variation Tip: You can serve with garlic sauce.
Nutritional Information per Serving: Calories: 481 | Fat: 20g | Sat Fat: 7g | Carbohydrates: 56g | Fiber: 4g | Sugar: 9g | Protein: 20g

French Toast Bites

Prep Time: 5 minutes | Cook Time: 10 minutes | Serves: 2

Ingredients:
- ½ loaf of brioche bread
- 3 eggs
- 1 tablespoon milk
- 1 teaspoon vanilla
- ½ teaspoon cinnamon

Preparation:
1. In a large mixing bowl, cut half a loaf of bread into cubes. 2. Combine the eggs, milk, vanilla, and cinnamon in a small mixing dish. 3. Pour the mixture over the slices and toss to coat. 4. In a greased air fry basket, arrange bread slices in a single layer. 5. Place on the Level 3 in the oven. 6. Turn on Ninja Foodi XL Pro Air Oven and select "Air Fry". 7. Select the timer for 10 minutes and the temperature for 390°F/200°C. 8. Remove from Ninja Foodi XL Pro Air Oven to serve.

Serving Suggestions: Top with maple syrup.
Variation Tip: Sprinkle sugar on top before placing it in the oven.
Nutritional Information per Serving: Calories: 107 | Fat: 6.8g | Sat Fat: 2.1g | Carbohydrates: 1.9g | Fiber: 0.3g | Sugar: 1.1g | Protein: 8.6g

Air Fryer Blueberry Bread

Prep Time: 5 minutes | Cook Time: 30 minutes | Serves: 2 to 4

Ingredients:
- 1 cup milk
- 3 cups all-purpose baking mix
- ¼ cup protein powder
- 3 eggs
- 1½ cups frozen blueberries

Preparation:
1. Select the AIR FRY function, 350°F/175°C, for 30 minutes. While the oven is preheating, prepare the ingredients. 2. Mix the milk, baking mix, protein powder, eggs, and blueberries in a large bowl. 3. Empty the mixture into a greased loaf pan. 4. When the unit beeps to signify it has preheated, open the oven. 5. Insert the greased loaf pan on wire rack into rails of Level 3 and air fry for about 30 minutes.

Serving Suggestion: Drizzle on a little honey before serving.
Variation Tip: You can try using Greek yogurt instead of protein powder.
Nutritional Information Per Serving: Calories: 140 | Fat: 5g | Sodium: 333mg | Carbs: 18g | Fiber: 17g | Sugar: 1g | Protein: 5g

Corn on the Cob

Prep Time: 5 minutes | Cook Time: 13 minutes | Serves: 2

Ingredients:

- 2 ears corn
- 2 tablespoons butter, melted
- ½ teaspoon dried parsley
- ¼ teaspoon sea salt
- 2 tablespoons parmesan cheese, shredded

Preparation:

1. Remove any silk from both ears of corn. If desired, cut corns in half. 2. In a mixing dish, combine melted butter, parsley, and sea salt. Using a pastry brush, evenly coat the corn. If used, wrap corn with foil. 3. Place corn inside the roast tray side by side. 4. Turn on Ninja Foodi XL Pro Air Oven and select "Air Roast". 5. Select the timer for 12 minutes and the temperature for 350°F/175°C. 6. When the unit beeps to signify it has preheated, slide the roast tray on the sheet pan into the rail of Level 3. Close the oven door and let it cook. 7. Remove from Ninja Foodi XL Pro Air Oven to serve hot.

Serving Suggestions: Top with fresh parsley.
Variation Tip: You can use any cheese.
Nutritional Information per Serving: Calories: 199 | Fat: 14g | Sat Fat: 8g | Carbohydrates: 17g | Fiber: 2g | Sugar: 4g | Protein: 5g

Air Fryer Sweet Potato Tots

Prep Time: 20 minutes | Cook Time: 1 hour | Serves: 4

Ingredients:

- 14 ounces sweet potatoes, peeled
- 1 tablespoon potato starch
- ⅛ teaspoon garlic powder
- 1¼ teaspoons kosher salt
- ¾ cup no-salt-added ketchup
- Cooking spray

Preparation:

1. Take a medium pot of water and boil it over high heat. Add the potatoes and cook for about 15 minutes. Transfer the potatoes to a plate and let them cool for about 15 minutes. 2. Using the large holes of a box grater, grate the potatoes into a medium bowl. Gently toss them with the potato starch, 1 teaspoon of salt, and garlic powder. Then, shape the mixture into tot-shaped cylinders. 3. Select the AIR FRY function, 400°F/200°C, for 14 minutes. 4. Coat the air fry basket with cooking spray. Lay half of the tots in the air fry basket in a single layer and spray with more cooking spray. 5. When the unit beeps to signify it has preheated, open the oven and insert the air fry basket in rail of Level 3. 6. Cook the tots for about 12 to 14 minutes, turning them halfway through the cooking time. Repeat the same with the remaining tots.

Serving Suggestion: Sprinkle with salt and serve with ketchup.
Variation Tip: You can try cumin or chives instead of garlic powder.
Nutritional Information Per Serving: Calories: 78 | Fat: 0g | Sodium: 335mg | Carbs: 19g | Fiber: 2g | Sugar: 2g | Protein: 1g

Air Fryer Pop-Tarts

Prep Time: 10 minutes | Cook Time: 11 minutes | Serves: 6

Ingredients:

- 1 (15-ounce) package refrigerated pie crust
- 6 tablespoons grape jelly
- 2 cups powdered sugar
- 2 to 4 tablespoons heavy cream
- 2 tablespoons butter, melted
- 1 teaspoon vanilla extract
- Sprinkles, as required

Preparation:

1. Select the AIR FRY function, 350°F/175°C, for 11 minutes. Select 2 LEVEL. While the oven is preheating, prepare the ingredients. 2. Cut out 12 equal-size rectangles from the pie crust. 3. Place 1 tablespoon of grape jelly in the center of 6 of the rectangles. Spread out the jelly to within ¼ inch of the edge. Moisten the outside using your fingers and some water. 4. Then, place the plain rectangles on top of the jelly rectangles, and press the edges together with a fork. 5. Use a knife to poke a few slits in the top of each pop-tart. 6. Spray the air fry basket and sheet pan with cooking spray. 7. Place the rectangles evenly on your air fry basket and sheet pan. 8. When the unit beeps to signify it has preheated, open the oven and insert the sheet pan on Level 1 and air fry basket on Level 3. Cook 2 pop-tarts in it at a time. 9. Take out the pop tarts and let them cool completely. 10. To make the icing, mix the powdered sugar, heavy cream, butter, and vanilla extract in a bowl until smooth. Spread over the cooled pop-tarts and then decorate with sprinkles. 11. Let the icing harden in the refrigerator before serving.

Serving Suggestion: Drizzle on some honey along with the sprinkles.
Variation Tip: You can use strawberry jam instead.
Nutritional Information Per Serving: Calories: 219 | Fat: 11g | Sodium: 174mg | Carbs: 26g | Fiber: 1g | Sugar: 9g | Protein: 3g

Cauliflower Poppers

Prep Time: 10 minutes | Cook Time: 20 minutes | Serves: 6

Ingredients:

- 3 tablespoons olive oil
- 1 teaspoon paprika
- ½ teaspoon ground cumin
- ¼ teaspoon ground turmeric
- Salt and ground black pepper, as required
- 1 medium head cauliflower, cut into florets

Preparation:

1. In a bowl, place all ingredients and toss to coat well. 2. Place the cauliflower mixture in the greased sheet pan. 3. Press "Power" button of Ninja Foodi XL Pro Air Oven and select the "Bake" function. 4. Press TEMP/SHADE +/- buttons to set the temperature at 450°F/230°C. 5. Now press TIME/SLICES +/- buttons to set the cooking time to 20 minutes. 6. Press "START/STOP" button to start. 7. When the unit beeps to show that it is preheated, open the lid and insert the sheet pan in oven. 8. Flip the cauliflower mixture once halfway through. 9. When cooking time is completed, open the lid and transfer the cauliflower poppers onto a platter. 10. Serve warm.

Serving Suggestions: Serve with a squeeze of lemon juice.
Variation Tip: Feel free to use spices of your choice.
Nutritional Information per Serving: Calories: 73 | Fat: 7.1g | Sat Fat: 1g | Carbohydrates: 2.7g | Fiber: 1.3g | Sugar: 1.1g | Protein: 1g

Vegan Dehydrated Cookies

Prep Time: 10 minutes | Cook Time: 6 hours | Serves: 5 to 8

Ingredients:

- 2 apples
- 4 tablespoons flax seeds
- 1 teaspoon ground cinnamon
- ½ cup almonds
- ½ cup dates
- 4 cups oats

Preparation:

1. Firstly, wash, core, and chop the apples. 2. Place all the ingredients, except the oats, into a food processor and blend for a few seconds. 3. Take a large mixing bowl and place the blended mixture in it, then add 2 cups of oats and blend again. Add the remaining oats and mix with a spoon or your hands. 4. Make the dough into cookies, put them in the air fry basket and place the basket on Level 3 in the oven. 5. Select the DEHYDRATE function, 115°F/45°C, for 6 hours. Turn the cookies over after 4 hours.

Serving Suggestion: Sprinkle some flax seeds on the cookies before serving.
Variation Tip: You can use nutmeg or allspice instead of cinnamon.
Nutritional Information Per Serving: Calories: 72 | Fat: 1.8g | Sodium: 1mg | Carbs: 12.3g | Fiber: 2g | Sugar: 3.6 | Protein: 2g

Salt and Vinegar Cucumber Chips

Prep Time: 10 minutes | Cook Time: 3 to 4 hours | Serves: 6

Ingredients:

- 2 medium cucumbers
- 1 tablespoon olive oil
- 1 teaspoon salt
- 2 teaspoons apple cider vinegar

Preparation:

1. Slice the cucumbers very thin. Pat dry the slices with power towels to remove their moisture. 2. Transfer the slices to a large bowl and add the olive oil, apple cider vinegar, and salt. Gently toss to combine. 3. Transfer to air fry basket. 4. Select the DEHYDRATE function on the oven and dehydrate the cucumber slices in the oven on Level 3 for about 3 to 4 hours at 175°F/80°C.

Serving Suggestion: Serve with sour cream or mayo.
Variation Tip: You can use white wine vinegar instead of apple cider vinegar.
Nutritional Information Per Serving: Calories: 29 | Fat: 2g | Sodium: 389mg | Carbs: 1g | Fiber: 1 | Sugar: 1g | Protein: 1g

Chapter 3 Poultry Mains Recipes

41	Chicken Kabobs	50	Crispy Chicken Thighs
41	Primavera Chicken	51	Herbed Duck Breast
41	Deviled Chicken	51	Oat Crusted Chicken Breasts
42	Roasted Duck	51	Lemony Chicken Thighs
42	Chinese Chicken Drumsticks	52	Buttermilk Whole Chicken
42	Blackened Chicken Bake	52	Cheesy Chicken Cutlets
43	Spanish Chicken Bake	52	Herbed Whole Chicken
43	Simple Turkey Wings	53	Breaded Chicken Tenderloins
43	Parmesan Chicken Meatballs	53	Molasses Glazed Duck Breast
44	Brine-Soaked Turkey	53	Crispy Roasted Chicken
44	Herbed Turkey Legs	54	Parmesan Chicken Tenders
44	Feta Turkey Burgers	54	Sweet and Sour Chicken Thighs
45	Chicken and Rice Casserole	54	Sweet and Spicy Chicken Drumsticks
45	Chicken Potato Bake	55	Honey-Glazed Chicken Drumsticks
46	Roasted Goose	55	Spiced Roasted Chicken
46	Creamy Chicken Casserole	55	Gingered Chicken Drumsticks
46	Bacon-Wrapped Chicken Breasts	56	Spicy Chicken Legs
47	Parmesan Crusted Chicken Breasts	56	Chicken Alfredo Bake
47	Herbed Chicken Thighs	56	Marinated Ranch Broiled Chicken
47	Spiced Chicken Breasts	57	Chicken Casserole
48	Chicken Kebabs	57	Tender Italian Baked Chicken
48	Duck a la Orange	57	Baked Honey Mustard Chicken
48	Baked Duck	58	Air Fryer Chicken Taco Pockets
49	Crispy Chicken Cutlets	58	Mushroom, Broccoli, and Cheese Stuffed Chicken
49	Marinated Spicy Chicken Legs		
49	Lemony Whole Chicken	58	Twice Baked Potatoes with Bacon
50	Crispy Chicken Drumsticks	59	Lasagna Stuffed Chicken
50	Cajun Spiced Whole Chicken	59	Oven-Baked Peri-Peri Chicken

Chicken Kabobs

Prep Time: 15 minutes | Cook Time: 9 minutes | Serves: 2

Ingredients:

- 1 (8-ounce) chicken breast, cut into medium-sized pieces
- 1 tablespoon fresh lemon juice
- 3 garlic cloves, grated
- 1 tablespoon fresh oregano, minced
- ½ teaspoon lemon zest, grated
- Salt and ground black pepper, as required
- 1 teaspoon plain Greek yogurt
- 1 teaspoon olive oil

Preparation:

1. In a large bowl, add the chicken, lemon juice, garlic, oregano, lemon zest, salt and black pepper and toss to coat well. 2. Cover the bowl and refrigerate overnight. 3. Remove the bowl from the refrigerator and stir in the yogurt and oil. 4. Thread the chicken pieces onto the metal skewers. 5. Press "Power" button of Ninja Foodi XL Pro Air Oven and select "Air Fry" function. 6. Press TEMP/SHADE +/- buttons to set the temperature at 350°F/175°C. 7. Now press TIME/SLICES +/- buttons to set the cooking time to 9 minutes. 8. Press "START/STOP" button to start. 9. When the unit beeps to show that it is preheated, open the lid and grease the air fry basket. 10. Place the skewers into the prepared air fry basket and insert in the oven. 11. Flip the skewers once halfway through. 12. When cooking time is completed, open the lid and serve hot.

Serving Suggestions: Serve alongside fresh salad.
Variation Tip: Feel free to add some seasoning as you like.
Nutritional Information per Serving: Calories: 167 | Fat: 5.5g | Sat Fat: 0.5g | Carbohydrates: 3.4g | Fiber: 0.5g | Sugar: 1.1g | Protein: 24.8g

Primavera Chicken

Prep Time: 15 minutes | Cook Time: 25 minutes | Serves: 4

Ingredients:

- 4 chicken breasts, boneless
- 1 zucchini, sliced
- 3 medium tomatoes, sliced
- 2 yellow bell peppers, sliced
- ½ red onion, sliced
- 2 tablespoons olive oil
- 1 teaspoon Italian seasoning
- Kosher salt, to taste
- Freshly ground black pepper, to taste
- 1 cup shredded mozzarella
- Freshly chopped parsley for garnish

Preparation:

1. Carve one side slit in the chicken breasts and stuff them with all the veggies. 2. Place these stuffed chicken breasts in a casserole dish, then drizzle oil, Italian seasoning, black pepper, salt, and Mozzarella over the chicken. 3. Transfer the dish to the 2nd rack position of Ninja Foodi XL Pro Air Oven and close the door. 4. Select the "Bake" Mode using FUNCTION +/- buttons and select Rack Level 2. 5. Set its cooking time to 25 minutes and temperature to 370°F/185°C, then press "START/STOP" to initiate cooking. 6. Garnish with parsley and serve warm.

Serving Suggestion: Serve chicken with a kale salad on the side.
Variation Tip: Brush the chicken with pesto before baking.
Nutritional Information Per Serving: Calories 445 | Fat 25g | Sodium 122mg | Carbs 13g | Fiber 0.4g | Sugar 1g | Protein 33g

Deviled Chicken

Prep Time: 15 minutes | Cook Time: 40 minutes | Serves: 8

Ingredients:

- 2 tablespoons butter
- 2 cloves garlic, chopped
- 1 cup Dijon mustard
- ½ teaspoon cayenne pepper
- 1½ cups panko breadcrumbs
- ¾ cup Parmesan, freshly grated
- ¼ cup chives, chopped
- 2 teaspoons paprika
- 8 small bone-in chicken thighs, skin removed

Preparation:

1. Toss the chicken thighs with crumbs, cheese, chives, butter, and spices in a bowl and mix well to coat. 2. Transfer the chicken along with its spice mix to a sheet pan. 3. Transfer the pan to the 3rd rack position of Ninja Foodi XL Pro Air Oven and close the door. 4. Select the "Air Fry" Mode using FUNCTION +/- buttons and select Rack Level 3. 5. Set its cooking time to 40 minutes and temperature to 375°F/190°C, then press "START/STOP" to initiate cooking. 6. Serve warm.

Serving Suggestion: Serve the chicken fried rice or sautéed vegetable.
Variation Tip: Coat the chicken with crushed cornflakes for a crispy texture.
Nutritional Information Per Serving: Calories 497 | Fat 14g | Sodium 364mg | Carbs 8g | Fiber 1g | Sugar 3g | Protein 32g

Roasted Duck

Prep Time: 15 minutes | Cook Time: 3 hours | Serves: 6

Ingredients:

6 pounds whole Pekin duck
Salt, to taste
Glaze
½ cup balsamic vinegar
1 lemon, juiced
5 garlic cloves chopped
1 lemon, chopped
¼ cup honey

Preparation:

1. Place the Pekin duck in a baking tray and add garlic, lemon, and salt on top. 2. Whisk honey, vinegar, and lemon juice in a bowl. 3. Brush this glaze over the duck liberally. Marinate overnight in the refrigerator. 4. Remove the duck from the marinade and move the duck to a sheet pan in the Ninja Foodi Air Fryer Oven. 5. Transfer the sandwich to the 1st rack position of Ninja Foodi XL Pro Air Oven and close the door. 6. Select the "Air Roast" Mode using FUNCTION +/- buttons and select Rack Level 1. 7. Set its cooking time to 3 hours and temperature to 350°F/175°C, then press "START/STOP" to initiate cooking. 8. Serve warm.
Serving Suggestion: Serve the duck with roasted green beans and mashed potatoes.
Variation Tip: Stuff the duck with the bread stuffing before baking.
Nutritional Information Per Serving: Calories 465 | Fat 5g | Sodium 422mg | Carbs 16g | Fiber 0g | Sugar 1g | Protein 25g

Chinese Chicken Drumsticks

Prep Time: 10 minutes | Cook Time: 20 minutes | Serves: 4

Ingredients:

1 tablespoon oyster sauce
1 teaspoon light soy sauce
½ teaspoon sesame oil
1 teaspoon Chinese five-spice powder
Salt and ground white pepper, as required
4 (6-ounce) chicken drumsticks
1 cup corn flour

Preparation:

1. In a bowl, mix the sauces, oil, five-spice powder, salt, and black pepper together. 2. Add the chicken drumsticks and generously coat with the marinade. 3. Refrigerate for at least 30-40 minutes. 4. In a shallow dish, place the corn flour. 5. Remove the chicken from marinade and lightly coat with corn flour. 6. Press "Power" button of Ninja Foodi XL Pro Air Oven and select "Air Fry" function. 7. Press TEMP/SHADE +/- buttons to set the temperature at 390°F/200°C. 8. Now press TIME/SLICES +/- buttons to set the cooking time to 20 minutes. 9. Press "START/STOP" button to start. 10. When the unit beeps to show that it is preheated, open the lid and grease the air fry basket. 11. Place the chicken drumsticks into the prepared air fry basket and insert in the oven. 12. When cooking time is completed, open the lid and serve hot.
Serving Suggestions: Serve with fresh greens.
Variation Tip: Add seasoning or sauces as you like.
Nutritional Information per Serving: Calories: 287 | Fat: 13.8g | Sat Fat: 7.1g | Carbohydrates: 1.6g | Fiber: 0.2g | Sugar: 0.1g | Protein: 38.3g

Blackened Chicken Bake

Prep Time: 15 minutes | Cook Time: 18 minutes | Serves: 4

Ingredients:

4 chicken breasts
Seasoning:
1½ tablespoons brown sugar
1 teaspoon paprika
1 teaspoon dried oregano
Garnish:
Chopped parsley
2 teaspoons olive oil
¼ teaspoons garlic powder
½ teaspoons salt and pepper

Preparation:

1. Mix olive oil with brown sugar, paprika, oregano, garlic powder, salt, and black pepper in a bowl. 2. Place the chicken breasts in the sheet pan of Ninja Foodi XL Pro Air Oven. 3. Transfer the sheet pan to the 2nd rack position of Ninja Foodi XL Pro Air Oven and close the door. 4. Select the "Bake" Mode using FUNCTION +/- buttons and select Rack Level 2. 5. Set its cooking time to 18 minutes and temperature to 425°F/220°C, then press "START/STOP" to initiate cooking. 6. Serve warm.
Serving Suggestion: Serve the chicken bake with roasted veggies.
Variation Tip: Sprinkle the breadcrumbs on top of the chicken before baking.
Nutritional Information Per Serving: Calories 419 | Fat 14g | Sodium 442mg | Carbs 23g | Fiber 0.4g | Sugar 2g | Protein 32.3g

Spanish Chicken Bake

Prep Time: 15 minutes | Cook Time: 25 minutes | Serves: 4

Ingredients:

- ½ onion, quartered
- ½ red onion, quartered
- ½ pound potatoes, quartered
- 4 garlic cloves
- 4 tomatoes, quartered
- ⅛ cup chorizo
- ¼ teaspoons paprika powder
- 4 chicken thighs, boneless
- ¼ teaspoons dried oregano
- ½ green bell pepper, julienned
- Salt, to taste
- Black pepper, to taste

Preparation:

1. Toss chicken, veggies, and all the ingredients in a roast tray. 2. Transfer the tray to the 2nd rack position of Ninja Foodi XL Pro Air Oven and close the door. 3. Select the "Bake" Mode using FUNCTION +/- buttons and select Rack Level 2. 4. Set its cooking time to 25 minutes and temperature to 425°F/220°C, then press "START/STOP" to initiate cooking. 5. Serve warm.

Serving Suggestion: Serve the chicken bake with warmed pita bread.
Variation Tip: Add canned corns to the casserole before cooking.
Nutritional Information Per Serving: Calories 478 | Fat 8g | Sodium 339mg | Carbs 28g | Fiber 1g | Sugar 2g | Protein 33g

Simple Turkey Wings

Prep Time: 10 minutes | Cook Time: 26 minutes | Serves: 4

Ingredients:

- 2 pounds turkey wings
- 4 tablespoons chicken rub
- 3 tablespoons olive oil

Preparation:

1. In a large bowl, add the turkey wings, chicken rub and olive oil and toss to coat well. 2. Press "Power" button of Ninja Foodi XL Pro Air Oven and select "Air Fry" function. 3. Press TEMP/SHADE +/- buttons to set the temperature at 380°F/195°C. 4. Now press TIME/SLICES +/- buttons to set the cooking time to 26 minutes. 5. Press "Start/Stop" button to start. 6. When the unit beeps to show that it is preheated, open the oven door. 7. Arrange the turkey wings into the greased air fry basket on Level 3. 8. Flip the turkey wings once halfway through. 9. When the cooking time is completed, open the oven door and serve hot.

Serving Suggestions: Serve alongside the yogurt sauce.
Variation Tip: You can use seasoning of your choice.
Nutritional Information per Serving:
Calories: 558 | Fat: 38.9g | Sat Fat: 1.5g | Carbohydrates: 3g | Fiber: 0g | Sugar: 0g | Protein: 46.6g

Parmesan Chicken Meatballs

Prep Time: 15 minutes | Cook Time: 12 minutes | Serves: 4

Ingredients:

- 1 pound ground chicken
- 1 large egg, beaten
- ½ cup Parmesan cheese, grated
- ½ cup pork rinds, ground
- **Crust:**
- ½ cup pork rinds, ground
- 1 teaspoon garlic powder
- 1 teaspoon paprika
- 1 teaspoon kosher salt
- ½ teaspoon pepper

Preparation:

1. Toss all the meatball ingredients in a bowl and mix well. 2. Make small meatballs out of this mixture and roll them in the pork rinds. 3. Place the coated meatballs in the air fry basket. 4. Transfer the basket to the 2nd rack position of Ninja Foodi XL Pro Air Oven and close the door. 5. Select the "Bake" Mode using FUNCTION +/- buttons and select Rack Level 2. 6. Set its cooking time to 12 minutes and temperature to 400°F/200°C, then press "START/STOP" to initiate cooking. 7. Serve warm.

Serving Suggestion: Serve the meatballs with fresh herbs on top and a bowl of steamed rice.
Variation Tip: Use crushed oats to the meatballs for a crispy texture.
Nutritional Information Per Serving: Calories 486 | Fat 13g | Sodium 611mg | Carbs 15g | Fiber 0g | Sugar g4 | Protein 26g

Brine-Soaked Turkey

Prep Time: 15 minutes | Cook Time: 60 minutes | Serves: 4

Ingredients:

7 pounds bone-in, skin-on turkey breast
Brine
½ cup salt
1 lemon
½ onion
3 cloves garlic, smashed
Turkey Breast
4 tablespoons butter, softened
½ teaspoon black pepper
½ teaspoon garlic powder
5 sprigs fresh thyme
3 bay leaves
black pepper

¼ teaspoon dried thyme
¼ teaspoon dried oregano

Preparation:

1. Mix the turkey brine ingredients in a pot and soak the turkey in the brine overnight. 2. The next day, remove the soaked turkey from the brine. 3. Whisk the butter, black pepper, garlic powder, oregano, and thyme. 4. Brush the butter mixture over the turkey, then place it in a roast tray. 5. Transfer the tray to the 2nd rack position of Ninja Foodi XL Pro Air Oven and close the door. 6. Select the "Air Roast" Mode using FUNCTION +/- buttons and select Rack Level 2. 7. Set its cooking time to 60 minutes and temperature to 375°F/190°C, then press "START/STOP" to initiate cooking. 8. Slice and serve warm.
Serving Suggestion: Serve the turkey with fresh cucumber and couscous salad.
Variation Tip: Brush the turkey with orange juice for a refreshing taste.
Nutritional Information Per Serving: Calories 553 | Fat 2.4g | Sodium 216mg | Carbs 18g | Fiber 2.3g | Sugar 1.2g | Protein 23.2g

Herbed Turkey Legs

Prep Time: 15 minutes | Cook Time: 30 minutes | Serves: 2

Ingredients:

1 tablespoon butter, melted
2 garlic cloves, minced
¼ teaspoon dried rosemary
¼ teaspoon dried thyme
¼ teaspoon dried oregano
Salt and ground black pepper, as required
2 turkey legs

Preparation:

1. In a large bowl, mix together the butter, garlic, herbs, salt, and black pepper. 2. Add the turkey legs and coat with mixture generously. 3. Press "Power" button of Ninja Foodi XL Pro Air Oven and select "Air Fry" function. 4. Press TEMP/SHADE +/- buttons to set the temperature at 350°F/175°C. 5. Now press TIME/SLICES +/- buttons to set the cooking time to 27 minutes. 6. Press "Start/Stop" button to start. 7. When the unit beeps to show that it is preheated, open the oven door. 8. Arrange the turkey wings into the greased air fry basket and insert into rail of Level 3. 9. When the cooking time is completed, open the oven door and serve hot.
Serving Suggestions: Serve with cabbage slaw.
Variation Tip: Use unsalted butter.
Nutritional Information per Serving: Calories: 592 | Fat: 22g | Sat Fat: 8.7g | Carbohydrates: 1.3g | Fiber: 0.3g | Sugar: 0g | Protein: 91.6g

Feta Turkey Burgers

Prep Time: 10 minutes | Cook Time: 15 minutes | Serves: 2

Ingredients:

8 ounces ground turkey breast
1½ tablespoons extra-virgin olive oil
2 garlic cloves, grated
2 teaspoons fresh oregano, chopped
½ teaspoon red pepper flakes, crushed
Salt, as required
¼ cup feta cheese, crumbled

Preparation:

1. In a large bowl, add all the ingredients except for cheese and mix until well combined. 2. Make 2 (½-inch-thick) patties from the mixture. 3. Press "Power" button of Ninja Foodi XL Pro Air Oven and select "Air Fry" function. 4. Press TEMP/SHADE +/- buttons to set the temperature at 360°F/180°C. 5. Now press TIME/SLICES +/- buttons to set the cooking time to 15 minutes. 6. Press "Start/Stop" button to start. 7. When the unit beeps to show that it is preheated, open the oven door. 8. Arrange the patties into the greased air fry basket and insert into the rail of Level 3. 9. Flip the turkey burgers once halfway through. 10. When the cooking time is completed, open the oven door and serve hot with the topping of feta.
Serving Suggestions: Serve with fresh greens.
Variation Tip: Try adding some dry breadcrumbs to the turkey mixture before you shape the patties.
Nutritional Information per Serving: Calories: 364 | Fat: 23.1g | Sat Fat: 6.7g | Carbohydrates: 3g | Fiber: 0.8g | Sugar: 0.9g | Protein: 35.6g

Spiced Turkey Breast

Prep Time: 10 minutes | Cook Time: 45 minutes | Serves: 8

Ingredients:

- 2 tablespoons fresh rosemary, chopped
- 1 teaspoon ground cumin
- 1 teaspoon ground cinnamon
- 1 teaspoon smoked paprika
- 1 teaspoon cayenne pepper
- Salt and ground black pepper, as required
- 1 (3-pound) turkey breast

Preparation:

1. In a bowl, mix together the rosemary, spices, salt and black pepper. 2. Rub the turkey breast with rosemary mixture evenly. 3. With kitchen twines, tie the turkey breast to keep it compact. 4. Press "Power" button of Ninja Foodi XL Pro Air Oven and select "Air Fry" function. 5. Press TEMP/SHADE +/- buttons to set the temperature at 360°F/180°C. 6. Now press TIME/SLICES +/- buttons to set the cooking time to 45 minutes. 7. Press "Start/Stop" button to start. 8. When the unit beeps to show that it is preheated, open the oven door. 10. Arrange the turkey breast into the greased air fry basket on Level 3. 11. When the cooking time is completed, open the oven door and place the turkey breast onto a platter for about 5-10 minutes before slicing. 12. With a sharp knife, cut the turkey breast into desired sized slices and serve.

Serving Suggestions: Serve alongside the cranberry sauce.
Variation Tip: Season the turkey breast generously.
Nutritional Information per Serving: Calories: 190 | Fat: 0.9g | Sat Fat: 0.1g | Carbohydrates: 0.9g | Fiber: 0.5g | Sugar: 6g | Protein: 29.5g

Chicken and Rice Casserole

Prep Time: 15 minutes | Cook Time: 25 minutes | Serves: 4

Ingredients:

- 2 pounds bone-in chicken thighs
- Salt and black pepper
- 1 teaspoon olive oil
- 5 cloves garlic, chopped
- 2 large onions, chopped
- 2 large red bell peppers, chopped
- 1 tablespoon sweet Hungarian paprika
- 1 teaspoon hot Hungarian paprika
- 2 tablespoons tomato paste
- 2 cups chicken broth
- 3 cups brown rice, thawed
- 2 tablespoons parsley, chopped
- 6 tablespoons sour cream

Preparation:

1. Season and rub the chicken with black pepper, salt, and olive oil. 2. Sear the chicken in a skillet for 5 minutes per side, then transfer to a casserole dish. 3. Sauté onion in the same skillet until soft. 4. Toss in garlic, peppers, and paprika, then sauté for 3 minutes. 5. Stir in tomato paste, chicken broth, and rice. 6. Mix well and cook until rice is soft, then add sour cream and parsley. 7. Spread the mixture over the chicken in the casserole dish. 8. Transfer the dish to the 2nd rack position of Ninja Foodi XL Pro Air Oven and close the door. 9. Transfer the sandwich to the 2nd rack position of Ninja Foodi XL Pro Air Oven and close the door. 10. Select the "Bake" Mode using FUNCTION +/- buttons and select Rack Level 2. 11. Set its cooking time to 10 minutes and temperature to 375°F/190°C, then press "START/STOP" to initiate cooking. 12. Serve warm.

Serving Suggestion: Serve the chicken casserole with toasted bread slices.
Variation Tip: Add corn kernels to the chicken casserole.
Nutritional Information Per Serving: Calories 454 | Fat 25g | Sodium 412mg | Carbs 22g | Fiber 0.2g | Sugar 1g | Protein 28.3g

Chicken Potato Bake

Prep Time: 15 minutes | Cook Time: 25 minutes | Serves: 4

Ingredients:

- 4 potatoes, diced
- 1 tablespoon garlic, minced
- 1.5 tablespoons olive oil
- ⅛ teaspoon salt
- ⅛ teaspoon pepper
- 1.5 pounds boneless skinless chicken
- ¾ cup mozzarella cheese, shredded
- parsley, chopped

Preparation:

1. Toss chicken and potatoes with all the spices and oil in a sheet pan. 2. Drizzle the cheese on top of the chicken and potato. 3. Transfer the pan to the 2nd rack position of Ninja Foodi XL Pro Air Oven and close the door. 4. Select the "Bake" Mode using FUNCTION +/- buttons and select Rack Level 2. 5. Set its cooking time to 25 minutes and temperature to 375°F/190°C, then press "START/STOP" to initiate cooking. 6. Serve warm.

Serving Suggestion: Serve the chicken potato bake with avocado guacamole.
Variation Tip: Add sliced eggplant instead of potatoes for a change of taste.
Nutritional Information Per Serving: Calories 462 | Fat 14g | Sodium 220mg | Carbs 16g | Fiber 0.2g | Sugar 1g | Protein 26g

Roasted Goose

Prep Time: 15 minutes | Cook Time: 40 minutes | Serves: 12

Ingredients:

8 pounds goose
Juice of a lemon
Salt and pepper
½ yellow onion, peeled and chopped
1 head garlic, peeled and chopped
½ cup wine
1 teaspoon dried thyme

Preparation:

1. Place the goose in a roast tray and whisk the rest of the ingredients in a bowl. 2. Pour this thick sauce over the goose and brush it liberally. 3. Transfer the goose to the 2nd rack position of Ninja Foodi XL Pro Air Oven and close the door. 4. Select the "Air Roast" Mode using FUNCTION +/- buttons and select Rack Level 2. 5. Set its cooking time to 40 minutes and temperature to 355°F/180°C, then press "START/STOP" to initiate cooking. 6. Serve warm.
Serving Suggestion: Serve the Goose with cucumber salad and toasted bread slices.
Variation Tip: Add butter sauce on top of the goose before cooking.
Nutritional Information Per Serving: Calories 449 | Fat 13g | Sodium 432mg | Carbs 31g | Fiber 3g | Sugar 1g | Protein 23g

Creamy Chicken Casserole

Prep Time: 15 minutes | Cook Time: 47 minutes | Serves: 4

Ingredients:

Chicken Mushroom Casserole
2½ pounds chicken breasts, sliced
1½ teaspoons salt
¼ teaspoon black pepper
1 cup all-purpose flour
Sauce
3 tablespoons unsalted butter
3 tablespoons all-purpose flour
1½ cups chicken broth/½ cup milk, optional
6 tablespoons olive oil
1 pound white mushrooms, sliced
1 medium onion, diced
3 garlic cloves, minced

1 tablespoon lemon juice
1 cup half and half cream

Preparation:

1. Butter a casserole dish and toss in chicken with mushrooms and all the casserole ingredients. 2. Prepare its sauce in a suitable pan. Add butter and melt over moderate heat. 3. Stir in flour and whisk well for 2 minutes, then pour in milk/chicken broth, lemon juice, and cream. 4. Mix well and pour this creamy white sauce over the chicken mix in the casserole dish. 5. Transfer the dish to the 2nd rack position of Ninja Foodi XL Pro Air Oven and close the door. 6. Select the "Bake" Mode using FUNCTION +/- buttons and select Rack Level 2. 7. Set its cooking time to 45 minutes and temperature to 350°F/175°C, then press "START/STOP" to initiate cooking. 8. Serve warm.
Serving Suggestion: Serve the creamy chicken casserole with steaming white rice.
Variation Tip: Drizzle breadcrumbs on top of the casserole before baking.
Nutritional Information Per Serving: Calories 601 | Fat 16g | Sodium 189mg | Carbs 32g | Fiber 0.3g | Sugar 0.1g | Protein 28.2g

Bacon-Wrapped Chicken Breasts

Prep Time: 10 minutes | Cook Time: 35 minutes | Serves: 2

Ingredients:

2 (5- to 6-ounce) boneless, skinless chicken breasts
½ teaspoon smoked paprika
½ teaspoon garlic powder
Salt and ground black pepper, as required
4 thin bacon slices

Preparation:

1. With a meat mallet, pound each chicken breast into ¾-inch thickness. 2. In a bowl, mix together the paprika, garlic powder, salt and black pepper. 3. Rub the chicken breasts with spice mixture evenly. 4. Wrap each chicken breast with bacon strips. 5. Press "Power" button of Ninja Foodi XL Pro Air Oven and select "Air Fry" function. 6. Press TEMP/SHADE +/- buttons to set the temperature at 400°F/200°C. 7. Now press TIME/SLICES +/- buttons to set the cooking time to 35 minutes. 8. Press "Start/Stop" button to start. 9. When the unit beeps to show that it is preheated, open the oven door. 10. Arrange the chicken pieces into the greased air fry basket and slide the basket into rail of Level 3. 11. When the cooking time is completed, open the oven door and serve hot.
Serving Suggestions: Serve with fresh baby greens.
Variation Tip: Secure the wrapping of bacon with toothpicks.
Nutritional Information per Serving: Calories: 293 | Fat: 17.4g | Sat Fat: 5.4g | Carbohydrates: 0.8g | Fiber: 0.1g | Sugar: 0.1g | Protein: 31.3g

Parmesan Crusted Chicken Breasts

Prep Time: 15 minutes | Cook Time: 15 minutes | Serves: 4

Ingredients:

- 2 large chicken breasts
- 1 cup mayonnaise
- 1 cup Parmesan cheese, shredded
- 1 cup panko breadcrumbs

Preparation:

1. Cut each chicken breast in half and then with a meat mallet pound each into even thickness. 2. Spread the mayonnaise on both sides of each chicken piece evenly. 3. In a shallow bowl, mix together the Parmesan and breadcrumbs. 4. Coat the chicken piece Parmesan mixture evenly. 5. Press "Power" button of Ninja Foodi XL Pro Air Oven and select "Air Fry" function. 6. Press TEMP/SHADE +/- buttons to set the temperature at 390°F/200°C. 7. Now press TIME/SLICES +/- buttons to set the cooking time to 15 minutes. 8. Press "Start/Stop" button to start. 9. When the unit beeps to show that it is preheated, open the oven door. 10. Arrange the chicken pieces into the greased air fry basket and slide the basket into the rail of Level 3. 11. After 10 minutes of cooking, flip the chicken pieces once. 12. When the cooking time is completed, open the oven door and serve hot.

Serving Suggestions: Serve with ranch dip.
Variation Tip: Use real mayonnaise.
Nutritional Information per Serving: Calories: 625 | Fat: 35.4g | Sat Fat: 9.4g | Carbohydrates: 18.8g | Fiber: 0.1g | Sugar: 3.8g | Protein: 41.6g

Herbed Chicken Thighs

Prep Time: 10 minutes | Cook Time: 20 minutes | Serves: 4

Ingredients:

- ½ tablespoon fresh rosemary, minced
- ½ tablespoon fresh thyme, minced
- Salt and ground black pepper, as required
- 4 (5-ounce) chicken thighs
- 2 tablespoons olive oil

Preparation:

1. In a large bowl, add the herbs, salt and black pepper and mix well. 2. Coat the chicken thighs with oil and then, rub with herb mixture. 3. Arrange the chicken thighs onto the greased sheet pan. 4. Press "Power" button of Ninja Foodi XL Pro Air Oven and select "Air Fry" function. 5. Press TEMP/SHADE +/- buttons to set the temperature at 400°F/200°C. 6. Now press TIME/SLICES +/- buttons to set the cooking time to 20 minutes. 7. Press "Start/Stop" button to start. 8. When the unit beeps to show that it is preheated, open the oven door and insert the sheet pan into rail of Level 3. 9. Flip the chicken thighs once halfway through. 10. When the cooking time is completed, open the oven door and serve hot.

Serving Suggestions: Serve with couscous salad.
Variation Tip: Cook the chicken thighs until it reaches an internal temperature of 165° F.
Nutritional Information per Serving: Calories: 332 | Fat: 17.6g | Sat Fat: 2.9g | Carbohydrates: 0.5g | Fiber: 0.3g | Sugar: 0g | Protein: 41.1g

Spiced Chicken Breasts

Prep Time: 10 minutes | Cook Time: 35 minutes | Serves: 4

Ingredients:

- 1½ tablespoons smoked paprika
- 1 teaspoon ground cumin
- Salt and ground black pepper, as required
- 2 (12-ounce) chicken breasts
- 1 tablespoon olive oil

Preparation:

1. In a small bowl, mix together the paprika, cumin, salt and black pepper. 2. Coat the chicken breasts with oil evenly and then season with the spice mixture generously. 3. Press "Power" button of Ninja Foodi XL Pro Air Oven and select "Air Fry" function. 4. Press TEMP/SHADE +/- buttons to set the temperature at 375°F/190°C. 5. Now press TIME/SLICES +/- buttons to set the cooking time to 35 minutes. 6. Press "Start/Stop" button to start. 7. When the unit beeps to show that it is preheated, open the oven door. 8. Arrange the chicken breasts into the air fry basket into the rail of Level 3. 9. When the cooking time is completed, open the oven door and place the chicken breasts onto a cutting board for about 5 minutes. 10. Cut each breast in 2 equal-sized pieces and serve.

Serving Suggestions: Serve with sautéed kale.
Variation Tip: Fat of chicken breasts should always be white or deep yellow and never pale or gray.
Nutritional Information per Serving: Calories: 363 | Fat: 16.6g | Sat Fat: 4g | Carbohydrates: 1.7g | Fiber: 1g | Sugar: 0.3g | Protein: 49.7g

Chicken Kebabs

Prep Time: 15 minutes. | Cook Time: 20 minutes | Serves: 6

Ingredients:

- 16 ounces skinless chicken breasts, cubed
- 2 tablespoons soy sauce
- ½ zucchini sliced
- 1 tablespoon chicken seasoning
- 1 teaspoon BBQ seasoning
- Salt and pepper to taste
- ½ green pepper sliced
- ½ red pepper sliced
- ½ yellow pepper sliced
- ¼ red onion sliced
- 4 cherry tomatoes
- Cooking spray

Preparation:

1. Toss chicken and veggies with all the spices and seasoning in a bowl. 2. Alternatively, thread them on skewers and place these skewers in the air fry basket. 3. Transfer the basket to the 3rd rack position of Ninja Foodi XL Pro Air Oven and close the door. 4. Select the "Air Fry" Mode using FUNCTION +/- buttons and select Rack Level 3. 5. Set its cooking time to 20 minutes and temperature to 350°F/175°C, then press "START/STOP" to initiate cooking. 6. Flip the skewers when cooked halfway through, then resume cooking. 7. Serve warm.

Serving Suggestion: Serve the kebabs with roasted veggies on the side.
Variation Tip: Add mozzarella balls to the skewers.
Nutritional Information Per Serving: Calories 434 | Fat 16g | Sodium 462mg | Carbs 13g | Fiber 0.4g | Sugar 3g | Protein 35.3g

Duck a la Orange

Prep Time: 15 minutes | Cook Time: 60 minutes | Serves: 8

Ingredients:

- 1 tablespoon salt
- 1 teaspoon ground coriander
- ½ teaspoon ground cumin
- 1 teaspoon black pepper
- 1 (5- to 6-pound) duck, skinned
- 1 juice orange, halved
- 4 fresh thyme sprigs
- 4 fresh marjoram sprigs
- 2 parsley sprigs
- 1 small onion, cut into wedges
- ½ cup dry white wine
- ½ cup chicken broth
- ½ carrot
- ½ celery rib

Preparation:

1. Place the Pekin duck in a roast tray and whisk orange juice and the rest of the ingredients in a bowl. 2. Pour the herb sauce over the duck and brush it liberally. 3. Transfer the duck to the 1st rack position of Ninja Foodi XL Pro Air Oven and close the door. 4. Select the "Air Fry" Mode using FUNCTION +/- buttons and select Rack Level 1. 5. Set its cooking time to 60 minutes and temperature to 350°F/175°C, then press "START/STOP" to initiate cooking. 6. Continue basting the duck during baking. 7. Serve warm.

Serving Suggestion: Serve the duck with chili garlic sauce.
Variation Tip: Add asparagus sticks around the duck and roast.
Nutritional Information Per Serving: Calories 531 | Fat 20g | Sodium 941mg | Carbs 30g | Fiber 0.9g | Sugar 1.4g | Protein 24.6g

Baked Duck

Prep Time: 15 minutes | Cook Time: 2 hours 20 minutes | Serves: 4

Ingredients:

- 1½ sprigs fresh rosemary
- ½ nutmeg
- Black pepper
- Juice from 1 orange
- 1 whole duck
- 4 cloves garlic, chopped
- 1½ red onions, chopped
- a few stalks celery
- 1½ carrot
- 2 cm piece fresh ginger
- 1½ bay leaves
- 2 pounds Piper potatoes
- 4 cups chicken stock

Preparation:

1. Place duck in a large cooking pot and add broth along with all the ingredients. 2. Cook this duck for 2 hours on a simmer, then transfer to the roast tray. 3. Transfer the roast tray to the 1st rack position of Ninja Foodi XL Pro Air Oven and close the door. 4. Select the "Air Fry" Mode using FUNCTION +/- buttons and select Rack Level 1. 5. Set its cooking time to 20 minutes and temperature to 350°F/175°C, then press "START/STOP" to initiate cooking. 6. Serve warm.

Serving Suggestion: Serve the duck with a fresh crouton salad.
Variation Tip: Stuff the duck with the bread stuffing and cheese.
Nutritional Information Per Serving: Calories 505 | Fat 7.9g | Sodium 581mg | Carbs 21.8g | Fiber 2.6g | Sugar 7g | Protein 37.2g

Crispy Chicken Cutlets

Prep Time: 15 minutes | Cook Time: 30 minutes | Serves: 4

Ingredients:
- ¾ cup flour
- 2 large eggs
- 1½ cups breadcrumbs
- ¼ cup Parmesan cheese, grated
- 1 tablespoon mustard powder
- Salt and ground black pepper, as required
- 4 (6-ounce) (¼-inch-thick) skinless, boneless chicken cutlets

Preparation:
1. In a shallow bowl, add the flour. 2. In a second bowl, crack the eggs and beat well. 3. In a third bowl, mix the breadcrumbs, cheese, mustard powder, salt, and black pepper together. 4. Season the chicken with salt, and black pepper. 5. Coat the chicken with flour, then dip into beaten eggs and finally coat with the breadcrumb mixture. 6. Press "Power" button of Ninja Foodi XL Pro Air Oven and select "Air Fry" function. 7. Press TEMP/SHADE +/- buttons to set the temperature at 355°F/180°C. 8. Now press TIME/SLICES +/- buttons to set the cooking time to 30 minutes. 9. Press "START/STOP" button to start. 10. When the unit beeps to show that it is preheated, open the lid and grease the air fry basket. 11. Place the chicken cutlets into the prepared air fry basket and insert in the oven. 12. When cooking time is completed, open the lid and serve hot.

Serving Suggestions: Serve with favorite greens.
Variation Tip: Parmesan cheese can be replaced with your favorite cheese.
Nutritional Information per Serving: Calories: 526 | Fat: 13g | Sat Fat: 4.2g | Carbohydrates: 48.6g | Fiber: 3g | Sugar: 3g | Protein: 51.7g

Marinated Spicy Chicken Legs

Prep Time: 10 minutes | Cook Time: 20 minutes | Serves: 4

Ingredients:
- 4 chicken legs
- 3 tablespoons fresh lemon juice
- 3 teaspoons ginger paste
- 3 teaspoons garlic paste
- Salt, as required
- 4 tablespoons plain yogurt
- 2 teaspoons red chili powder
- 1 teaspoon ground cumin
- 1 teaspoon ground coriander
- 1 teaspoon ground turmeric
- Ground black pepper, as required

Preparation:
1. In a bowl, mix the chicken legs, lemon juice, ginger, garlic, and salt together. Set aside for about 15 minutes. 2. Meanwhile, in another bowl, mix the yogurt and spices together. 3. Add the chicken legs and coat with the spice mixture generously. 4. Cover the bowl and refrigerate for at least 10-12 hours. 5. Press "Power" button of Ninja Foodi XL Pro Air Oven and select "Air Fry" function. 6. Press TEMP/SHADE +/- buttons to set the temperature at 440°F/225°C. 7. Now press TIME/SLICES +/- buttons to set the cooking time to 20 minutes. 8. Press "START/STOP" button to start. 9. When the unit beeps to show that it is preheated, open the lid and grease the air fry basket. 10. Place the chicken legs into the prepared air fry basket and insert in the oven. 11. When cooking time is completed, open the lid and serve hot.

Serving Suggestions: Serve with fresh greens.
Variation Tip: Lemon juice can be replaced with vinegar.
Nutritional Information per Serving: Calories: 461 | Fat: 17.6g | Sat Fat: 5g | Carbohydrates: 4.3g | Fiber: 0.9g | Sugar: 1.5g | Protein: 67.1g

Lemony Whole Chicken

Prep Time: 15 minutes | Cook Time: 1 hour 20 minutes | Serves: 8

Ingredients:
- 1 (5-pound) whole chicken, neck and giblets removed
- Salt and ground black pepper, as required
- 2 fresh rosemary sprigs
- 1 small onion, peeled and quartered
- 1 garlic clove, peeled and cut in half
- 4 lemon zest slices
- 1 tablespoon extra-virgin olive oil
- 1 tablespoon fresh lemon juice

Preparation:
1. Rub the inside and outside of chicken with salt and black pepper evenly. 2. Place the rosemary sprigs, onion quarters, garlic halves and lemon zest in the cavity of the chicken. 3. With kitchen twine, tie off wings and legs. 4. Arrange the chicken onto a greased baking pan and drizzle with oil and lemon juice. 5. Press "Power" button of Ninja Foodi XL Pro Air Oven and select "Bake" function. 6. Press TEMP/SHADE +/- buttons to set the temperature at 400°F/200°C. 7. Now press TIME/SLICES +/- buttons to set the cooking time to 20 minutes. 8. Press "START/STOP" button to start. 9. When the unit beeps to show that it is preheated, open the lid. 10. Arrange the pan over the wire rack and insert in the oven. 11. After 20 minutes of cooking, set the temperature to 375°F/190°C for 60 minutes. 12. When cooking time is completed, open the lid and place the chicken onto a platter for about 10 minutes before carving. 13. Cut into desired sized pieces and serve.

Serving Suggestions: Serve alongside the steamed veggies.
Variation Tip: Lemon can be replaced with lime.
Nutritional Information per Serving: Calories: 448 | Fat: 10.4g | Sat Fat: 2.7g | Carbohydrates: 1g | Fiber: 0.4g | Sugar: 0.2g | Protein: 82g

Crispy Chicken Drumsticks

Prep Time: 15 minutes | Cook Time: 25 minutes | Serves: 4

Ingredients:

- 4 chicken drumsticks
- 1 tablespoon adobo seasoning
- Salt, as required
- 1 tablespoon onion powder
- 1 tablespoon garlic powder
- ½ tablespoon paprika
- Ground black pepper, as required
- 2 eggs
- 2 tablespoons milk
- 1 cup all-purpose flour
- ¼ cup cornstarch

Preparation:

1. Season chicken drumsticks with adobo seasoning and a pinch of salt. 2. Set aside for about 5 minutes. 3. In a small bowl, add the spices, salt and black pepper and mix well. 4. In a shallow bowl, add the eggs, milk and 1 teaspoon of spice mixture and beat until well combined. 5. In another shallow bowl, add the flour, cornstarch and remaining spice mixture. 6. Coat the chicken drumsticks with flour mixture completely and tap off the excess. 7. Now, dip the chicken drumsticks in egg mixture. 8. Again coat the chicken drumsticks with flour mixture. 9. Arrange the chicken drumsticks onto a wire rack lined baking sheet and set aside for about 15 minutes. 10. Now, arrange the chicken drumsticks onto a sheet pan and spray the chicken with cooking spray lightly. 11. Press "Power" button of Ninja Foodi XL Pro Air Oven and select "Air Fry" function. 12. Press TEMP/SHADE +/- buttons to set the temperature at 350°F/175°C. 13. Now press TIME/SLICES +/- buttons to set the cooking time to 25 minutes. 14. Press "START/STOP" button to start. 15. When the unit beeps to show that it is preheated, open the lid and grease the air fry basket. 16. Place the chicken drumsticks into the prepared air fry basket and insert in the oven. 17. When cooking time is completed, open the lid and serve hot.

Serving Suggestions: Serve with French fries.
Variation Tip: Feel free to add some seasoning as you like.
Nutritional Information per Serving: Calories: 483 | Fat: 12.5g | Sat Fat: 3.4g | Carbohydrates: 35.1g | Fiber: 1.6g | Sugar: 1.8g | Protein: 53.7g

Cajun Spiced Whole Chicken

Prep Time: 15 minutes | Cook Time: 1 hour 10 minutes | Serves: 6

Ingredients:

- ¼ cup butter, softened
- 2 teaspoons dried rosemary
- 2 teaspoons dried thyme
- 1 tablespoon Cajun seasoning
- 1 tablespoon onion powder
- 1 tablespoon garlic powder
- 1 tablespoon paprika
- 1 teaspoon cayenne pepper
- Salt, as required
- 1 (3-pound) whole chicken, neck and giblets removed

Preparation:

1. In a bowl, add the butter, herbs, spices and salt and mix well. 2. Rub the chicken with spicy mixture generously. 3. With kitchen twine, tie off wings and legs. 4. Press "Power" button of Ninja Foodi XL Pro Air Oven and select "Bake" function. 5. Press TEMP/SHADE +/- buttons to set the temperature at 380°F/195°C. 6. Now press TIME/SLICES +/- buttons to set the cooking time to 70 minutes. 7. Press "START/STOP" button to start. 8. When the unit beeps to show that it is preheated, open the lid. 9. Arrange the chicken over the wire rack and insert in the oven. 10. When cooking time is completed, open the lid and place the chicken onto a platter for about 10 minutes before carving. 11. Cut into desired sized pieces and serve.

Serving Suggestions: Serve alongside a fresh green salad.
Variation Tip: You can adjust the ratio of spices according to your choice.
Nutritional Information per Serving: Calories: 421 | Fat: 14.8g | Sat Fat: 6.9g | Carbohydrates: 2.3g | Fiber: 0.9g | Sugar: 0.5g | Protein: 66.3g

Crispy Chicken Thighs

Prep Time: 15 minutes | Cook Time: 25 minutes | Serves: 4

Ingredients:

- ½ cup all-purpose flour
- 1½ tablespoons Cajun seasoning
- 1 teaspoon seasoning salt
- 1 egg
- 4 (4-ounce) skin-on chicken thighs

Preparation:

1. In a shallow bowl, mix the flour, Cajun seasoning, and salt together. 2. In another bowl, crack the egg and beat well. 3. Coat each chicken thigh with the flour mixture, then dip into beaten egg and finally, coat with the flour mixture again. 4. Shake off the excess flour thoroughly. 5. Press "Power" button of Ninja Foodi XL Pro Air Oven and select "Air Fry" function. 6. Press TEMP/SHADE +/- buttons to set the temperature at 390°F/200°C. 7. Now press TIME/SLICES +/- buttons to set the cooking time to 25 minutes. 8. Press "START/STOP" button to start. 9. When the unit beeps to show that it is preheated, open the lid and grease the air fry basket. 10. Place the chicken thighs into the prepared air fry basket and insert in the oven. 11. When cooking time is completed, open the lid and serve hot.

Serving Suggestions: Serve with ketchup.
Variation Tip: Feel free to use seasoning of your choice.
Nutritional Information per Serving: Calories: 288 | Fat: 9.6g | Sat Fat: 2.7g | Carbohydrates: 12g | Fiber: 0.4g | Sugar: 0.1g | Protein: 35.9g

Herbed Duck Breast

Prep Time: 15 minutes | Cook Time: 20 minutes | Serves: 2

Ingredients:

- 1 (10-ounce) duck breast
- Olive oil cooking spray
- ½ tablespoon fresh thyme, chopped
- ½ tablespoon fresh rosemary, chopped
- 1 cup chicken broth
- 1 tablespoon fresh lemon juice
- Salt and ground black pepper, as required

Preparation:

1. Spray the duck breast with cooking spray evenly. 2. In a bowl, mix well the remaining ingredients. 3. Add the duck breast and coat with the marinade generously. 4. Refrigerate, covered for about 4 hours. 5. With a piece of foil, cover the duck breast. 6. Press "Power" button of Ninja Foodi XL Pro Air Oven and select "Air Fry" function. 7. Press TEMP/SHADE +/- buttons to set the temperature at 390°F/200°C. 8. Now press TIME/SLICES +/- buttons to set the cooking time to 15 minutes. 9. Press "START/STOP" button to start. 10. When the unit beeps to show that it is preheated, open the lid and grease the air fry basket. 11. Place the duck breast into the prepared air fry basket and insert in the oven. 12. After 15 minutes of cooking, set the temperature to 355°F/180°C for 5 minutes. 13. When cooking time is completed, open the lid and serve hot.

Serving Suggestions: Serve with spiced potatoes.
Variation Tip: Feel free to add some seasoning as you like.
Nutritional Information per Serving: Calories: 209 | Fat: 6.6g | Sat Fat: 0.3g | Carbohydrates: 1.6g | Fiber: 0.6g | Sugar: 0.5g | Protein: 33.8g

Oat Crusted Chicken Breasts

Prep Time: 15 minutes | Cook Time: 12 minutes | Serves: 2

Ingredients:

- 2 (6-ounce) chicken breasts
- Salt and ground black pepper, as required
- ¾ cup oats
- 2 tablespoons mustard powder
- 1 tablespoon fresh parsley
- 2 medium eggs

Preparation:

1. Check the meat "best by" date. Place the chicken breasts onto a cutting board and with a meat mallet, flatten each into even thickness. 2. Then, cut each breast in half. 3. Sprinkle the chicken pieces with salt and black pepper and set aside. 4. In a blender, add the oats, mustard powder, parsley, salt and black pepper and pulse until a coarse breadcrumb-like mixture is formed. 5. Transfer the oat mixture into a shallow bowl. 6. In another bowl, crack the eggs and beat well. 7. Coat the chicken with oats mixture and then, dip into beaten eggs and again, coat with the oats mixture. 8. Press "Power" button of Ninja Foodi XL Pro Air Oven and select "Air Fry" function. 9. Press TEMP/SHADE +/- buttons to set the temperature at 350°F/175°C. 10. Now press TIME/SLICES +/- buttons to set the cooking time to 12 minutes. 11. Press "START/STOP" button to start. 12. When the unit beeps to show that it is preheated, open the lid and grease the air fry basket. 13. Place the chicken breasts into the prepared air fry basket and insert in the oven. 14. Flip the chicken breasts once halfway through. 15. When cooking time is completed, open the lid and serve hot.

Serving Suggestions: Serve with mashed potatoes.
Variation Tip: Feel free to add some seasoning as you like.
Nutritional Information per Serving: Calories: 556 | Fat: 22.2g | Sat Fat: 5.3g | Carbohydrates: 25.1g | Fiber: 4.8g | Sugar: 1.4g | Protein: 61.6g

Lemony Chicken Thighs

Prep Time: 15 minutes | Cook Time: 20 minutes | Serves: 6

Ingredients:

- 6 (6-ounce) chicken thighs
- 2 tablespoons olive oil
- 2 tablespoons fresh lemon juice
- 1 tablespoon Italian seasoning
- Salt and ground black pepper, as required
- 1 lemon, sliced thinly

Preparation:

1. In a large bowl, add all the ingredients except for lemon slices and toss to coat well. 2. Refrigerate to marinate for 30 minutes to overnight. 3. Remove the chicken thighs and let any excess marinade drip off. 4. Press "Power" button of Ninja Foodi XL Pro Air Oven and select "Air Fry" function. 5. Press TEMP/SHADE +/- buttons to set the temperature at 350°F/175°C. 6. Now press TIME/SLICES +/- buttons to set the cooking time to 20 minutes. 7. Press "START/STOP" button to start. 8. When the unit beeps to show that it is preheated, open the lid and grease the air fry basket. 9. Place the chicken thighs into the prepared air fry basket and insert in the oven. 10. After 10 minutes of cooking, flip the chicken thighs. 11. When cooking time is completed, open the lid and serve hot alongside the lemon slices.

Serving Suggestions: Serve alongside your favorite dipping sauce.
Variation Tip: Select chicken with a pinkish hue.
Nutritional Information per Serving: Calories: 472 | Fat: 18g | Sat Fat: 4.3g | Carbohydrates: 0.6g | Fiber: 0.1g | Sugar: 0.4g | Protein: 49.3g

Buttermilk Whole Chicken

Prep Time: 15 minutes | Cook Time: 50 minutes | Serves: 6

Ingredients:

- 2 cups buttermilk
- ¼ cup olive oil
- 1 teaspoon garlic powder
- Salt, as required
- 1 (3-pound) whole chicken, neck and giblets removed
- Ground black pepper, as required

Preparation:

1. In a large resealable bag, mix together the buttermilk, oil, garlic powder and 1 tablespoon of salt. 2. Add the whole chicken and seal the bag tightly. 3. Refrigerate to marinate for 24 hours up to 2 days. 4. Remove the chicken from bag and pat dry with paper towels. 5. Season the chicken with salt and black pepper. 6. With kitchen twine, tie off wings and legs. 7. Press "Power" button of Ninja Foodi XL Pro Air Oven and select "Air Fry" function. 8. Press TEMP/SHADE +/- buttons to set the temperature at 380°F/195°C. 9. Now press TIME/SLICES +/- buttons to set the cooking time to 50 minutes. 10. Press "Start/Stop" button to start. 11. When the unit beeps to show that it is preheated, open the oven door. 12. Arrange the chicken into the greased air fry basket, breast-side down on sheet pan into rails of Level 3. 13. When the cooking time is completed, open the oven door and place the chicken onto a cutting board for about 10 minutes before carving. 14. With a sharp knife, cut the chicken into desired sized pieces and serve.

Serving Suggestions: Serve with steamed veggies
Variation Tip: Kitchen shears are very useful for trimming excess fat from the chicken's cavity.
Nutritional Information per Serving: Calories: 449 | Fat: 16g | Sat Fat: 3.6g | Carbohydrates: 68.5g | Fiber: 4.3g | Sugar: 0.1g | Protein: 4g

Cheesy Chicken Cutlets

Prep Time: 10 minutes | Cook Time: 30 minutes | Serves: 2

Ingredients:

- 1 large egg
- 6 tablespoons flour
- ¾ cup panko breadcrumbs
- 2 tablespoons parmesan cheese, grated
- 2 chicken cutlets, skinless and boneless
- ½ tablespoon mustard powder
- Salt and black pepper, to taste

Preparation:

1. Take a shallow bowl, add the flour. 2. In a second bowl, crack the egg and beat well. 3. Take a third bowl and mix together breadcrumbs, cheeses, mustard powder, salt and black pepper. 4. Season the chicken with salt and black pepper. 5. Coat the chicken with flour, then dip into beaten egg and then finally coat with the breadcrumbs mixture. 6. Turn on your Ninja Foodi XL Pro Air Oven and select "Air Fry". 7. Select the timer for about 30 minutes and temperature for 355°F/180°C. Press START/STOP to begin preheating. 8. When the unit beeps to signify it has preheated, open the oven and slide an air fry basket into the rail of Level 3. 9. Grease the air fry basket and place the chicken cutlets into the prepared basket. Close the oven and let it cook. 10. Remove from the oven and serve on a platter. 11. Serve hot and enjoy!

Serving Suggestions: Serve with a topping of lemon slices.
Variation Tip: You can also use mozzarella cheese instead.
Nutritional Information per Serving: Calories: 510 | Fat: 16.3g | Sat Fat: 7.5g | Carbohydrates: 26.2g | Fiber: 1.2g | Sugar: 0.5g | Protein: 41.4g

Herbed Whole Chicken

Prep Time: 15 minutes | Cook Time: 1 hour | Serves: 8

Ingredients:

- 1 tablespoon fresh basil, chopped
- 1 tablespoon fresh oregano, chopped
- 1 tablespoon fresh thyme, chopped
- Salt and ground black pepper, as required
- 1 (4½-pound) whole chicken, necks and giblets removed
- 3 tablespoons olive oil, divided

Preparation:

1. In a bowl, mix together the herbs, salt and black pepper. 2. Coat the chicken with 2 tablespoons of oil and then, rub inside, outside and underneath the skin with half of the herb mixture generously. 3. Press "Power" button of Ninja Foodi XL Pro Air Oven and select "Air Fry" function. 4. Press TEMP/SHADE +/- buttons to set the temperature at 360°F/180°C. 5. Now press TIME/SLICES +/- buttons to set the cooking time to 60 minutes. 6. Press "Start/Stop" button to start. 7. When the unit beeps to show that it is preheated, open the oven door. 8. Arrange the chicken into the greased air fry basket, breast-side down and slide the basket into rails of Level 3. 9. After 30 minutes of cooking, arrange the chicken, breast-side up and coat with the remaining oil. 10. Then rub with the remaining herb mixture. 11. When the cooking time is completed, open the oven door and place the chicken onto a cutting board for about 10 minutes before carving. 12. With a sharp knife, cut the chicken into desired sized pieces and serve.

Serving Suggestions: Serve with roasted vegetables.
Variation Tip: Dried herbs can be used instead of fresh herbs.
Nutritional Information per Serving: Calories: 533 | Fat: 24.3g | Sat Fat: 6g | Carbohydrates: 0.6g | Fiber: 0.4g | Sugar: 0g | Protein: 73.9g

Breaded Chicken Tenderloins

Prep Time: 10 minutes | Cook Time: 15 minutes | Serves: 2

Ingredients:

- 4 chicken tenderloins, skinless and boneless
- ½ egg, beaten
- 1 tablespoon vegetable oil
- ¼ cup breadcrumbs

Preparation:

1. Take a shallow dish and add the beaten egg. 2. Take another dish and mix together oil and breadcrumbs until you have a crumbly mixture. 3. Dip the chicken tenderloins into the beaten egg and then coat with the breadcrumbs mixture. 4. Shake off the excess coating. 5. Turn on your Ninja Foodi XL Pro Air Oven and select "Air Fry". 6. Select the timer for about 15 minutes and temperature for 355°F/180°C. Press START/STOP to begin preheating. 7. When the unit beeps to signify it has preheated, open the oven and place an air fry basket on Level 3. 8. Grease the air fry basket and place the chicken tenderloins into the prepared basket. Close the oven and let it cook. 9. Remove from the oven and serve on a platter. 10. Serve hot and enjoy!

Serving Suggestions: Serve with red chili sauce or ketchup.
Variation Tip: You can use foil to cover the chicken.
Nutritional Information per Serving: Calories: 409 | Fat: 16.6g | Sat Fat: 4.8g | Carbohydrates: 9.8g | Fiber: 0.6g | Sugar: 0.9g | Protein: 53.2g

Molasses Glazed Duck Breast

Prep Time: 15 minutes | Cook Time: 44 minutes | Serves: 3

Ingredients:

- 2 cups fresh pomegranate juice
- 2 tablespoons fresh lemon juice
- 3 tablespoons brown sugar
- 1 pound boneless duck breast
- Salt and ground black pepper, as required

Preparation:

1. For pomegranate molasses: in a medium saucepan, add the pomegranate juice, lemon and brown sugar over medium heat and bring to a boil. 2. Reduce the heat to low and simmer for about 25 minutes until the mixture is thick. 3. Remove from the hat and set aside to cool slightly 4. Meanwhile, with a knife, make the slit on the duck breast. 5. Season the duck breast with salt and black pepper generously. 6. Press "Power" button of Ninja Foodi XL Pro Air Oven and select "Air Fry" function. 7. Press TEMP/SHADE +/- buttons to set the temperature at 400°F/200°C. 8. Now press TIME/SLICES +/- buttons to set the cooking time to 14 minutes. 9. Press "Start/Stop" button to start. 10. When the unit beeps to show that it is preheated, open the oven door. 11. Arrange the duck breast into the greased air fry basket, skin side up and insert in the rail of Level 3. 12. After 6 minutes of cooking, flip the duck breast. 13. When the cooking time is completed, open the oven door and place the duck breast onto a platter for about 5 minutes before slicing. 14. With a sharp knife, cut the duck breast into desired sized slices and transfer onto a platter. 15. Drizzle with warm molasses and serve.

Serving Suggestions: Serve alongside the garlicky sweet potatoes.
Variation Tip: You can also use store-bought pomegranate molasses.
Nutritional Information per Serving: Calories: 332 | Fat: 6.1g | Sat Fat: 0.1g | Carbohydrates: 337g | Fiber: 0g | Sugar: 31.6g | Protein: 34g

Crispy Roasted Chicken

Prep Time: 15 minutes | Cook Time: 40 minutes | Serves: 8

Ingredients:

- 1 (3½-pound) whole chicken, cut into 8 pieces
- Salt and ground black pepper, as required
- 2 cups buttermilk
- 2 cups all-purpose flour
- 1 tablespoon ground mustard
- 1 tablespoon garlic powder
- 1 tablespoon onion powder
- 1 tablespoon paprika

Preparation:

1. Rub the chicken pieces with salt and black pepper. 2. In a large bowl, add the chicken pieces and buttermilk and refrigerate to marinate for at least 1 hour. 3. Meanwhile, in a large bowl, place the flour, mustard, spices, salt and black pepper and mix well. 4. Remove the chicken pieces from bowl and drip off the excess buttermilk. 5. Coat the chicken pieces with the flour mixture, shaking any excess off. 6. Insert wire rack on Level 2. Press "Power" button of Ninja Foodi XL Pro Air Oven and select "Air Fry" function. Select 2 Level. 7. Press TEMP/SHADE +/- buttons to set the temperature at 390°F/200°C. 8. Now press TIME/SLICES +/- buttons to set the cooking time to 20 minutes. 9. Press "Start/Stop" button to start. 10. When the unit beeps to show that it is preheated, open the oven door and grease air fry basket. 11. Arrange half of the chicken pieces into air fry basket and insert into the rail of Level 4. And the other on roast tray over wire rack into the rail of Level 2. 12. When the cooking time is completed, open the oven door and serve immediately.

Serving Suggestions: Serve alongside the French fries.
Variation Tip: Adjust the ratio of spices according to your taste.
Nutritional Information per Serving: Calories: 518 | Fat: 8.5g | Sat Fat: 2.4g | Carbohydrates: 33.4g | Fiber: 1.8 | Sugar: 4.3g | Protein: 72.6g

Parmesan Chicken Tenders

Prep Time: 15 minutes | Cook Time: 15 minutes | Serves: 4

Ingredients:

½ cup flour
Salt and ground black pepper, as required
2 eggs, beaten
¾ cup panko breadcrumbs
¾ cup Parmesan cheese, grated finely
1 teaspoon Italian seasoning
8 chicken tenders

Preparation:

1. In a shallow dish, mix together the flour, salt and black pepper. 2. In a second shallow dish, place the beaten eggs. 3. In a third shallow dish, mix together the breadcrumbs, parmesan cheese and Italian seasoning. 4. Coat the chicken tenders with flour mixture, then dip into the beaten eggs and finally coat with breadcrumb mixture. 5. Arrange the tenders onto a greased sheet pan in a single layer and a greased air fryer basket. 6. Insert wire rack into rail of Level 2. Press "Power" button of Ninja Foodi XL Pro Air Oven and select "Air Fry" function. 7. Press TEMP/SHADE +/- buttons to set the temperature at 360°F/180°C. 8. Now press TIME/SLICES +/- buttons to set the cooking time to 15 minutes. 9. Press "Start/Stop" button to start. 10. When the unit beeps to show that it is preheated, open the oven door and slide the basket on Level 4 and the sheet pan over wire rack on Level 2. 11. When the cooking time is completed, open the oven door and serve hot.
Serving Suggestions: Serve with blue cheese dip.
Variation Tip: Use dry breadcrumbs.
Nutritional Information per Serving: Calories: 435 | Fat: 16.1g | Sat Fat: 5.4g | Carbohydrates: 15.3g | Fiber: 0g | Sugar: 0.5g | Protein: 0.4g

Sweet and Sour Chicken Thighs

Prep Time: 10 minutes | Cook Time: 20 minutes | Serves: 1

Ingredients:

¼ tablespoon soy sauce
¼ tablespoon rice vinegar
½ teaspoon sugar
½ garlic, minced
½ scallion, finely chopped
¼ cup corn flour
1 chicken thigh, skinless and boneless
Salt and black pepper, to taste

Preparation:

1. Take a bowl and mix all the ingredients together except chicken and corn flour. 2. Add the chicken thigh to the bowl to coat well. 3. Take another bowl and add corn flour. 4. Remove the chicken thighs from marinade and lightly coat with corn flour. 5. Turn on your Ninja Foodi XL Pro Air Oven and select "Air Fry". 6. Select the timer for about 10 minutes and temperature for 390°F/200°C. Press START/STOP to begin preheating. 7. When the unit beeps to signify it has preheated, open the oven and place an air fry basket on Level 3. 8. Grease the air fry basket and place the chicken thighs into the prepared basket. Close the oven and let it cook. 9. Air fry for about 10 minutes and then for another to 10 minutes at 355°F/180°C. 10. Remove from the oven and serve on a platter. 11. Serve hot and enjoy!
Serving Suggestions: Serve with red chili sauce.
Variation Tip: You can add lemon juice on top.
Nutritional Information per Serving: Calories: 262 | Fat: 5.2g | Sat Fat: 1.7g | Carbohydrates: 25.8g | Fiber: 2.4g | Sugar: 2.5g | Protein: 27.5g

Sweet and Spicy Chicken Drumsticks

Prep Time: 10 minutes | Cook Time: 20 minutes | Serves: 2

Ingredients:

2 chicken drumsticks
½ garlic clove, crushed
1 teaspoon ginger, crushed
1 teaspoon brown sugar
½ tablespoon mustard
½ teaspoon red chili powder
½ teaspoon cayenne pepper
½ tablespoon vegetable oil
Salt and black pepper, to taste

Preparation:

1. Take a bowl and mix together mustard, ginger, brown sugar, oil and spices. 2. Add chicken drumsticks to the bowl for well coating. 3. Refrigerate for at least 20 to 30 minutes. 4. Turn on your Ninja Foodi XL Pro Air Oven and select "Air Fry". 5. Select the timer for about 10 minutes and temperature for 390°F/200°C. 6. When the unit beeps to signify it has preheated, open the oven and slide the air fry basket into the rail of Level 3. 7. Grease the air fry basket and place the drumsticks into the prepared basket. Close the oven and let it cook. 8. Air fry for about 10 minutes and then 10 more minutes at 300°F/150°C. 9. Remove from the oven and serve on a platter. 10. Serve hot and enjoy!
Serving Suggestions: Serve with red chili sauce.
Variation Tip: You can add lemon juice to enhance taste.
Nutritional Information per Serving: Calories: 131 | Fat: 7g | Sat Fat: 1.4g | Carbohydrates: 3.3g | Fiber: 0.8g | Sugar: 1.8g | Protein: 13.5g

Honey-Glazed Chicken Drumsticks

Prep Time: 10 minutes | Cook Time: 22 minutes | Serves: 2

Ingredients:

½ tablespoon fresh thyme, minced
2 tablespoons Dijon mustard
½ tablespoon honey
1 tablespoon olive oil
1 teaspoon fresh rosemary, minced
2 chicken drumsticks, boneless
Salt and black pepper, to taste

Preparation:

1. Take a bowl and mix together mustard, honey, herbs, salt, oil and black pepper. 2. Add chicken drumsticks to the bowl and coat them well with the mixture. 3. Cover and refrigerate overnight. 4. Turn on your Ninja Foodi XL Pro Air Oven and select "Air Fry". 5. Select the timer for about 12 minutes and temperature for 320°F/160°C. 6. When the unit beeps to signify it has preheated, open the oven and slide an air fry basket on Level 3. 7. Grease the air fry basket and place the drumsticks into the prepared basket. Close the oven and let it cook. 8. Air fry for about 12 minutes and then for about 10 more minutes at 355°F/180°C. 9. Remove from the oven and serve on a platter. 10. Serve hot and enjoy!

Serving Suggestions: Serve with red chili sauce.
Variation Tip: You can add lemon juice to enhance taste.
Nutritional Information per Serving: Calories: 301 | Fat: 19.8g | Sat Fat: 4.4g | Carbohydrates: 6.1g | Fiber: 1g | Sugar: 4.5g | Protein: 23.8g

Spiced Roasted Chicken

Prep Time: 10 minutes | Cook Time: 1 hour | Serves: 3

Ingredients:

1 teaspoon paprika
½ teaspoon cayenne pepper
½ teaspoon ground white pepper
½ teaspoon garlic powder
1 teaspoon dried thyme
½ teaspoon onion powder
Salt and black pepper, to taste
2 tablespoons oil
½ whole chicken, necks and giblets removed

Preparation:

1. Take a bowl and mix together the thyme and spices. 2. Coat the chicken with oil and rub it with the spice mixture. 3. Turn on your Ninja Foodi XL Pro Air Oven and select "Air Fry". 4. Select the timer for about 30 minutes and temperature for 350°F/175°C. 5. Place the chicken in the air fry basket on Level 3 in oven and air fry for 30 minutes. 6. After that, take out the chicken, flip it over and let it air fry for another 30 minutes. 7. When cooked, let it sit for 10 minutes on a large plate and then carve to desired pieces. 8. Serve and enjoy!

Serving Suggestions: Top with chopped celery leaves and hot sauce.
Variation Tip: You can also add shredded mozzarella cheese on top.
Nutritional Information per Serving: Calories: 113 | Fat: 8.7g | Sat Fat: 1.4g | Carbohydrates: 1.9g | Fiber: 0.7g | Sugar: 0.4g | Protein: 7.1g

Gingered Chicken Drumsticks

Prep Time: 10 minutes | Cook Time: 25 minutes | Serves: 3

Ingredients:

¼ cup full-fat coconut milk
2 teaspoons fresh ginger, minced
2 teaspoons galangal, minced
2 teaspoons ground turmeric
Salt, as required
3 (6-ounce) chicken drumsticks

Preparation:

1. Place the coconut milk, galangal, ginger, and spices in a large bowl and mix well. 2. Add the chicken drumsticks and coat with the marinade generously. 3. Refrigerate to marinate for at least 6-8 hours. 4. Now press TIME/SLICES +/- buttons to set the cooking time to 25 minutes. 5. Press "Power" button of Ninja Foodi XL Pro Air Oven and select "Air Fry" function. 6. Press TEMP/SHADE +/- buttons to set the temperature at 375°F/190°C. 7. Press "START/STOP" button to start. 8. When the unit beeps to show that it is preheated, open the lid and grease the air fry basket. 9. Place the chicken drumsticks into the prepared air fry basket and insert in the oven. 10. When cooking time is completed, open the lid and serve hot.

Serving Suggestions: Serve alongside the lemony couscous.
Variation Tip: Coconut milk can be replaced with cream.
Nutritional Information per Serving: Calories: 347 | Fat: 14.8g | Sat Fat: 6.9g | Carbohydrates: 3.8g | Fiber: 1.1g | Sugar: 0.8g | Protein: 47.6g

Spicy Chicken Legs

Prep Time: 20 minutes | Cook Time: 25 minutes | Serves: 6

Ingredients:

- 6 chicken legs
- 4 cups white flour
- 2 cups buttermilk
- 2 teaspoons onion powder
- 2 teaspoons garlic powder
- 2 teaspoons paprika
- 2 teaspoons ground cumin
- Salt and black pepper, to taste
- 2 tablespoons olive oil

Preparation:

1. Take a bowl, add chicken legs and buttermilk. Refrigerate for about 2 hours. 2. Take another bowl, mix together flour and spices. 3. Remove the chicken legs from buttermilk and coat them with the flour mixture. 4. Do it again until we have a fine coating. 5. Turn on your Ninja Foodi XL Pro Air Oven and select "Air Fry". 6. Select the timer for about 20 to 25 minutes and temperature for 360°F/180°C. 7. Place an air fry basket on Level 3. Grease the air fry basket and arrange the chicken legs on it. 8. Take it out when chicken legs are brown enough and serve onto a serving platter.

Serving Suggestions: Add hot sauce on top.
Variation Tip: You can also add dried basil.
Nutritional Information per Serving: Calories: 653 | Fat: 16.9g | Sat Fat: 4.1g | Carbohydrates: 69.5g | Fiber: 2.7g | Sugar: 4.7g | Protein: 52.3g

Chicken Alfredo Bake

Prep Time: 8 minutes | Cook Time: 25 minutes | Serves: 2

Ingredients:

- ¼ cup heavy cream
- ½ cup milk
- 1 tablespoon flour, divided
- ½ clove garlic, minced
- 1 cup penne pasta
- ½ tablespoon butter
- ½ cup cubed rotisserie chicken
- ½ cup Parmigiano-Reggiano cheese, freshly grated
- ½ pinch ground nutmeg

Preparation:

1. Take a large pot of lightly salted water and bring it to a boil. 2. Add penne and cook for about 11 minutes. 3. Insert a wire rack on Level 3. Turn on your Ninja Foodi XL Pro Air Oven and select "Bake". 4. Set time to 10 to 12 minutes and temperature to 375°F/190°C. Press START/STOP to begin preheating. 5. In the meanwhile, take a sauce pan and melt butter over medium heat and cook garlic for about a minute. 6. Add in flour and whisk continuously until you have a paste. 7. Pour in milk and cream, whisking continuously. 8. Stir in cheese and nutmeg. 9. Now add drained penne pasta and cooked chicken. 10. Pour the mixture into an oven-safe dish. 11. Sprinkle cheese on top. 12. When the unit beeps to signify that it has preheated, add the dish on the wire rack in Ninja Foodi XL Pro Air Oven. 13. Close the oven and bake in the preheated Ninja Foodi XL Pro Air Oven for about 10 to 12 minutes at 375°F/190°C. 14. Serve and enjoy!

Serving Suggestions: Serve with garlic bread.
Variation Tip: Add salt and black pepper according to taste.
Nutritional Information per Serving: Calories: 403 | Fat: 16.2g | Sat Fat: 8.3g | Carbohydrates: 43g | Fiber: 0.1g | Sugar: 3.1g | Protein: 22g

Marinated Ranch Broiled Chicken

Prep Time: 5 minutes | Cook Time: 15 minutes | Serves: 1

Ingredients:

- 1 tablespoon olive oil
- ½ tablespoon red wine vinegar
- 2 tablespoons dry Ranch-style dressing mix
- 1 chicken breast half, skinless and boneless

Preparation:

1. Take a bowl and mix together dressing mix, oil and vinegar. 2. Add chicken in it and toss to coat well. 3. Refrigerate for about an hour. 4. Turn on your Ninja Foodi XL Pro Air Oven and select "Broil". 5. Set timer for 15 minutes and temperature level to HI. Press START/STOP button to begin preheating. 6. When the unit beeps to signify that it has preheated, place chicken onto the roast tray on sheet pan into Level 3 and broil for about 15 minutes until chicken is cooked through. 7. Serve warm and enjoy!

Serving Suggestions: Serve with some rice.
Variation Tip: You can use any type of vinegar.
Nutritional Information per Serving: Calories: 372 | Fat: 28g | Sat Fat: 5.5g | Carbohydrates: 1.1g | Fiber: 0g | Sugar: 0g | Protein: 25g

Chicken Casserole

Prep Time: 15 minutes | Cook Time: 1 hour 50 minutes | Serves: 4

Ingredients:

- Extra-virgin olive oil
- 2 cups white rice
- 1 large onion, chopped
- 2 cups low-sodium chicken broth
- 10½ ounces cream of mushroom soup
- Kosher salt, to taste
- Freshly ground black pepper, to taste
- 2 pounds large bone-in, skin-on chicken thighs
- 2 tablespoons butter, melted
- 2 teaspoons fresh thyme
- 1 clove garlic, minced

Preparation:

1. Insert a wire rack in oven on Level 3. Select the BAKE function, 350°F/175°C, for 1 hour and 30 minutes. While the oven is preheating, grease the sheet pan and prepare the ingredients. 2. Add the onion, soup, broth, and rice to a bowl, then season with salt and pepper. 3. Put the chicken thighs in the rice mixture, skin side up. Brush with the butter. Sprinkle with thyme and garlic, then season with salt and pepper. Place the mixture in the sheet pan. 4. Cover with foil. When the unit beeps to signify it has preheated, open the oven and place the sheet pan onto wire rack and bake for 1 hour. Uncover and bake for an additional 30 minutes. 5. Select the BROIL function on HI and broil it for about 3 to 5 minutes.

Serving Suggestion: Garnish with freshly chopped parsley before serving.
Variation Tip: You can try replacing the low-sodium chicken broth with vegetable stock.
Nutritional Information Per Serving: Calories: 1025 | Fat: 50g | Sodium: 1340g | Carbs: 94g | Fiber: 3g | Sugar: 3g | Protein: 44g

Tender Italian Baked Chicken

Prep Time: 10 minutes | Cook Time: 20 minutes | Serves: 4

Ingredients:

- ¾ cup mayonnaise
- ½ cup grated parmesan cheese
- ¾ teaspoon garlic powder
- ¾ cup Italian seasoned breadcrumbs
- 4 skinless, boneless chicken breast halves

Preparation:

1. Insert a wire rack in oven on Level 3. Select the BAKE function, 425°F/220°C, for 20 minutes. While the oven preheats, prepare the ingredients. 2. Take a bowl, and mix the parmesan cheese, mayonnaise, and garlic powder. In a separate bowl, place the breadcrumbs. 3. Dip the chicken in the mayonnaise mixture and then coat it into the breadcrumbs. Arrange the chicken on the sheet pan. 4. When the unit beeps to signify it has preheated, open the oven and insert the sheet pan on wire rack. 5. Bake the coated chicken for about 20 minutes.

Serving Suggestion: Serve with a sauce of your choice or mustard.
Variation Tip: Try experimenting with different flavored breadcrumbs.
Nutritional Information Per Serving: Calories: 553 | Fat: 39.6g | Sodium: 768.3 | Carbs: 17.1g | Fiber: 0.8g | Sugar: 1.3g | Protein: 3.6g

Baked Honey Mustard Chicken

Prep Time: 15 minutes | Cook Time: 45 minutes | Serves: 6

Ingredients:

- 6 skinless, boneless chicken breast halves
- Salt and pepper, to taste
- ½ cup honey
- ½ cup mustard
- 1 teaspoon dried basil
- 1 teaspoon paprika
- ½ teaspoon dried parsley

Preparation:

1. Insert a wire rack in oven on Level 3. Select the BAKE function, 350°F/175°C, for 45 minutes. Prepare a greased oven-safe baking dish. While the oven is preheating, prepare the ingredients. 2. Season the chicken with salt and pepper and place it in the baking dish. 3. Take a small bowl, and combine the mustard, paprika, honey, parsley, and basil. Mix well. Pour half of the honey-mustard mixture over the chicken, then brush to cover. 4. When the unit beeps to signify it has preheated, open the oven and place the baking dish on wire rack. 5. Bake the chicken for about 30 minutes, turn over, brush with the remaining honey-mustard mixture, and bake for 10 to 15 more minutes. 6. Let the chicken cool for 10 minutes before serving.

Serving Suggestion: You can serve it on a bed of rice alongside some veggies.
Variation Tip: You can try using almond cream instead of mustard.
Nutritional Information Per Serving: Calories: 232 | Fat: 3.7g | Sodium: 296mg | Carbs: 24.8g | Fiber: 1g | Sugar: 23.4g | Protein: 25.6g

Air Fryer Chicken Taco Pockets

Prep Time: 5 minutes | Cook Time: 25 minutes | Serves: 8

Ingredients:

- 2 8-ounce tubes of crescent rolls
- ½ cup salsa
- ½ cup sour cream
- 2 tablespoons taco seasoning
- 1 cup rotisserie chicken, shredded
- 1 cup cheddar cheese, shredded

Preparation:

1. Select the AIR FRY function, 375°F/190°C, for 15 minutes. While the oven is preheating, prepare the ingredients. 2. Unroll 1 tube of crescent roll, separate it into 2 rectangles, and press the perforation to seal. Repeat for the other tube. 3. Take a bowl, and combine the sour cream, salsa, and taco seasoning. Place some shredded chicken on the left sides of the rectangles and top them with the salsa mixture. Sprinkle with the cheese and fold the dough over the filling, then pinch the edges to seal. 4. Transfer the pockets to the air fry basket. When the unit beeps to signify it has preheated, open the oven and slide the air fry basket into rails of Level 3. 5. Close the oven and cook for about 13 to 15 minutes. Cut in half and serve.

Serving Suggestion: Serve with salsa and a topping of your choice.
Variation Tip: You can add shredded lettuce and guacamole to the recipe.
Nutritional Information Per Serving: Calories: 393 | Fat: 24g | Sodium: 896 | Carbs: 29g | Fiber: 0g | Sugar: 7g | Protein: 16g

Mushroom, Broccoli, and Cheese Stuffed Chicken

Prep Time: 10 minutes | Cook Time: 40 minutes | Serves: 4

Ingredients:

- 2 cups broccoli florets, chopped
- 2 tablespoons water
- ½ cup pepper jack cheese
- ¼ cup mayonnaise
- 4 small button mushrooms
- 1 teaspoon garlic powder
- 4 large skinless, boneless chicken breasts
- 1 teaspoon paprika
- Salt and ground black pepper, to taste

Preparation:

1. Insert a wire rack in oven on Level 3. Select the BAKE function, 400°F/200°C, for 35 minutes. While the oven is preheating, prepare the ingredients. 2. Take a microwave-safe bowl and mix the broccoli with the water. Cook for 2 minutes in the microwave on high power. Drain. 3. Combine the pepper jack cheese, mushrooms, broccoli, mayonnaise, and garlic powder in a large bowl. 4. Then, season the chicken breasts with salt, paprika, and pepper. Cut a slice through the middle of each with a sharp knife, creating a deep pocket. Make sure you don't cut all the way through. 5. Stuff the chicken breasts with the broccoli mixture and lay them on the sheet pan. 6. When the unit beeps to signify it has preheated, open the oven and insert the sheet pan on wire rack. 7. Bake the chicken for about 35 minutes.

Serving Suggestion: Serve the chicken on a bed of rice along with some greens.
Variation Tip: You are free to experiment with different combinations of veggies.
Nutritional Information Per Serving: Calories: 579 | Fat: 36.6g | Sodium: 650mg | Carbs: 18.8g | Fiber: 2g | Sugar: 1.3g | Protein: 43.2g

Twice Baked Potatoes with Bacon

Prep Time: 15 minutes | Cook Time: 1 hour 15 minutes | Serves: 8

Ingredients:

- 4 large baking potatoes
- 8 slices bacon
- 1 cup sour cream
- ½ cup milk
- 4 tablespoons butter
- ½ teaspoon salt
- ½ teaspoon pepper
- 1 cup cheddar cheese, shredded
- 8 green onions, sliced

Preparation:

1. Insert a wire rack in oven on Level 3. Select the BAKE function, 350°F/175°C, for 1 hour and 15 minutes. Allow the oven to preheat. 2. Place the potatoes on sheet pan. 3. When the unit beeps to signify it has preheated, open the oven and place the sheet pan on wire rack. Close the oven door and bake the potatoes for about 1 hour. 4. Meanwhile, take a large, deep skillet, place the bacon in it, and cook over medium-high heat. Drain, crumble, and keep it aside. 5. Once the potatoes are done, let them cool down. Slice the cooled potatoes in half lengthwise, scoop the flesh into a large bowl, and save the skins. 6. Add the milk, salt, pepper, sour cream, butter, ½ cup of cheese, and ½ the green onions. Mix well and spoon the mixture into the potato skins. 7. Top them with the remaining cheese, bacon, and green onions. 8. Bake for about 15 minutes.

Serving Suggestion: Sprinkle some cheese and greens on top before serving.
Variation Tip: You can try mushrooms instead of bacon to give this a vegetarian twist.
Nutritional Information Per Serving: Calories: 422 | Fat: 29.5g | Sodium: 537mg | Carbs: 29.3g | Fiber: 2g | Sugar: 3.26g | Protein: 11g

Lasagna Stuffed Chicken

Prep Time: 10 minutes | Cook Time: 35 minutes | Serves: 3

Ingredients:

- 3 large boneless, skinless chicken breasts
- 1 tablespoon olive oil
- 1½ teaspoons Italian seasoning
- 1 teaspoon garlic powder
- 1 teaspoon salt
- 1 cup ricotta cheese
- 1½ cups mozzarella, grated
- 2 teaspoons parsley
- ½ cup marinara sauce

Preparation:

1. Insert a wire rack in oven on Level 3. Select the BAKE function, 375°F/190°C, for 35 minutes. While the oven is preheating, prepare a baking dish with non-stick spray and get the rest of the ingredients ready. 2. Using a sharp knife, cut a deep slit into the side of each chicken breast. 3. Drizzle the chicken breasts with olive oil and season with the garlic powder, ½ teaspoon of Italian seasoning, and ½ teaspoon of salt. 4. In a mixing bowl, combine ½ cup of the mozzarella, the ricotta, ½ teaspoon of parsley, 1 teaspoon of Italian seasoning, and ½ teaspoon of salt. 5. Stuff the ricotta mixture into the chicken breasts. Then place them in the prepared dish. 6. Spoon the marinara over the chicken breasts. 7. When the unit beeps to signify it has preheated, open the oven and place the dish on wire rack. 8. Bake them for about 30 minutes, sprinkle 1 cup of mozzarella over the top, and bake for another 5 minutes.

Serving Suggestion: Sprinkle with the rest of the parsley before serving.
Variation Tip: You can use oregano instead of Italian seasoning.
Nutritional Information Per Serving: Calories: 374 | Fat: 18g | Sodium: 987mg | Carbs: 5g | Fiber: 1g | Sugar: 3g | Protein: 50g

Oven-Baked Peri-Peri Chicken

Prep Time: 5 minutes | Cook Time: 45 minutes Marinate Time: 1 hour | Serves: 4

Ingredients:

- 3 cloves garlic
- Juice and zest of 1 lemon
- Juice of 1 orange
- ¼ cup olive oil
- 2 teaspoons sweet paprika
- ¼ teaspoon black pepper
- ½ teaspoon red pepper flakes
- 1 teaspoon dried oregano
- 2.2 pounds skin-on chicken pieces
- ½ teaspoon salt

Preparation:

1. Insert a wire rack in oven on Level 3. Select the BAKE function, 390°F/200°C, for 45 minutes. 2. Combine the lemon juice, orange juice, minced garlic, and olive oil in a large plastic bowl. 3. Add the sweet paprika, chili flakes, lemon zest, and oregano and combine well. 4. Add the chicken pieces and leave them to marinate for about 1 hour in the refrigerator. 5. Place the chicken pieces on a baking dish. Sprinkle them with salt, place the mixture onto a sheet pan. 6. When the unit beeps to signify it has preheated, open the oven and place the sheet pan on wire rack. 7. Close the oven door and bake for 45 minutes. 8. Pour the pan juices carefully over the chicken before serving.

Serving Suggestion: Add fresh chopped parsley before serving. Serve alongside garlic rice.
Variation Tip: Add more chili flakes to make it spicier, and you can also try Italian seasoning.
Nutritional Information Per Serving: Calories: 638 | Fat: 41g | Sodium: 1037mg | Carbs: 6g | Fiber: 2g | Sugar: 2g | Protein: 61g

Chapter 4 Beef, Pork, and Lamb Recipes

61	Garlicky Lamb Steaks	70	Simple Beef Tenderloin
61	Steak with Bell Peppers	70	Herbed Chuck Roast
61	Lamb Kebabs	71	Lamb Burgers
62	Sauce Glazed Meatloaf	71	Glazed Beef Short Ribs
62	Herb-Crumbed Rack of Lamb	71	Buttered Strip Steak
62	Garlicky Lamb Chops	72	Crispy Sirloin Steaks
63	Lamb Chops with Rosemary Sauce	72	Simple Pork Chops
63	Beef Short Ribs	72	Balsamic Beef Top Roast
63	Garlic Braised Ribs	73	Herbed Leg of Lamb
64	Mint Lamb with Toasted Hazelnuts	73	Lamb Chops with Carrots
64	Greek lamb Farfalle	73	Mustard Lamb Loin Chops
64	Lamb Rack with Lemon Crust	74	Herbed Lamb Loin Chops
65	Beef Zucchini Shashliks	74	Baked Pork Chops
65	Minced Lamb Casserole	74	Herby Pork Bake
65	Pork Chops with Cashew Sauce	75	Czech Roast Pork
66	Za'atar Chops	75	Roast Beef and Yorkshire Pudding
66	Bacon-Wrapped Pork Tenderloin	75	Savory Pork Roast
66	Spiced Pork Shoulder	76	Ground Beef Casserole
67	Tarragon Beef Shanks	76	Baked Beef Stew
67	Zucchini Beef Meatloaf	76	Italian Baked Meatballs
67	Rosemary Lamb Chops	77	Lamb Chops
68	Seasoned Sirloin Steak	77	Air Fryer Beef Taquitos
68	Breaded Pork Chops	77	Roast Sirloin of Beef and Port Gravy
68	Citrus Pork Chops	78	Air Fryer Low-Carb Taco Casserole
69	BBQ Pork Chops	78	Stuffed Pork Tenderloin
69	Pork Stuffed Bell Peppers	78	Breaded Air Fryer Pork Chops
69	Simple New York Strip Steak	79	Glazed Pork Tenderloin
70	American Roast Beefn		

Garlicky Lamb Steaks

Prep Time: 15 minutes | Cook Time: 15 minutes | Serves: 4

Ingredients:

½ onion, roughly chopped
5 garlic cloves, peeled
1 tablespoon fresh ginger, peeled
1 teaspoon ground fennel
½ teaspoon ground cumin

½ teaspoon ground cinnamon
½ teaspoon cayenne pepper
Salt and ground black pepper, as required
1½ pounds boneless lamb sirloin steaks

Preparation:

1. In a blender, add the onion, garlic, ginger, and spices and pulse until smooth. 2. Transfer the mixture into a large bowl. 3. Add the lamb steaks and coat with the mixture generously. 4. Refrigerate to marinate for about 24 hours. 5. Press "Power" button of Ninja Foodi XL Pro Air Oven and select "Air Fry" function. 6. Press TEMP/SHADE +/- buttons to set the temperature at 330°F/165°C. 7. Now press TIME/SLICES +/- buttons to set the cooking time to 15 minutes. 8. Press "START/STOP" button to start. 9. When the unit beeps to show that it is preheated, open the lid and grease the air fry basket. 10. Allow the lamb steaks to reach room temperature before cooking. Place the lamb steaks into the prepared air fry basket and insert in the oven. 11. Flip the steaks once halfway through. 12. When cooking time is completed, open the lid and serve hot.
Serving Suggestions: Serve with your favorite greens.
Variation Tip: Feel free to add some seasoning as you like.
Nutritional Information per Serving: Calories: 336 | Fat: 12.8g | Sat Fat: 4.5g | Carbohydrates: 4.2g | Fiber: 1g | Sugar: 0.7g | Protein: 8.4g

Steak with Bell Peppers

Prep Time: 15 minutes | Cook Time: 11 minutes | Serves: 4

Ingredients:

1 teaspoon dried oregano, crushed
1 teaspoon onion powder
1 teaspoon garlic powder
1 teaspoon red chili powder
1 teaspoon paprika
Salt, as required

1¼ pounds flank steak, cut into thin strips
3 green bell peppers, seeded and cubed
1 red onion, sliced
2 tablespoons olive oil
3-4 tablespoons feta cheese, crumbled

Preparation:

1. In a large bowl, mix the oregano and spices together. 2. Add the steak strips, bell peppers, onion, and oil and mix until well combined. 3. Press "Power" button of Ninja Foodi XL Pro Air Oven and select "Air Fry" function. 4. Press TEMP/SHADE +/- buttons to set the temperature at 390°F/200°C. 5. Now press TIME/SLICES +/- buttons to set the cooking time to 11 minutes. 6. Press "START/STOP" button to start. 7. When the unit beeps to show that it is preheated, open the lid and grease the air fry basket. 8. Place the steak mixture into the prepared air fry basket and insert in the oven. 9. When cooking time is completed, open the lid and transfer the steak mixture onto serving plates. 10. Serve immediately with the topping of feta.
Serving Suggestions: Serve with plain rice.
Variation Tip: Adjust the ratio of spices according to your taste.
Nutritional Information per Serving: Calories: 732 | Fat: 35g | Sat Fat: 12.9g | Carbohydrates: 11.5g | Fiber: 2.5g | Sugar: 6.5g | Protein: 89.3g

Lamb Kebabs

Prep Time: 15 minutes | Cook Time: 20 minutes | Serves: 4

Ingredients:

18 ounces lamb mince
1 teaspoon chili powder
1 teaspoon cumin powder

1 egg
2 ounces onion, chopped
2 teaspoons sesame oil

Preparation:

1. Whisk onion with egg, chili powder, oil, cumin powder, and salt in a bowl. 2. Add lamb to coat well, then thread it on the skewers. 3. Place these lamb skewers in the air fry basket. 4. Transfer the basket to the 3rd rack position of Ninja Foodi XL Pro Air Oven and close the door. 5. Select the "Air Fry" Mode using FUNCTION +/- buttons and select Rack Level 3. 6. Set its cooking time to 20 minutes and temperature to 395°F/200°C, then press "START/STOP" to initiate cooking. 7. Serve warm.
Serving Suggestion: Serve the lamb kebabs with garlic bread slices and fresh herbs on top.
Variation Tip: Add chopped green chilis to the meat mixture.
Nutritional Information Per Serving: Calories 405 | Fat 22.7g | Sodium 227mg | Carbs 6.1g | Fiber 1.4g | Sugar 0.9g | Protein 45.2g

Sauce Glazed Meatloaf

Prep Time: 15 minutes | Cook Time: 60 minutes | Serves: 6

Ingredients:

- 1 pound ground beef
- ½ onion chopped
- 1 egg
- 1½ garlic clove, minced
- 1½ tablespoons ketchup
- 1½ tablespoons fresh parsley, chopped

Glaze
- ¾ cup ketchup
- 1½ teaspoons white vinegar
- 2½ tablespoons brown sugar
- 1 teaspoon garlic powder
- ¼ cup breadcrumbs
- 2 tablespoons milk
- Salt to taste
- 1½ teaspoons herb seasoning
- ¼ teaspoon black pepper
- ½ teaspoon ground paprika
- ½ teaspoon onion powder
- ¼ teaspoon ground black pepper
- ¼ teaspoon salt

Preparation:

1. Thoroughly mix ground beef with egg, onion, garlic, crumbs, and all the ingredients in a bowl. 2. Grease a meatloaf pan with oil or butter and spread the minced beef in the pan. 3. Transfer the pan to the 3rd rack position of Ninja Foodi XL Pro Air Oven and close the door. 4. Select the "Air Fry" Mode using FUNCTION +/- buttons and select Rack Level 3. 5. Set its cooking time to 40 minutes and temperature to 375°F/190°C, then press "START/STOP" to initiate cooking. 6. Meanwhile, prepare the glaze by whisking its ingredients in a suitable saucepan. 7. Stir cook for 5 minutes until it thickens. 8. Brush this glaze over the meatloaf and bake it again for 15 minutes. 9. Slice and serve.

Serving Suggestion: Serve the meatloaf with mashed potatoes.
Variation Tip: Wrap the bacon over the meatloaf before baking.
Nutritional Information Per Serving: Calories 435 | Fat 25g | Sodium 532mg | Carbs 23g | Fiber 0.4g | Sugar 2g | Protein 28.3g

Herb-Crumbed Rack of Lamb

Prep Time: 15 minutes | Cook Time: 30 minutes | Serves: 5

Ingredients:

- 1 tablespoon butter, melted
- 1 garlic clove, finely chopped
- 1¾ pounds rack of lamb
- Salt and ground black pepper, as required
- 1 egg
- ½ cup panko breadcrumbs
- 1 tablespoon fresh thyme, minced
- 1 tablespoon fresh rosemary, minced

Preparation:

1. In a bowl, mix the butter, garlic, salt, and black pepper together. 2. Coat the rack of lamb evenly with garlic mixture. 3. In a shallow dish, beat the egg. 4. In another dish, mix the breadcrumbs and herbs together. 5. Dip the rack of lamb in beaten egg and then coat with breadcrumbs mixture. 6. Press "Power" button of Ninja Foodi XL Pro Air Oven and select "Air Fry" function. 7. Press TEMP/SHADE +/- buttons to set the temperature at 215°F/100°C. 8. Now press TIME/SLICES +/- buttons to set the cooking time to 25 minutes. 9. Press "START/STOP" button to start. 10. When the unit beeps to show that it is preheated, open the lid and grease the air fry basket. 11. Place the rack of lamb into the prepared air fry basket and insert in the oven. 12. After 25 minutes of cooking, flip the rack of lamb. 13. When cooking time is completed, open the lid and set the temperature at 390°F/200°C for 5 minutes. 14. When cooking time is completed, open the lid and place the rack of lamb onto a cutting board for about 5-10 minutes for a more delicious taste. 15. With a sharp knife, cut the rack of lamb into individual chops and serve.

Serving Suggestions: Serve with a drizzling of lemon juice.
Variation Tip: Add some seasoning as you like.
Nutritional Information per Serving: Calories: 331 | Fat: 17.2g | Sat Fat: 6.7g | Carbohydrates: 2.6g | Fiber: 0.5g | Sugar: 0g | Protein: 32.7g

Garlicky Lamb Chops

Prep Time: 15 minutes | Cook Time: 45 minutes | Serves: 8

Ingredients:

- 8 medium lamb chops
- ¼ cup olive oil
- 3 thin lemon slices
- 2 garlic cloves, crushed
- 1 teaspoon dried oregano
- 1 teaspoon salt
- ½ teaspoon black pepper

Preparation:

1. Place the lamb chops in a suitable baking tray and rub them with olive oil. 2. Add garlic, lemon slices, salt, oregano, and black pepper on top of the lamb chops. 3. Transfer the tray to the 2nd rack position of Ninja Foodi XL Pro Air Oven and close the door. 4. Select the "Air Roast" Mode using FUNCTION +/- buttons and select Rack Level 2. 5. Set its cooking time to 45 minutes and temperature to 400°F/200°C, then press "START/STOP" to initiate cooking. 6. Serve warm.

Serving Suggestion: Serve the chops with boiled rice or cucumber salad.
Variation Tip: Cook the lamb chops with potatoes and asparagus
Nutritional Information Per Serving: Calories 461 | Fat 16g | Sodium 515mg | Carbs 3g | Fiber 0.1g | Sugar 1.2g | Protein 21.3g

Lamb Chops with Rosemary Sauce

Prep Time: 15 minutes | Cook Time: 45 minutes | Serves: 8

Ingredients:

8 lamb loin chops
1 small onion, peeled and chopped
For Sauce:
1 onion, peeled and chopped
1 tablespoon rosemary leaves
1 ounce butter
1 ounce plain flour

Salt and black pepper, to taste

6 ounces milk
6 ounces vegetable stock
2 tablespoons cream, whipping
Salt and black pepper, to taste

Preparation:

1. Place the lamb loin chops and onion in a roast tray, then drizzle salt and black pepper on top. 2. Transfer the tray to the 2nd rack position of Ninja Foodi XL Pro Air Oven and close the door. 3. Select the "Air Fry" Mode using FUNCTION +/- buttons and select Rack Level 2. 4. Set its cooking time to 45 minutes and temperature to 350°F/175°C, then press "START/STOP" to initiate cooking. 5. Prepare the white sauce by melting butter in a suitable saucepan, then stir in onions. 6. Sauté for 5 minutes, then stir flour and stir cook for 2 minutes. 7. Stir in the rest of the sauce ingredients and mix well. 8. Pour its sauce over baked chops and serve.

Serving Suggestion: Serve the chops with a fresh green's salad.
Variation Tip: Wrap the lamb chops with a foil sheet before baking for a rich taste.
Nutritional Information Per Serving: Calories 450 | Fat 20g | Sodium 686mg | Carbs 3g | Fiber 1g | Sugar 1.2g | Protein 31g

Beef Short Ribs

Prep Time: 15 minutes | Cook Time: 35 minutes | Serves: 4

Ingredients:

1⅔ pounds short ribs
Salt and black pepper, to taste
1 teaspoon grated garlic
½ teaspoon salt
1 teaspoon cumin seeds

¼ cup panko crumbs
1 teaspoon ground cumin
1 teaspoon avocado oil
½ teaspoon orange zest
1 egg, beaten

Preparation:

1. Place the beef ribs in a baking tray and pour the whisked egg on top. 2. Whisk the rest of the crusting ingredients in a bowl and spread over the beef. 3. Transfer the tray to the 2nd rack position of Ninja Foodi XL Pro Air Oven and close the door. 4. Select the "Air Fry" Mode using FUNCTION +/- buttons and select Rack Level 2. 5. Set its cooking time to 35 minutes and temperature to 350°F/175°C, then press "START/STOP" to initiate cooking. 6. Serve warm.

Serving Suggestion: Serve the short ribs with white rice or warmed bread.
Variation Tip: Add orange juice to the marinade for a refreshing taste.
Nutritional Information Per Serving: Calories 425 | Fat 14g | Sodium 411mg | Carbs 44g | Fiber 0.3g | Sugar 1g | Protein 23g

Garlic Braised Ribs

Prep Time: 15 minutes | Cook Time: 20 minutes | Serves: 8

Ingredients:

2 tablespoons vegetable oil
5 pounds bone-in short ribs
Salt and black pepper, to taste
2 heads garlic, halved
1 medium onion, chopped
4 ribs celery, chopped
2 medium carrots, chopped

3 tablespoons tomato paste
¼ cup dry red wine
¼ cup beef stock
4 sprigs thyme
1 cup parsley, chopped
½ cup chives, chopped
1 tablespoon lemon zest, grated

Preparation

1. Toss everything in a large bowl, then add short ribs. 2. Mix well to soak the ribs and marinate for 30 minutes. 3. Transfer the soaked ribs to the baking pan and add the marinade around them. 4. Transfer the pan to the 2nd rack position of Ninja Foodi XL Pro Air Oven and close the door. 5. Select the "Air Fry" Mode using FUNCTION +/- buttons and select Rack Level 2. 6. Set its cooking time to 20 minutes and temperature to 400°F/200°C, then press "START/STOP" to initiate cooking. 7. Serve warm.

Serving Suggestion: Serve the ribs with mashed potatoes.
Variation Tip: Add barbecue sauce to season the ribs.
Nutritional Information Per Serving: Calories 441 | Fat 5g | Sodium 88mg | Carbs 13g | Fiber 0g | Sugar 0g | Protein 24g

Mint Lamb with Toasted Hazelnuts

Prep Time: 15 minutes | Cook Time: 25 minutes | Serves: 2

Ingredients:

- ¼ cup hazelnuts, toasted
- ⅔ pound shoulder lamb, cut into strips
- 1 tablespoon hazelnut oil
- 2 tablespoons mint leaves, chopped
- ½ cup frozen peas
- ¼ cup of water
- ½ cup white wine
- Salt and black pepper to taste

Preparation:

1. Toss lamb with hazelnuts, spices, and all the ingredients in a baking pan. 2. Transfer the pan to the 3rd rack position of Ninja Foodi XL Pro Air Oven and close the door. 3. Select the "Air Fry" Mode using FUNCTION +/- buttons and select Rack Level 3. 4. Set its cooking time to 25 minutes and temperature to 370°F/185°C, then press "START/STOP" to initiate cooking. 5. Serve warm.
Serving Suggestion: Serve the lamb with carrots and potatoes on the side.
Variation Tip: Use chimichurri sauce to season the lamb.
Nutritional Information Per Serving: Calories 445 | Fat 36g | Sodium 272mg | Carbs 1g | Fiber 0.2g | Sugar 0.1g | Protein 22.5g

Greek lamb Farfalle

Prep Time: 15 minutes | Cook Time: 20 minutes | Serves: 6

Ingredients:

- 1 tablespoon olive oil
- 1 onion, chopped
- 2 garlic cloves, chopped
- 2 teaspoons dried oregano
- 1 pound pack lamb mince
- ¾ pound tin tomatoes, chopped
- ¼ cup black olives pitted
- ½ cup frozen spinach, defrosted
- 2 tablespoons dill, removed and chopped
- 9 ounces farfalle, boiled
- 1 ball half-fat mozzarella, torn

Preparation:

1. Sauté onion and garlic with oil in a pan over moderate heat for 5 minutes. 2. Stir in tomatoes, spinach, dill, oregano, lamb, and olives, then stir cook for 5 minutes. 3. Spread the lamb in a casserole dish and toss in the boiled Farfelle pasta. 4. Top the pasta lamb mix with mozzarella cheese. 5. Transfer the dish to the 2nd rack position of Ninja Foodi XL Pro Air Oven and close the door. 6. Select the "Air Fry" Mode using FUNCTION +/- buttons and select Rack Level 2. 7. Set its cooking time to 10 minutes and temperature to 350°F/175°C, then press "START/STOP" to initiate cooking. 8. Serve warm.
Serving Suggestion: Serve the lamb farfalle with fresh green and mashed potatoes.
Variation Tip: Add shredded cheddar cheese to the meat mixture, then bake.
Nutritional Information Per Serving: Calories 461 | Fat 5g | Sodium 340mg | Carbs 24.7g | Fiber 1.2g | Sugar 1.3g | Protein 15.3g

Lamb Rack with Lemon Crust

Prep Time: 15 minutes | Cook Time: 25 minutes | Serves: 3

Ingredients:

- 1⅔ pounds frenched rack of lamb
- Salt and black pepper, to taste
- ¼ pound dry breadcrumbs
- 1 teaspoon garlic, grated
- ½ teaspoon salt
- 1 teaspoon cumin seeds
- 1 teaspoon ground cumin
- 1 teaspoon oil
- ½ teaspoon grated lemon rind
- 1 egg, beaten

Preparation:

1. Place the lamb rack in a baking tray and pour the whisked egg on top. 2. Whisk the rest of the crusting ingredients in a bowl and spread over the lamb. 3. Transfer the baking tray to the 2nd rack position of Ninja Foodi XL Pro Air Oven and close the door. 4. Select the "Air Fry" Mode using FUNCTION +/- buttons and select Rack Level 2. 5. Set its cooking time to 25 minutes and temperature to 350°F/175°C, then press "START/STOP" to initiate cooking. 6. Serve warm.
Serving Suggestion: Serve the Lamb rack with sautéed green beans and mashed potatoes.
Variation Tip: Drizzle parmesan cheese on top before cooking.
Nutritional Information Per Serving: Calories 455 | Fat 9.5g | Sodium 655mg | Carbs 13.4g | Fiber 0.4g | Sugar 0.4g | Protein 28.3g

Beef Zucchini Shashliks

Prep Time: 15 minutes | Cook Time: 25 minutes | Serves: 4

Ingredients:

- 1 pound beef, boned and diced
- 1 lime, juiced, and chopped
- 3 tablespoons olive oil
- 20 garlic cloves, chopped
- 1 handful rosemary, chopped
- 3 green peppers, cubed
- 2 zucchinis, cubed
- 2 red onions, cut into wedges

Preparation:

1. Toss the beef with the rest of the skewer's ingredients in a bowl. 2. Thread the beef, peppers, zucchini, and onion on the skewers. 3. Place these beef skewers in the air fry basket. 4. Transfer the basket to the 3rd rack position of Ninja Foodi XL Pro Air Oven and close the door. 5. Select the "Air Fry" Mode using FUNCTION +/- buttons and select Rack Level 3. 6. Set its cooking time to 25 minutes and temperature to 370°F/185°C, then press "START/STOP" to initiate cooking. 7. Flip the skewers when cooked halfway through, then resume cooking. 8. Serve warm.

Serving Suggestion: Serve the shashlik with crispy bacon and sautéed vegetables.
Variation Tip: Season the beef with yogurt and spice marinade.
Nutritional Information Per Serving: Calories 416 | Fat 21g | Sodium 476mg | Carbs 22g | Fiber 3g | Sugar 4g | Protein 20g

Minced Lamb Casserole

Prep Time: 15 minutes | Cook Time: 31 minutes | Serves: 6

Ingredients:

- 2 tablespoons olive oil
- 1 medium onion, chopped
- ½ pound ground lamb
- 4 fresh mushrooms, sliced
- 1 cup small pasta shells, cooked
- 2 cups bottled marinara sauce
- 1 teaspoon butter
- 4 teaspoons flour
- 1 cup milk
- 1 egg, beaten
- 1 cup cheddar cheese, grated

Preparation:

1. Put a wok on moderate heat and add oil to heat. 2. Toss in onion and sauté until soft. 3. Stir in mushrooms and lamb, then cook until meat is brown. 4. Add marinara sauce and cook it to a simmer. 5. Stir in pasta, then spread this mixture in a casserole dish. 6. Prepare its sauce by melting butter in a suitable saucepan over moderate heat. 7. Stir in flour and whisk well, pour in the milk. 8. Mix well and whisk ¼ cup sauce with egg, then return it to its saucepan. 9. Stir, cook for 1 minute, then pour this sauce over the lamb. 10. Drizzle cheese over the lamb casserole. 11. Transfer the dish to the 2nd rack position of Ninja Foodi XL Pro Air Oven and close the door. 12. Select the "Bake" Mode using FUNCTION +/- buttons and select Rack Level 2. 13. Set its cooking time to 30 minutes and temperature to 350°F/175°C, then press "START/STOP" to initiate cooking. 14. Serve warm.

Serving Suggestion: Serve the lamb casserole with quinoa salad.
Variation Tip: Add shredded cheese to the casserole for a cheesy taste.
Nutritional Information Per Serving: Calories 448 | Fat 23g | Sodium 350mg | Carbs 18g | Fiber 6.3g | Sugar 1g | Protein 40.3g

Pork Chops with Cashew Sauce

Prep Time: 15 minutes | Cook Time: 52 minutes | Serves: 8

Ingredients:

- 8 pork loin chops
- 1 small onion, peeled and chopped
- **For Sauce:**
- ¼ cup cashews, finely chopped
- 1 cup cashew butter
- 1 ounce wheat flour
- 6 fl. oz. milk
- Salt and black pepper, to taste
- 6 fl. oz. beef stock
- 2 tablespoons coconut cream, whipping
- Salt and black pepper, to taste

Preparation:

1. Place the pork loin chops and onion in a baking tray, then drizzle salt and black pepper on top. 2. Transfer the tray to the 2nd rack position of Ninja Foodi XL Pro Air Oven and close the door. 3. Select the "Bake" Mode using FUNCTION +/- buttons and select Rack Level 2. 4. Set its cooking time to 45 minutes and temperature to 375°F/190°C, then press "START/STOP" to initiate cooking. 5. Prepare the white sauce by first melting butter in a suitable saucepan, then stir in cashews. 6. Sauté for 5 minutes, then stir flour and stir cook for 2 minutes. 7. Stir in the rest of its sauce ingredients and mix well. 8. Pour its sauce over baked chops and serve.

Serving Suggestion: Serve the pork chops with sautéed vegetables and toasted bread slices.
Variation Tip: Add crushed cashews on top before baking.
Nutritional Information Per Serving: Calories 309 | Fat 25g | Sodium 463mg | Carbs 9g | Fiber 0.3g | Sugar 0.3g | Protein 18g

Za'atar Chops

Prep Time: 15 minutes | Cook Time: 20 minutes | Serves: 8

Ingredients:

- 8 pork loin chops, bone-in
- 1 tablespoon Za'atar
- 3 garlic cloves, crushed
- 1 teaspoon avocado oil
- 2 tablespoons lemon juice
- 1 ¼ teaspoons salt
- Black pepper, to taste

Preparation:

1. Rub the pork chops with oil, za'atar, salt, lemon juice, garlic, and black pepper. 2. Place these chops in the air fry basket. 3. Transfer the basket to the 2nd rack position of Ninja Foodi XL Pro Air Oven and close the door. 4. Select the "Air Fry" Mode using FUNCTION +/- buttons and select Rack Level 2. 5. Set its cooking time to 20 minutes and temperature to 400°F/200°C, then press "START/STOP" to initiate cooking. 6. Flip the chops when cooked halfway through, then resume cooking. 7. Serve warm.

Serving Suggestion: Serve the chops with mashed potatoes.
Variation Tip: Add dried herbs to season the chops.
Nutritional Information Per Serving: Calories 437 | Fat 20g | Sodium 719mg | Carbs 5.1g | Fiber 0.9g | Sugar 1.4g | Protein 37.8g

Bacon-Wrapped Pork Tenderloin

Prep Time: 15 minutes | Cook Time: 30 minutes | Serves: 4

Ingredients:

- 1 (1½-pound) pork tenderloin
- 2 tablespoons Dijon mustard
- 1 tablespoon honey
- 4 bacon strips

Preparation:

1. Coat the tenderloin with mustard and honey. 2. Wrap the pork tenderloin with bacon strips. 3. Press "Power" button of Ninja Foodi XL Pro Air Oven and select "Air Fry" function. 4. Press TEMP/SHADE +/- buttons to set the temperature at 360°F/180°C. 5. Now press TIME/SLICES +/- buttons to set the cooking time to 30 minutes. 6. Press "START/STOP" button to start. 7. When the unit beeps to show that it is preheated, open the lid and grease the air fry basket. 8. Place the pork tenderloin into the prepared air fry basket and insert in the oven. 9. Flip the pork tenderloin once halfway through. 10. When cooking time is completed, open the lid and place the pork loin onto a cutting board for about 10 minutes before slicing. 11. With a sharp knife, cut the tenderloin into desired sized slices and serve.

Serving Suggestions: Enjoy with mashed potatoes.
Variation Tip: Make sure to remove the silver skin from the tenderloin.
Nutritional Information per Serving: Calories: 386 | Fat: 16.1g | Sat Fat: 5.7g | Carbohydrates: 4.8g | Fiber: 0.3g | Sugar: 4.4g | Protein: 52g

Spiced Pork Shoulder

Prep Time: 15 minutes | Cook Time: 55 minutes | Serves: 4

Ingredients:

- 1 teaspoon ground cumin
- 1 teaspoon cayenne pepper
- ½ teaspoon garlic powder
- ½ teaspoon onion powder
- Salt and ground black pepper, as required
- 2 pounds skin-on pork shoulder

Preparation:

1. In a small bowl, place the spices, salt and black pepper and mix well. 2. Arrange the pork shoulder onto a cutting board, skin-side down. 3. Season the inner side of pork shoulder with salt and black pepper. 4. With kitchen twines, tie the pork shoulder into a long round cylinder shape. 5. Season the outer side of pork shoulder with spice mixture. 6. Press "Power" button of Ninja Foodi XL Pro Air Oven and select the "Air Roast" function. 7. Press TEMP/SHADE +/- buttons to set the temperature at 350°F/175°C. 8. Now press TIME/SLICES +/- buttons to set the cooking time to 55 minutes. 9. Press "START/STOP" button to start. 10. When the unit beeps to show that it is preheated, open the lid and grease the air fry basket. 11. Arrange the pork shoulder into air fry basket and insert in the oven. 12. When cooking time is completed, open the lid and place the pork shoulder onto a platter for about 10 minutes before slicing. 13. With a sharp knife, cut the pork shoulder into desired sized slices and serve.

Serving Suggestions: Choose a pork shoulder with pinkish-red color. Serve with southern-style grits.
Variation Tip: Add some seasoning of your choice.
Nutritional Information per Serving: Calories: 445 | Fat: 32.5g | Sat Fat: 11.9g | Carbohydrates: 0.7g | Fiber: 0.2g | Sugar: 0.2g | Protein: 35.4g

Tarragon Beef Shanks

Prep Time: 15 minutes | Cook Time: 15 minutes | Serves: 4

Ingredients:

- 2 tablespoons olive oil
- 2 pounds beef shank
- Salt and black pepper to taste
- 1 onion, diced
- 2 stalks celery, diced
- 1 cup Marsala wine
- 2 tablespoons dried tarragon

Preparation:

1. Place the beef shanks in a baking pan. 2. Whisk the rest of the ingredients in a bowl and pour over the shanks. 3. Place these shanks in the air fry basket. 4. Transfer the basket to the 2nd rack position of Ninja Foodi XL Pro Air Oven and close the door. 5. Select the "Air Fry" Mode using FUNCTION +/- buttons and select Rack Level 2. 6. Set its cooking time to 15 minutes and temperature to 375°F/190°C, then press "START/STOP" to initiate cooking. 7. Serve warm.

Serving Suggestion: Serve the beef shanks with sweet potato casserole.
Variation Tip: Cook the beef shanks with the mushrooms sauce.
Nutritional Information Per Serving: Calories 425 | Fat 15g | Sodium 345mg | Carbs 12.3g | Fiber 1.4g | Sugar 3g | Protein 23.3g

Zucchini Beef Meatloaf

Prep Time: 15 minutes | Cook Time: 40 minutes | Serves: 4

Ingredients:

- 2 pounds ground beef
- 1 cup zucchini, shredded
- 2 eggs
- ½ cup onion, chopped
- 3 garlic cloves, minced
- 3 tablespoons Worcestershire sauce
- 3 tablespoons fresh parsley, chopped
- ¾ cup Panko breadcrumbs
- ⅓ cup beef broth
- Salt to taste
- ¼ teaspoon ground black pepper
- ½ teaspoon ground paprika

Preparation:

1. Thoroughly mix ground beef with egg, zucchini, onion, garlic, crumbs, and all the ingredients in a bowl. 2. Grease a meatloaf pan with oil and spread the minced beef in the pan. 3. Transfer the pan to the 2nd rack position of Ninja Foodi XL Pro Air Oven and close the door. 4. Select the "Air Fry" Mode using FUNCTION +/- buttons and select Rack Level 2. 5. Set its cooking time to 40 minutes and temperature to 375°F/190°C, then press "START/STOP" to initiate cooking. 6. Slice and serve.

Serving Suggestion: Serve the meatloaf with toasted bread slices.
Variation Tip: Add crumbled bacon on top for a crispy texture.
Nutritional Information Per Serving: Calories 325 | Fat 16g | Sodium 431mg | Carbs 22g | Fiber 1.2g | Sugar 4g | Protein 23g

Rosemary Lamb Chops

Prep Time: 10 minutes | Cook Time: 6 minutes | Serves: 2

Ingredients:

- 1 tablespoon olive oil, divided
- 2 garlic cloves, minced
- 1 tablespoon fresh rosemary, chopped
- Salt and ground black pepper, as required
- 4 (4-ounce) fresh lamb chops

Preparation:

1. In a large bowl, mix the oil, garlic, rosemary, salt and black pepper together. 2. Dry out the edges of lamb chops. Coat the chops with half of the garlic mixture. 3. Press "Power" button of Ninja Foodi XL Pro Air Oven and select "Air Fry" function. 4. Press TEMP/SHADE +/- buttons to set the temperature at 390°F/200°C. 5. Now press TIME/SLICES +/- buttons to set the cooking time to 6 minutes. 6. Press "START/STOP" button to start. 7. When the unit beeps to show that it is preheated, open the lid and grease the air fry basket. 8. Place the lamb chops into the prepared air fry basket and insert in the oven. 9. Flip the chops once halfway through. 10. When cooking time is completed, open the lid and serve hot with the topping of the remaining garlic mixture.

Serving Suggestions: Serve with yogurt sauce.
Variation Tip: Feel free to add some seasoning of your choice.
Nutritional Information per Serving: Calories: 492 | Fat: 23.9g | Sat Fat: 7.1g | Carbohydrates: 2.1g | Fiber: 0.8g | Sugar: 0g | Protein: 64g

Seasoned Sirloin Steak

Prep Time: 10 minutes | Cook Time: 12 minutes | Serves: 2

Ingredients:

2 (7-ounce) top sirloin steaks
1 tablespoon steak seasoning

Salt and ground black pepper, as required

Preparation:

1. Make sure the surface of the steak be moist but not wet or sticky. 2. Season each steak with steak seasoning, salt and black pepper. 3. Arrange the steaks onto the greased cooking pan. 4. Press "Power" button of Ninja Foodi XL Pro Air Oven and select "Air Fry" function. 5. Press TEMP/SHADE +/- buttons to set the temperature at 400°F/200°C. 6. Now press TIME/SLICES +/- buttons to set the cooking time to 12 minutes. 7. Press "START/STOP" button to start. 8. When the unit beeps to show that it is preheated, open the lid and insert the baking pan in the oven. 9. Flip the steaks once halfway through. 10. When cooking time is completed, open the lid and serve hot.
Serving Suggestions: Serve with cheesy scalloped potatoes.
Variation Tip: Feel free to add some seasoning of your choice.
Nutritional Information per Serving: Calories: 369 | Fat: 12.4g | Sat Fat: 4.7g | Carbohydrates: 0g | Fiber: 0g | Sugar: 0g | Protein: 60.2g

Breaded Pork Chops

Prep Time: 15 minutes | Cook Time: 15 minutes | Serves: 3

Ingredients:

3 (6-ounce) pork chops
Salt and ground black pepper, as required
¼ cup plain flour

1 egg
4 ounces seasoned breadcrumbs
1 tablespoon canola oil

Preparation:

1. Season each pork chop with salt and black pepper. 2. In a shallow bowl, place the flour. 3. In a second bowl, crack the egg and beat well. 4. In a third bowl, add the breadcrumbs and oil and mix until a crumbly mixture forms. 5. Coat the pork chop with flour, then dip into beaten egg and finally, coat with the breadcrumbs mixture. 6. Press "Power" button of Ninja Foodi XL Pro Air Oven and select "Air Fry" function. 7. Press TEMP/SHADE +/- buttons to set the temperature at 400°F/200°C. 8. Now press TIME/SLICES +/- buttons to set the cooking time to 15 minutes. 9. Press "START/STOP" button to start. 10. When the unit beeps to show that it is preheated, open the lid and grease the air fry basket. 11. Place the lamb chops into the prepared air fry basket and insert in the oven. 12. Flip the chops once halfway through. 13. When cooking time is completed, open the lid and serve hot.
Serving Suggestions: Don't cook chops straight from the refrigerator. Serve with your favorite dipping sauce.
Variation Tip: Replace the black pepper with some other peppers of your choice.
Nutritional Information per Serving: Calories: 413 | Fat: 20.2g | Sat Fat: 4.4g | Carbohydrates: 31g | Fiber: 1.6g | Sugar: 0.1g | Protein: 28.3g

Citrus Pork Chops

Prep Time: 15 minutes | Cook Time: 15 minutes | Serves: 6

Ingredients:

½ cup olive oil
1 teaspoon fresh orange zest, grated
3 tablespoons fresh orange juice
1 teaspoon fresh lime zest, grated
3 tablespoons fresh lime juice
8 garlic cloves, minced

1 cup fresh cilantro, chopped finely
¼ cup fresh mint leaves, chopped finely
1 teaspoon dried oregano, crushed
1 teaspoon ground cumin
Salt and ground black pepper, as required
6 thick-cut pork chops

Preparation:

1. In a bowl, place the oil, orange zest, orange juice, lime zest, lime juice, garlic, fresh herbs, oregano, cumin, salt and black pepper and beat until well combined. 2. In a small bowl, reserve ¼ cup of the marinade. 3. In a large zip lock bag, place the remaining marinade and pork chops. 4. Seal the bag and shake to coat well. 5. Refrigerate to marinate overnight. 6. Remove the pork chops from the bag and shake off to remove the excess marinade. 7. Press "Power" button of Ninja Foodi XL Pro Air Oven and select the "Broil" function. 8. Press TEMP/SHADE button to select HI. 9. Now press TIME/SLICES +/- buttons to set the cooking time to 15 minutes. 10. Press "Start/Stop" button to start. 11. When the unit beeps to show that it is preheated, open the oven door. 12. Place the pork chops over the wire rack on Level 3. 13. After 8 minutes of cooking, flip the chops once. 14. When the cooking time is completed, open the oven door and serve hot.
Serving Suggestions: Serve with steamed broccoli.
Variation Tip: Use fresh orange juice and zest.
Nutritional Information per Serving: Calories: 700 | Fat: 59.3g | Sat Fat: 18.3g | Carbohydrates: 2.1g | Fiber: 0.4g | Sugar: 0.3g | Protein: 38.7g

BBQ Pork Chops

Prep Time: 10 minutes | Cook Time: 16 minutes | Serves: 6

Ingredients:

- 6 (8-ounce) pork loin chops
- Salt and ground black pepper, as required
- ½ cup BBQ sauce

Preparation:

1. With a meat tenderizer, tenderize the chops completely. 2. Sprinkle the chops with a little salt and black pepper. 3. In a large bowl, add the BBQ sauce and chops and mix well. 4. Refrigerate, covered for about 6-8 hours. 5. Press "Power" button of Ninja Foodi XL Pro Air Oven and select "Air Fry" function. Select 2 LEVEL. 6. Press TEMP/SHADE +/- buttons to set the temperature at 355°F/180°C. 7. Now press TIME/SLICES +/- buttons to set the cooking time to 16 minutes. 8. Press "Start/Stop" button to start. 9. When the unit beeps to show that it is preheated, open the oven door. 10. Arrange the pork chops into the greased air fry basket on Level 4 and sheet pan over wire rack on Level 2. 11. Flip the chops once halfway through. 12. When the cooking time is completed, open the oven door and serve hot.

Serving Suggestions: Serve with roasted veggies.
Variation Tip: Make sure to use good quality BBQ sauce.
Nutritional Information per Serving:
Calories: 757 | Fat: 56.4g | Sat Fat: 21.1g | Carbohydrates: 7.6g | Fiber: 0.1g | Sugar: 5.4g | Protein: 51g

Pork Stuffed Bell Peppers

Prep Time: 20 minutes | Cook Time: 1 hour 10 minutes | Serves: 4

Ingredients:

- 4 medium green bell peppers
- ⅔ pound ground pork
- 2 cups cooked white rice
- 1½ cups marinara sauce, divided
- 1 teaspoon Worcestershire sauce
- 1 teaspoon Italian seasoning
- Salt and ground black pepper, as required
- ½ cup mozzarella cheese, shredded

Preparation:

1. Cut the tops from bell peppers and then carefully remove the seeds. 2. Heat a large skillet over medium heat and cook the pork for about 6-8 minutes, breaking into crumbles. 3. Add the rice, ¾ cup of marinara sauce, Worcestershire sauce, Italian seasoning, salt and black pepper and stir to combine. 4. Remove from the heat. 5. Arrange the bell peppers into the greased baking pan. 6. Carefully, stuff each bell pepper with the pork mixture and top each with the remaining sauce. 7. Press "Power" button of Ninja Foodi XL Pro Air Oven and select the "Bake" function. 8. Press TEMP/SHADE +/- buttons to set the temperature at 350°F/175°C. 9. Now press TIME/SLICES +/- buttons to set the cooking time to 60 minutes. 10. Press "START/STOP" button to start. 11. When the unit beeps to show that it is preheated, open the lid. 12. Insert the baking pan in oven. 13. After 50 minutes of cooking, top each bell pepper with cheese. 14. When cooking time is completed, open the lid and transfer the bell peppers onto a platter. 15. Serve warm.

Serving Suggestions: Serve with baby greens.
Variation Tip: Feel free to add some seasoning as you like.
Nutritional Information per Serving: Calories: 580 | Fat: 7.1g | Sat Fat: 2.2g | Carbohydrates: 96.4g | Fiber: 5.2g | Sugar: 14.8g | Protein: 30.3g

Simple New York Strip Steak

Prep Time: 5 minutes | Cook Time: 8 minutes | Serves: 1

Ingredients:

- ½ teaspoon olive oil
- ½ New York strip steak
- Kosher salt and ground black pepper, to taste

Preparation:

1. Coat the steak with oil and then, generously season with salt and black pepper. 2. Grease an air fry basket. 3. Place steak into the prepared air fry basket on Level 3 in oven. 4. Turn on your Ninja Foodi XL Pro Air Oven and select "Air Fry". 5. Select the timer for about 7 to 8 minutes and temperature for 400°F/200°C. 6. Remove from the oven and place the steak onto a cutting board for about 10 minutes before slicing. 7. Cut the steak into desired-size slices and transfer onto serving plates. 8. Serve immediately.

Serving Suggestions: Add your favorite sauce or mushroom sauce on top.
Variation Tip: You can also add chopped rosemary.
Nutritional Information per Serving: Calories: 245 | Fat: 16.3g | Sat Fat: 5.8g | Carbohydrates: 0g | Fiber: 0g | Sugar: 0g | Protein: 25g

American Roast Beefn

Prep Time: 5 minutes | Cook Time: 1 hour | Serves: 3

Ingredients:

- 1½ pounds beef eye of round roast
- ¼ teaspoon kosher salt
- ⅛ teaspoon black pepper, freshly ground
- ¼ teaspoon garlic powder

Preparation:

1. Turn on your Ninja Foodi XL Pro Air Oven and select "Air Roast". 2. Set the timer for 60 minutes and temperature for 375°F/190°C. 3. Press START/STOP to begin preheating. 4. When the unit beeps to signify it has preheated, place beef in a sheet pan on Level 3 and season with salt, garlic powder and pepper. 5. Roast in oven for about an hour. 6. Remove from oven and set aside for 10 minutes before slicing. 7. Serve warm and enjoy!

Serving Suggestions: Serve it with mashed potatoes.
Variation Tip: You can add onions on top for a little flavoring.
Nutritional Information per Serving: Calories: 382 | Fat: 11.1g | Sat Fat: 4g | Carbohydrates: 0.2g | Fiber: 0g | Sugar: 0.1g | Protein: 65.8g

Simple Beef Tenderloin

Prep Time: 10 minutes | Cook Time: 50 minutes | Serves: 10

Ingredients:

- 1 (3½-pound) beef tenderloin, trimmed
- 2 tablespoons olive oil
- Salt and ground black pepper, as required

Preparation:

1. With kitchen twine, tie the tenderloin. 2. Rub the tenderloin with oil and season with salt and black pepper. 3. Place the tenderloin into the greased baking pan. 4. Press "Power" button of Ninja Foodi XL Pro Air Oven and select the "Air Roast" function. 5. Press TEMP/SHADE +/- buttons to set the temperature at 400°F/200°C. 6. Now press TIME/SLICES +/- buttons to set the cooking time to 50 minutes. 7. Press "START/STOP" button to start. 8. When the unit beeps to show that it is preheated, open the lid and insert the baking pan in the oven. 9. When cooking time is completed, open the lid and place the tenderloin onto a platter for about 10 minutes before slicing. 10. With a sharp knife, cut the tenderloin into desired sized slices and serve.

Serving Suggestions: Serve with lemony herbed couscous.
Variation Tip: Add some seasoning as you like.
Nutritional Information per Serving: Calories: 351 | Fat: 17.3g | Sat Fat: 5.9g | Carbohydrates: 0g | Fiber: 0g | Sugar: 0g | Protein: .46g

Herbed Chuck Roast

Prep Time: 10 minutes | Cook Time: 45 minutes | Serves: 6

Ingredients:

- 1 (2-pound) beef chuck roast
- 1 tablespoon olive oil
- 1 teaspoon dried rosemary, crushed
- 1 teaspoon dried thyme, crushed
- Salt, as required

Preparation:

1. In a bowl, add the oil, herbs and salt and mix well. 2. Coat the beef roast with herb mixture generously. 3. Arrange the beef roast onto the greased cooking pan. 4. Press "Power" button of Ninja Foodi XL Pro Air Oven and select "Air Fry" function. 5. Press TEMP/SHADE +/- buttons to set the temperature at 360°F/180°C. 6. Now press TIME/SLICES +/- buttons to set the cooking time to 45 minutes. 7. Press "START/STOP" button to start. 8. When the unit beeps to show that it is preheated, open the lid and insert the baking pan in the oven. 9. When cooking time is completed, open the lid and place the roast onto a cutting board. 10. With a piece of foil, cover the beef roast for about 20 minutes before slicing. 11. With a sharp knife, cut the beef roast into desired size slices and serve.

Serving Suggestions: Serve with roasted Brussels sprouts.
Variation Tip: Dried herbs can be replaced with fresh herbs.
Nutritional Information per Serving: Calories: 304 | Fat: 14g | Sat Fat: 4.5g | Carbohydrates: 0.2g | Fiber: 0.2g | Sugar: 0g | Protein: 41.5g

Lamb Burgers

Prep Time: 10 minutes | Cook Time: 8 minutes | Serves: 6

Ingredients:

- 2 pounds ground lamb
- ½ tablespoon onion powder
- ½ tablespoon garlic powder
- ¼ teaspoon ground cumin
- Salt and ground black pepper, as required

Preparation:

1. In a bowl, add all the ingredients and mix well. 2. Make 6 equal-sized patties from the mixture. 3. Arrange the patties onto the greased sheet pan in a single layer. 4. Press "Power" button of Ninja Foodi XL Pro Air Oven and select "Air Fry" function. 5. Press TEMP/SHADE +/- buttons to set the temperature at 360°F/180°C. 6. Now press TIME/SLICES +/- buttons to set the cooking time to 8 minutes. 7. Press "START/STOP" button to start. 8. When the unit beeps to show that it is preheated, open the lid. 9. Insert the sheet pan in oven. 10. Flip the burgers once halfway through. 11. When cooking time is completed, open the lid and serve hot.

Serving Suggestions: Serve with fresh salad.
Variation Tip: Feel free to add some seasoning or sauces of your choice.
Nutritional Information per Serving: Calories: 286 | Fat: 11.1g | Sat Fat: 4g | Carbohydrates: 1g | Fiber: 0.1g | Sugar: 0.4g | Protein: 42.7g

Glazed Beef Short Ribs

Prep Time: 15 minutes | Cook Time: 8 minutes | Serves: 4

Ingredients:

- 2 pounds bone-in beef short ribs
- 3 tablespoons scallions, chopped
- ½ tablespoon fresh ginger, finely grated
- ½ cup low-sodium soy sauce
- ¼ cup balsamic vinegar
- ½ tablespoon Sriracha
- 1 tablespoon sugar
- ½ teaspoon ground black pepper

Preparation:

1. In a resealable bag, place all the ingredients. 2. Seal the bag and shake to coat well. 3. Refrigerate overnight. 4. Press "Power" button of Ninja Foodi XL Pro Air Oven and select "Air Fry" function. 5. Press TEMP/SHADE +/- buttons to set the temperature at 380°F/195°C. 6. Now press TIME/SLICES +/- buttons to set the cooking time to 8 minutes. 7. Press "Start/Stop" button to start. 8. When the unit beeps to show that it is preheated, open the oven door. 9. Place the ribs into the greased roast tray on sheet pan and place them into rail of Level 3. 10. Flip the ribs once halfway through. 11. When the cooking time is completed, open the oven door and serve hot.

Serving Suggestions: Serve with cucumber salad.
Variation Tip: Brown sugar can also be used in this recipe.
Nutritional Information per Serving: Calories: 496 | Fat: 20.5g | Sat Fat: 7.8g | Carbohydrates: 6.5g | Fiber: 0.3g | Sugar: 5.2g | Protein: 67.7g

Buttered Strip Steak

Prep Time: 10 minutes | Cook Time: 15 minutes | Serves: 4

Ingredients:

- 2 (14-ounce) New York strip steaks
- 2 tablespoons butter, melted
- Salt and ground black pepper, as required

Preparation:

1. Brush each steak with the melted butter evenly and then season with salt and black pepper. 2. Press "Power" button of Ninja Foodi XL Pro Air Oven and select the "Broil" function. 3. Press the TEMP/SHADE +/- buttons to select HI. 4. Now press TIME/SLICES +/- buttons to set the cooking time to 15 minutes. 5. Press "Start/Stop" button to start. 6. When the unit beeps to show that it is preheated, open the oven door. 7. Place the steaks on the sheet pan over the wire rack and insert into the rail of Level 3. 8. When cooking time is completed, open the oven door and place the steaks onto a cutting board for about 5 minutes before slicing. 9. Cut each steak into 2 portions and serve.

Serving Suggestions: Serve alongside the spiced potatoes.
Variation Tip: Use freshly ground black pepper.
Nutritional Information per Serving: Calories: 296 | Fat: 12.7g | Sat Fat: 6.6g | Carbohydrates: 0g | Fiber: 0g | Sugar: 0g | Protein: 44.5g

Crispy Sirloin Steaks

Prep Time: 10 minutes | Cook Time: 14 minutes | Serves: 2

Ingredients:

- ½ cup flour
- Salt and ground black pepper, as required
- 2 eggs
- ¾ cup breadcrumbs
- 3 (6-ounce) sirloin steaks, pounded

Preparation:

1. In a shallow bowl, place the flour, salt and black pepper and mix well. 2. In a second shallow bowl, beat the eggs. 3. In a third shallow bowl, place the breadcrumbs. 4. Coat the steak with flour, then dip into eggs, and finally coat with the panko mixture. 5. Press "Power" button of Ninja Foodi XL Pro Air Oven and select "Air Fry" function. 6. Press TEMP/SHADE +/- buttons to set the temperature at 360°F/180°C. 7. Now press TIME/SLICES +/- buttons to set the cooking time to 14 minutes. 8. Press "Start/Stop" button to start. 9. When the unit beeps to show that it is preheated, open the oven door. 10. Arrange the steaks into the greased air fry basket and insert into the rail of Level 3. 11. When the cooking time is completed, open the oven door and serve hot.

Serving Suggestions: Serve with your favorite dipping sauce.
Variation Tip: Feel free to use breadcrumbs of your choice.
Nutritional Information per Serving: Calories: 540 | Fat: 15.2g | Sat Fat: 5.3g | Carbohydrates: 35.6g | Fiber: 1.8g | Sugar: 2g | Protein: 61g

Simple Pork Chops

Prep Time: 10 minutes | Cook Time: 18 minutes | Serves: 2

Ingredients:

- 2 (6-ounce) (½-inch thick) pork chops
- Salt and ground black pepper, as required

Preparation:

1. Season the pork chops with salt and black pepper evenly. 2. Arrange the pork chops onto a greased sheet pan. 3. Press "Power" button of Ninja Foodi XL Pro Air Oven and select the "Broil" function. 4. Press the TEMP/SHADE +/- buttons to select HI. 5. Now press TIME/SLICES +/- buttons to set the cooking time to 18 minutes. 6. Press "Start/Stop" button to start. 7. When the unit beeps to show that it is preheated, open the oven door and insert the sheet pan over wire rack into the rail of Level 3. 8. After 12 minutes of cooking, flip the chops once. 9. When cooking time is completed, open the oven door and serve hot.

Serving Suggestions: Serve alongside the mashed potato.
Variation Tip: Season the chops generously.
Nutritional Information per Serving: Calories: 544 | Fat: 42.3g | Sat Fat: 15.8g | Carbohydrates: 0g | Fiber: 0g | Sugar: 0g | Protein: 38.2g

Balsamic Beef Top Roast

Prep Time: 10 minutes | Cook Time: 45 minutes | Serves: 10

Ingredients:

- 1 tablespoon butter, melted
- 1 tablespoon balsamic vinegar
- ½ teaspoon ground cumin
- ½ teaspoon smoked paprika
- ½ teaspoon red pepper flakes, crushed
- Salt and ground black pepper, as required
- 3 pounds beef top roast

Preparation:

1. In a bowl, add butter, vinegar, spices, salt and black pepper and mix well. 2. Coat the roast with spice mixture generously. 3. With kitchen twines, tie the roast to keep it compact. 4. Arrange the roast onto the greased sheet pan and greased air fry basket. 5. Press "Power" button of Ninja Foodi XL Pro Air Oven and select "Air Fry" function. Select 2 LEVEL. 6. Press TEMP/SHADE +/- buttons to set the temperature at 360°F/180°C. 7. Now press TIME/SLICES +/- buttons to set the cooking time to 45 minutes. 8. Press "Start/Stop" button to start. 9. When the unit beeps to show that it is preheated, open the oven door and insert the sheet pan over wire rack on Level 2 and air fry basket on Level 4. 10. When the cooking time is completed, open the oven door and place the roast onto a cutting board for about 10 minutes before slicing. 11. With a sharp knife, cut the roast into desired sized slices and serve.

Serving Suggestions: Serve alongside the buttered green beans.
Variation Tip: Use unsalted butter.
Nutritional Information per Serving: Calories: 305 | Fat: 17.1g | Sat Fat: 6.1g | Carbohydrates: 0.1g | Fiber: 0.1g | Sugar: 0g | Protein: 35.1g

Herbed Leg of Lamb

Prep Time: 10 minutes | Cook Time: 1¼ hours | Serves: 6

Ingredients:

- 2¼ pounds boneless leg of lamb
- 2 tablespoons olive oil
- Salt and ground black pepper, as required
- 2 fresh rosemary sprigs
- 2 fresh thyme sprigs

Preparation:

1. Coat the leg of lamb with oil and sprinkle with salt and black pepper. 2. Wrap the leg of lamb with herb sprigs. 3. Press "Power" button of Ninja Foodi XL Pro Air Oven and select "Air Fry" function. 4. Press TEMP/SHADE +/- buttons to set the temperature at 300°F/150°C. 5. Now press TIME/SLICES +/- buttons to set the cooking time to 75 minutes. 6. Press "Start/Stop" button to start. 7. When the unit beeps to show that it is preheated, open the oven door. 8. Arrange the leg of lamb into the greased air fry basket on Level 3. 9. Immediately set the temperature at 355°F/180°C. 10. When the cooking time is completed, open the oven door and place the leg of lamb onto a cutting board for about 10 minutes. 11. Cut the leg of lamb into desired-sized pieces and serve.

Serving Suggestions: Serve alongside the roasted Brussels sprout.
Variation Tip: Always slice the meat against the grain.
Nutritional Information per Serving: Calories: 360 | Fat: 17.3g | Sat Fat: 5.2g | Carbohydrates: 0.7g | Fiber: 0.5g | Sugar: 0g | Protein: 47.8g

Lamb Chops with Carrots

Prep Time: 15 minutes | Cook Time: 10 minutes | Serves: 4

Ingredients:

- 2 tablespoons fresh rosemary, minced
- 2 tablespoons fresh mint leaves, minced
- 1 garlic clove, minced
- 3 tablespoons olive oil
- Salt and ground black pepper, as required
- 4 (6-ounce) lamb chops
- 2 large carrots, peeled and cubed

Preparation:

1. In a large bowl, mix together the herbs, garlic, oil, salt, and black pepper. 2. Add the chops and generously coat with mixture. 3. Refrigerate to marinate for about 3 hours. 4. In a large pan of water, soak the carrots for about 15 minutes. 5. Drain the carrots completely. 6. Press "Power" button of Ninja Foodi XL Pro Air Oven and select "Air Fry" function. 7. Press TEMP/SHADE +/- buttons to set the temperature at 390°F/200°C. 8. Now press TIME/SLICES +/- buttons to set the cooking time to 10 minutes. 9. Press "Start/Stop" button to start. 10. When the unit beeps to show that it is preheated, open the oven door. 11. Arrange chops into the greased air fry basket in a single layer and insert into the rail of Level 3. 12. After 2 minutes of cooking, arrange carrots into the air fry basket and top with the chops in a single layer. 13. Insert the basket in oven. 14. When the cooking time is completed, open the oven door and transfer the chops and carrots onto serving plates. 15. Serve hot.

Serving Suggestions: Serve with fresh greens.
Variation Tip: You can use herbs of your choice.
Nutritional Information per Serving: Calories: 429 | Fat: 23.2g | Sat Fat: 6.1g | Carbohydrates: 5.1g | Fiber: 1.8g | Sugar: 1.8g | Protein: 48.3g

Mustard Lamb Loin Chops

Prep Time: 10 minutes | Cook Time: 15 minutes | Serves: 2

Ingredients:

- 1 tablespoon Dijon mustard
- ½ tablespoon white wine vinegar
- 1 teaspoon olive oil
- ½ teaspoon dried tarragon
- Salt and ground black pepper, as required
- 4 (4-ounce) lamb loin chops

Preparation:

1. In a large bowl, mix together the mustard, vinegar, oil, tarragon, salt, and black pepper. 2. Add the chops and coat with the mixture generously. 3. Arrange the chops onto the greased sheet pan. 4. Press "Power" button of Ninja Foodi XL Pro Air Oven and select "Bake" function. 5. Press TEMP/SHADE +/- buttons to set the temperature at 390°F/200°C. 6. Now press TIME/SLICES +/- buttons to set the cooking time to 15 minutes. 7. Press "Start/Stop" button to start. 8. When the unit beeps to show that it is preheated, open the oven door and insert the sheet pan into rail of Level 3. 9. When the cooking time is completed, open the oven door and serve hot.

Serving Suggestions: Serve alongside the feta spinach.
Variation Tip: Remember to bring the chops to room temperature.
Nutritional Information per Serving: Calories: 44 | Fat: 19.3g | Sat Fat: 6.3g | Carbohydrates: 0.5g | Fiber: 0.3g | Sugar: 0.1g | Protein: 64.1g

Herbed Lamb Loin Chops

Prep Time: 10 minutes | Cook Time: 12 minutes | Serves: 2

Ingredients:

- 4 (4-ounce) (½-inch-thick) lamb loin chops
- 1 teaspoon fresh thyme, minced
- 1 teaspoon fresh rosemary, minced
- 1 teaspoon fresh oregano, minced
- 2 garlic cloves, crushed
- Salt and ground black pepper, as required

Preparation:

1. In a large bowl, place all ingredients and mix well. 2. Refrigerate to marinate overnight. 3. Arrange the chops onto the greased sheet pan. 4. Press "Power" button of Ninja Foodi XL Pro Air Oven and select "Bake" function. 5. Press TEMP/SHADE +/- buttons to set the temperature at 400°F/200°C. 6. Now press TIME/SLICES +/- buttons to set the cooking time to 12 minutes. 7. Press "Start/Stop" button to start. 8. When the unit beeps to show that it is preheated, open the oven door and insert the sheet pan over wire rack into rail of Level 3. 9. Flip the chops once halfway through. 10. When the cooking time is completed, open the oven door and serve hot.

Serving Suggestions: Serve with steamed cauliflower.
Variation Tip: Season the chops nicely.
Nutritional Information per Serving: Calories: 432 | Fat: 16.9g | Sat Fat: 6g | Carbohydrates: 2.2g | Fiber: 0.8g | Sugar: 0.1g | Protein: 64g

Baked Pork Chops

Prep Time: 5 minutes | Cook Time: 20 minutes | Serves: 2

Ingredients:

- 2 boneless pork chops
- ½ tablespoon olive oil
- ¾ tablespoon brown sugar
- ½ teaspoon onion powder
- 1 teaspoon paprika
- ½ teaspoon dried thyme
- ¼ teaspoon black pepper
- ½ teaspoon salt

Preparation:

1. Turn on your Ninja Foodi XL Pro Air Oven and select "Bake". 2. Take a dish and line sheet pan with parchment paper. 3. Arrange the pork chops on the prepared dish. 4. Take a small bowl and combine the brown sugar, onion powder, dried thyme, salt, pepper and paprika. 5. Rub the prepared mixture over pork chops evenly. 6. Place the sheet pan on Level 3 in oven. 7. Select the timer for 20 minutes and temperature for 425°F/220°C. 8. Bake the pork chops in the preheated Ninja Foodi XL Pro Air Oven for 20 minutes at 425°F/220°C. 9. After done, set them aside for 5 minutes and then serve. 10. Enjoy!

Serving Suggestions: Serve with mashed potatoes and salad.
Variation Tip: Be careful not to overcook the pork chops or they may dry out.
Nutritional Information per Serving: Calories: 171 | Fat: 6.7g | Sat Fat: 1.6g | Carbohydrates: 4.7g | Fiber: 0.6g | Sugar: 3.6g | Protein: 22.5g

Herby Pork Bake

Prep Time: 10 minutes | Cook Time: 40 minutes | Serves: 2

Ingredients:

- 1 pork loin steak, cut into bite-sized pieces
- ½ red onion, cut into wedges
- 1 potato, halved
- ½ carrot, halved
- ½ tablespoon olive oil
- 1 tablespoon mixed dried herbs
- 4 tablespoons Cider Pour Over Sauce

Preparation:

1. Turn on your Ninja Foodi XL Pro Air Oven and select "Bake". 2. Select the timer for 25 minutes and temperature for 420°F/215°C. 3. Take a roast tray and toss pork, onion, potatoes and carrots with herbs and olive oil. 4. When the unit beeps to signify it has preheated, open the oven and place the roast tray on sheet pan into rail of Level 3. 5. Bake for about 25 minutes in preheated Ninja Foodi XL Pro Air Oven at 420°F/215°C. 6. Remove from the oven and add sauce on top. 7. Bake for 5 more minutes so that you have a bubbling sauce. 8. Serve and enjoy!

Serving Suggestions: Serve with garlic bread.
Variation Tip: You can also add tomatoes to your like.
Nutritional Information per Serving: Calories: 269 | Fat: 9.6g | Sat Fat: 2.6g | Carbohydrates: 32g | Fiber: 3.3g | Sugar: 4g | Protein: 14.7g

Czech Roast Pork

Prep Time: 20 minutes | Cook Time: 3 hours and 30 minutes | Serves: 4

Ingredients:

- 1 tablespoon caraway seeds
- ½ tablespoon garlic powder
- 1 tablespoon vegetable oil
- ½ tablespoon prepared mustard
- ½ tablespoon salt
- 1½ medium onions, chopped
- 2 pounds pork shoulder blade roast
- 1 teaspoon ground black pepper
- ¼ cup beer

Preparation:

1. Take a bowl and add garlic powder, mustard, vegetable oil, caraway seeds, salt and pepper to form a paste. 2. Rub the paste over pork roast and let it sit for about 30 minutes. 3. Turn on your Ninja Foodi XL Pro Air Oven and select "Air Roast". 4. Select the timer for 60 minutes and temperature for 350°F/175°C. 5. Take a roast tray and add onions, pour in the beer and place pork. 6. Cover it with a foil. 7. When the unit beeps to signify it has preheated, open the oven and place the roast tray on a sheet pan into rail of Level 3. 8. Roast for about an hour in preheated Ninja Foodi XL Pro Air Oven at 350°F/175°C. 9. Remove foil, turn roast and let it roast for 2 hours and 30 minutes more. 10. Remove from oven and set aside for 10 minutes before slicing. 11. Serve warm and enjoy!

Serving Suggestions: Serve it with the sprinkle of herbs.
Variation Tip: Do not skip the beer.
Nutritional Information per Serving: Calories: 722 | Fat: 44.3g | Sat Fat: 15.4g | Carbohydrates: 6.4g | Fiber: 1.8g | Sugar: 2g | Protein: 69.8g

Roast Beef and Yorkshire Pudding

Prep Time: 20 minutes | Cook Time: 1 hour 50 minutes | Serves: 2

Ingredients:

- 1 egg, beaten
- ½ cup milk
- ½ cup flour
- ⅛ teaspoon salt
- Salt, to taste
- Freshly ground pepper, to taste
- 1 pound rump roast
- Garlic powder, to taste

Preparation:

1. Turn on your Ninja Foodi XL Pro Air Oven and select "Air Roast". 2. Preheat by selecting the timer for 3 minutes and temperature for 375°F/190°C. 3. Place beef in a sheet pan on Level 3 in oven and season with salt, garlic powder and pepper. 4. Roast in oven for about 90 minutes until the thickest part of the beef is at 135°F/55°C. 5. Remove from oven, reserving drippings. 6. Take a small bowl, beat egg until foamy. 7. Take another bowl, stir salt and flour. Pour in the beaten egg and add milk. 8. Now, preheat by selecting the timer for 3 minutes and temperature for 400°F/200°C on "Air Roast" mode. 9. Pour the reserved drippings to a tin. Place in the preheated oven for about 3 minutes. 10. Remove from oven, add the flour mixture into the hot drippings. 11. Return to oven and set the timer for 20 minutes or until brown. 12. Serve warm and enjoy!

Serving Suggestions: Serve it with your favorite sauce.
Variation Tip: You can add an extra egg if you like.
Nutritional Information per Serving: Calories: 582 | Fat: 17.4g | Sat Fat: 1.5g | Carbohydrates: 27.2g | Fiber: 0.9g | Sugar: 3g | Protein: 78.4g

Savory Pork Roast

Prep Time: 10 minutes | Cook Time: 1 hour | Serves: 3

Ingredients:

- ¼ teaspoon dried thyme
- 1 tablespoon fresh rosemary, divided
- 1 teaspoon garlic salt
- ⅛ teaspoon black pepper, freshly ground
- 1½ pounds pork loin roast, boneless

Preparation:

1. Turn on your Ninja Foodi XL Pro Air Oven and select "Air Roast". 2. Select the timer for 60 minutes and temperature for 350°F/175°C. 3. Take a bowl mix well rosemary, garlic salt, thyme, and pepper together. 4. Now add pork to coat well. 5. Take a roast tray and place coated pork on it. 6. When the unit beeps to signify it has preheated, open the oven and place the roast tray on sheet pan on Level 3. Close the oven and let it cook. 7. Roast pork for about an hour in preheated Ninja Foodi XL Pro Air Oven at 350°F/175°C. 8. Serve and enjoy!

Serving Suggestions: Serve with juice and salad.
Variation Tip: Use foil to avoid dryness.
Nutritional Information per Serving: Calories: 331 | Fat: 8.2g | Sat Fat: 2.8g | Carbohydrates: 1.4g | Fiber: 0.6g | Sugar: 0.2g | Protein: 59.6g

Ground Beef Casserole

Prep Time: 8 minutes | Cook Time: 25 minutes | Serves: 3

Ingredients:

- ¼ medium onion, chopped
- ½ pound extra lean ground beef
- ½ pound penne
- ½ tablespoon olive oil
- ½ clove garlic, minced
- ½ cup marinara sauce
- 1 cup cheddar cheese, shredded
- Salt and pepper to taste

Preparation:

1. Take a large pot with lightly salted water and bring it to a boil. Add penne and let it cook for about 10 minutes. 2. Take a pan and add oil, beef and onion. 3. Fry for about 10 minutes over medium-high heat and add garlic. 4. Stir in the marinara sauce and add salt and pepper according to taste. 5. Drain the pasta and pour into the sheet pan. 6. Add the beef-marinara mixture on top of the penne pasta. Lastly, add cheese with cheese. 7. Insert a wire rack on Level 3. Turn on your Ninja Foodi XL Pro Air Oven and select "Bake". 8. Select the timer for 10 minutes and temperature for 400°F/200°C. 9. When the unit beeps to signify it has preheated, open the oven and place the sheet pan on wire rack. 10. Close the oven and bake for about 10 minutes in preheated Ninja Foodi XL Pro Air Oven until the cheese is nicely melted. 11. Serve immediately.

Serving Suggestions: Serve it with your favorite soda.
Variation Tip: You can add more marinara sauce if you want.
Nutritional Information per Serving: Calories: 560 | Fat: 22.6g | Sat Fat: 11.1g | Carbohydrates: 48.6g | Fiber: 1.3g | Sugar: 4.3g | Protein: 38.7g

Baked Beef Stew

Prep Time: 15 minutes | Cook Time: 2 hours | Serves: 4

Ingredients:

- 1 pound beef-stew, cut into cubes
- ½ cup water
- 2 tablespoons instant tapioca
- ½ can dried tomatoes with juice
- 1 teaspoon white sugar
- ½ tablespoon beef bouillon granules
- ¾ teaspoon salt
- ⅛ teaspoon ground black pepper
- 1 strip celery, cut into ¾ inch pieces
- ½ onion, chopped
- 2 carrots, cut into 1-inch pieces
- ½ slice bread, cubed
- 2 potatoes, peeled and cubed

Preparation:

1. Insert a wire rack on Level 3. Turn on your Ninja Foodi XL Pro Air Oven and select "Bake". 2. Select the timer for 2 hours and temperature for 375°F/190°C. 3. Grease a sheet pan. 4. Take a large pan over medium heat and brown the stew meat. 5. Meanwhile, take a bowl and mix together tomatoes, water, tapioca, beef bouillon granules, sugar, salt and pepper. 6. Add prepared brown beef, celery, potatoes, carrots, onion and bread cubes. 7. Pour in the greased sheet pan. 8. When the unit beeps to signify it has preheated, open the oven and place the sheet pan on the wire rack. 9. Close the oven and bake for about 2 hours in preheated Ninja Foodi Air Fryer at 375°F/190°C. 10. Remove from oven and set aside for 2 minutes. 11. Serve warm and enjoy!

Serving Suggestions: Serve warm with rice.
Variation Tip: You can also add few tablespoons of cornstarch.
Nutritional Information per Serving: Calories: 378 | Fat: 7.6g | Sat Fat: 2.7g | Carbohydrates: 30.1g | Fiber: 3.9g | Sugar: 5.6g | Protein: 44.8g

Italian Baked Meatballs

Prep Time: 20 minutes | Cook Time: 30 minutes | Serves: 6

Ingredients:

- 1 cup Italian-seasoned breadcrumbs
- ¼ cup Romano cheese, grated
- 2 tablespoons fresh parsley, chopped
- ½ teaspoon salt
- ½ teaspoon ground black pepper
- ½ teaspoon garlic powder
- ½ teaspoon onion powder
- ½ cup water
- 2 eggs
- 1½ pounds ground beef

Preparation:

1. Insert a wire rack in oven on Level 3. 2. Select the BAKE function, 350°F/175°C, for 30 minutes. While the oven is preheating, prepare the ingredients. 3. Mix the Romano cheese, salt, pepper, breadcrumbs, parsley, garlic powder, and onion powder. Then combine the mixture with the water and eggs. 4. Add the ground beef and mix well. Shape the mixture into balls and put them on the sheet pan greased with some non-stick cooking spray. 5. When the unit beeps to signify it has preheated, open the oven and place the sheet pan on wire rack. 6. Bake the meatballs for about 30 minutes.

Serving Suggestion: Serve the meatballs with tomato sauce.
Variation Tip: Try using parmesan cheese instead of Romano cheese.
Nutritional Information Per Serving: Calories: 343 | Fat: 20.4g | Sodium: 611mg | Carbs: 14g | Fiber: 0.8g | Sugar: 1g | Protein: 24.4g

Lamb Chops

Prep Time: 5 minutes | Cook Time: 16 minutes | Serves: 4

Ingredients:

4 medium lamb chops
2 tablespoons olive oil
1 garlic clove, crushed
3 thin lemon slices
½ teaspoon dried oregano
¼ teaspoon black pepper, freshly ground
½ teaspoon kosher salt

Preparation:

1. Take a dish and mix together salt, pepper, olive oil, lemon slices, garlic, and oregano. 2. Add lamb in the dish and marinate for about 4 hours. 3. Insert a wire rack on Level 3. Turn on your Ninja Foodi XL Pro Air Oven and select "Bake". 4. Select the timer for 10 minutes and temperature for 400°F/200°C. 5. Meanwhile, take a pan and add oil and heat over medium heat and cook each side of lamb for 3 minutes until brown. 6. When the unit beeps to signify it has preheated, open the oven and place the lamb in a sheet pan on wire rack. Bake for about 8 to 10 minutes in preheated Ninja Foodi XL Pro Air Oven at 400°F/200°C. 7. Remove from oven and set aside for 2 minutes. 8. Serve warm and enjoy!
Serving Suggestions: Serve with roasted carrots.
Variation Tip: You can also use foil.
Nutritional Information per Serving: Calories: 302 | Fat: 18.5g | Sat Fat: 4.3g | Carbohydrates: 0.5g | Fiber: 0.1g | Sugar: 0g | Protein: 32.6g

Air Fryer Beef Taquitos

Prep Time: 10 minutes | Cook Time: 20 minutes | Serves: 4 to 6

Ingredients:

1 pound ground beef
14 medium-sized corn and flour blend tortillas
1½ cups Mexican blend cheese, shredded
1 teaspoon kosher salt
1 teaspoon oregano
1 teaspoon garlic powder
¾ teaspoon cumin
¼ teaspoon ground pepper
Cooking oil spray

Preparation:

1. Select the AIR FRY function, 350°F/175°C, for 8 minutes. 2. Add the oregano, salt, pepper, garlic powder, and cumin seasoning to the ground beef in a large bowl. Mix well. 3. Add this beef filling to the tortillas, then add the cheese and roll tightly. Use toothpicks to secure the ends. 4. Spray the taquitos with the cooking oil spray on all sides. 5. Place the taquitos in the air fry basket, toothpick side down. 6. When the unit beeps to signify it has preheated, open the oven and slide the air fry basket into rail of Level 3 in oven. 7. Close the oven door and cook for 8 minutes.
Serving Suggestion: You can serve the taquitos with any dip or salsa of your choice.
Variation Tip: You can try using ricotta cheese instead of Mexican blend shredded cheese.
Nutritional Information Per Serving: Calories: 217 | Fat: 12g | Sodium: 477mg | Carbs: 16g | Fiber: 1g | Sugar: 1g | Protein: 11g

Roast Sirloin of Beef and Port Gravy

Prep Time: 10 minutes | Cook Time: 2 hours 30 minutes | Serves: 6

Ingredients:

3 garlic cloves, finely chopped
2 tablespoons thyme leaves
For the Gravy:
1 garlic clove
1 bay leaf
Few thyme sprigs
2 tablespoons olive oil
4.8 pounds rolled sirloin of beef

5 tablespoons port
1½ cups red wine
¾ cup beef stock

Preparation:

1. Mix the thyme, olive oil, black pepper, and garlic in a bowl. Rub the beef with the mixture and leave for at least 1 hour. 2. Place the beef mixture onto a roast tray. Season the beef with salt and pepper. 3. Select the AIR ROAST function, 395°F/200°C, for 30 minutes. When the oven has preheated, place the roast tray on sheet pan into rail of Level 3. 4. Roast the beef for about 30 minutes. 5. Turn the heat down to 360°F and cook the beef for another 10 to 15 minutes. 6. Take the beef out when cooked and let it rest, loosely wrapped, for about 30 minutes. 7. Meanwhile, prepare the gravy. Take a roasting tin and place it on high heat. Add the garlic, bay leaves, and thyme. Then splash in the port, use a wooden spoon to stir, loosen any residue, and let it bubble until almost completely reduced. 8. Next, add the red wine and reduce it by three quarters. Put the stock in and bring it to a boil, then season to taste. Pour any remaining resting juices into the tin. 9. Transfer the gravy to a warm jug, carve the meat and serve it with the gravy.
Serving Suggestion: Serve with roasted potatoes and veggies.
Variation Tip: Double the quantity of stock if you want it to be alcohol-free.
Nutritional Information Per Serving: Calories: 431 | Fat: 22g | Sodium: 128mg | Carbs: 2g | Fiber: 0g | Sugar: 2g | Protein: 52g

Air Fryer Low-Carb Taco Casserole

Prep Time: 15 minutes | Cook Time: 25 minutes | Serves: 4

Ingredients:

- 1 pound 95% lean ground beef
- 2 tablespoons taco seasoning
- ¼ cup of water
- 10 ounces canned diced tomatoes
- 2 green chilies, seeded and chopped
- ¼ cup reduced-fat cheddar cheese, shredded
- 4 large eggs
- ¼ cup light sour cream
- ⅓ cup heavy cream

Preparation:

1. Prepare a baking dish by lightly spraying it with a non-stick cooking spray. Set it aside. 2. Take a medium skillet and place it over medium heat. Add the ground beef and cook it in the skillet for about 5 to 6 minutes. Drain the grease. 3. Then, add the taco seasoning, diced tomatoes, water, and green chilies to the skillet and simmer for about 5 minutes. 4. Transfer the beef mixture to the prepared dish. 5. Take a bowl, and whisk together the sour cream, eggs, and heavy cream. Pour it over to the beef mixture, and top with shredded cheese. Transfer the dish to the air fry basket. 6. Select the AIR FRY function, 300°F/150°C, for 20 minutes. 7. When the unit beeps to signify it has preheated, open the oven and slide the air fry basket with the dish on Level 3. 8. Close the oven and cook the casserole.

Serving Suggestion: Serve with some greens.
Variation Tip: Colby cheese can be a great substitute for cheddar cheese.
Nutritional Information Per Serving: Calories: 441 | Fat: 24g | Sodium: 593mg | Carbs: 8g | Fiber: 1g | Sugar: 5g | Protein: 47g

Stuffed Pork Tenderloin

Prep Time: 10 minutes | Cook Time: 30 minutes | Serves: 6

Ingredients:

- 1 tablespoon extra-virgin olive oil
- 1 tablespoon yellow onion, finely chopped
- A dash of vinegar
- ⅓ cup breadcrumbs
- 3 tablespoons parsley, chopped
- 1 whole orange
- Orange zest, grated
- 2 tablespoons Dijon mustard
- 2 tablespoons honey
- A dash of black pepper
- 2 lean pork tenderloins

Preparation:

1. Butterfly the pork tenderloins by cutting them in half lengthwise but not all the way through. 2. Take a non-stick skillet to heat the olive oil over medium heat. Add the onions and sauté for about 20 minutes, stirring frequently. Stir in the vinegar, pepper, and salt, then cook for 5 minutes. Remove from the heat. Stir in the breadcrumbs, orange zest, and parsley. Set it aside. 3. Place the filling along the length of one tenderloin, then top it with another tenderloin and tie it with string. Place it on the rack in the oven set over a foil-lined roasting pan. 4. Prepare the glaze: Take a small bowl, combine pepper, honey, and mustard, then brush over pork. 5. Select the AIR ROAST function and roast the pork at 375°F/190°C for about 40 minutes on Level 3. 6. Cover it and let it rest for about 10 minutes before carving it into slices.

Serving Suggestion: The pork slices can be served with mustard or cream.
Variation Tip: Horseradish sauce can be an excellent substitute for Dijon mustard.
Nutritional Information Per Serving: Calories: 203 | Fat: 4.5g | Sodium: 218mg | Carbs: 15g | Fiber: 1.7g | Sugar: 7.7g | Protein: 26.7g

Breaded Air Fryer Pork Chops

Prep Time: 10 minutes | Cook Time: 10 minutes | Serves: 4

Ingredients:

- 4 boneless and center-cut pork chops
- 1 teaspoon Cajun seasoning
- 1½ cups cheese and garlic-flavored croutons
- 2 eggs
- Cooking spray

Preparation:

1. Select the AIR FRY function, 390°F/200°C, for 10 minutes. While the oven preheats, prepare the ingredients. 2. Use the Cajun seasoning to season both sides of the pork chops. 3. Blend the croutons in a small food processor and transfer them to a shallow dish. 4. Take a shallow dish and lightly beat the eggs in it. Dip the pork chops into the eggs and then coat them with the crouton breading. Spray them with the cooking spray. 5. Place the pork chops in the air fry basket. Cook in batches if needed. 6. When the unit beeps to signify it has preheated, open the oven and slide the air fry basket into rail of Level 3. 7. Cook the pork chops for about 5 minutes, flip, and mist with cooking spray, then cook for another 5 minutes.

Serving Suggestion: Garnish the pork chops with some lemon slices and serve alongside a sauce of your choice.
Variation Tip: You can try using Italian seasoning instead of Cajun seasoning.
Nutritional Information Per Serving: Calories: 393 | Fat: 18g | Sodium: 428mg | Carbs: 10g | Fiber: 0.8g | Sugar: 1g | Protein: 44.7g

Glazed Pork Tenderloin

Prep Time: 15 minutes | Cook Time: 30 minutes | Serves: 6

Ingredients:

- 2 tablespoons olive oil
- 2 pork tenderloins
- ¼ teaspoon salt
- ¼ teaspoon freshly ground black pepper
- 1 cup peach, chopped
- 2 tablespoons balsamic vinegar
- 2 tablespoons Dijon mustard
- 2 tablespoons brown sugar

Preparation:

1. Select the AIR ROAST function, 350°F/175°C, for 30 minutes. While the oven is preheating, prepare the ingredients. 2. Take a large skillet and heat the olive oil in it over medium heat. 3. Trim the excess fat and silver skin from the pork, and then season with salt and pepper. Sear on all sides for about 6 to 8 minutes, and transfer to a roast tray. 4. Combine the remaining ingredients in a saucepan. Bring them to a simmer. Remove from the heat and keep it aside. 5. Place the roast tray on sheet pan on Level 3 and cook in the preheated oven for about 12 minutes. Take the glaze mixture and brush the pork generously with it. Continue to roast for another 5 to 10 minutes.

Serving Suggestion: Season with salt and pepper and serve it with the remaining glaze.

Variation Tip: You can use grill seasoning instead of salt and pepper to season the pork.

Nutritional Information Per Serving:
Calories: 357 | Fat: 9g | Sodium: 369mg | Carbs: 39g | Fiber: 0g | Sugar: 28g | Protein: 30g

Chapter 5 Fish and Seafood Recipes

81	Herbed Shrimp	89	Parmesan Flounder
81	Lemony Salmon	90	Tangy Sea Bass
81	Spicy Bay Scallops	90	Salmon with Prawns
82	Seafood Casserole	90	Cod Burgers
82	Buttered Crab Shells	91	Maple Bacon Salmon
82	Nuts Crusted Salmon	91	Spiced Shrimp
83	Scallops with Capers Sauce	91	Crispy Catfish
83	Buttered Trout	92	Baked Sardines with Garlic and Oregano
83	Cod Parcel	92	Cod with Sauce
84	Scallops with Spinach	92	Garlic Shrimp with Lemon
84	Cajun Salmon	93	Garlic Butter Salmon Bites
84	Crab Cakes	93	Seafood Medley Mix
85	Salmon & Asparagus Parcel	93	Tilapia with Herbs and Garlic
85	Rum-Glazed Shrimp	94	Shrimp Fajitas
85	Pesto Salmon	94	Air Fried Fish Sticks
86	Crispy Flounder	94	Breaded Shrimp
86	Lobster Tail Casserole	95	Air Fried Fish Cakes
86	Beer-Battered Fish	95	Lobster Tails with Lemon-Garlic Butter
87	Crispy Cod	95	Greek Baked Bonito with Herbs and Potatoes
87	Fish Newburg with Haddock	96	Lemon Pepper Shrimp
87	Salmon Burgers	96	Brown Sugar and Garlic Air Fryer Salmon
88	Prawns in Butter Sauce	96	Crispy Air Fryer Fish Tacos
88	Spicy Salmon	97	Baked Sole with Mint and Ginger
88	Fish in Yogurt Marinade	97	Air Fryer Tuna Patties
89	Salmon with Broccoli	97	Scallops with Chanterelles
89	Baked Tilapia with Buttery Crumb Topping		

Herbed Shrimp

Prep Time: 15 minutes | Cook Time: 7 minutes | Serves: 3

Ingredients:

- 4 tablespoons salted butter, melted
- 1 tablespoon fresh lemon juice
- 1 tablespoon garlic, minced
- 2 teaspoons red pepper flakes, crushed
- 1 pound shrimp, peeled and deveined
- 2 tablespoons fresh basil, chopped
- 1 tablespoon fresh chives, chopped
- 2 tablespoons chicken broth

Preparation:

1. In a 7-inch-round baking pan, place butter, lemon juice, garlic, and red pepper flakes and mix well. 2. Press "Power" button of Ninja Foodi XL Pro Air Oven and select the "Air Fry" function. 3. Press TEMP/SHADE +/- buttons to set the temperature at 325°F/160°C. 4. Now press TIME/SLICES +/- buttons to set the cooking time to 7 minutes. 5. Press "Start/Stop" button to start. 6. When the unit beeps to show that it is preheated, open the oven door and place the pan over wire rack on Level 3. 7. Insert the wire rack in oven. 8. After 2 minutes of cooking in the pan, stir in the shrimp, basil, chives and broth. 9. When cooking time is completed, open the oven door and stir the mixture. 10. Serve hot.
Serving Suggestions: Serve with the garnishing of scallion.
Variation Tip: Use fresh shrimp.
Nutritional Information per Serving: Calories: 327 | Fat: 18.3g | Sat Fat: 10.6g | Carbohydrates: 4.2g | Fiber: 0.5g | Sugar: 0.3g | Protein: 35.3g

Lemony Salmon

Prep Time: 10 minutes | Cook Time: 8 minutes | Serves: 3

Ingredients:

- 1½ pounds salmon
- ½ teaspoon red chili powder
- Salt and ground black pepper, as required
- 1 lemon, cut into slices
- 1 tablespoon fresh dill, chopped

Preparation:

1. Season the salmon with chili powder, salt, and black pepper. 2. Press "Power" button of Ninja Foodi XL Pro Air Oven and select "Air Fry" function. 3. Press TEMP/SHADE +/- buttons to set the temperature at 375°F/190°C. 4. Now press TIME/SLICES +/- buttons to set the cooking time to 8 minutes. 5. Press "Start/Stop" button to start. 6. When the unit beeps to show that it is preheated, open the oven door. 7. Arrange the salmon fillets into the greased air fry basket and slide the basket into the rail of Level 3. 8. When cooking time is completed, open the oven door and serve hot with the garnishing of fresh dill.
Serving Suggestions: Serve with the topping of cheese.
Variation Tip: Make sure to pat dry the salmon completely before seasoning.
Nutritional Information per Serving: Calories: 305 | Fat: 14.1g | Sat Fat: 2g | Carbohydrates: 1.3g | Fiber: 0.4g | Sugar: 0.2g | Protein: 44.3g

Spicy Bay Scallops

Prep Time: 15 minutes | Cook Time: 8 minutes | Serves: 4

Ingredients:

- 1 pound bay scallops rinsed and patted dry
- 2 teaspoons smoked paprika
- 2 teaspoons chili powder
- 2 teaspoons olive oil
- 1 teaspoon garlic powder
- ¼ teaspoon ground black pepper
- ⅛ teaspoon cayenne red pepper

Preparation:

1. Scallops with paprika, chili powder, olive oil, garlic powder, black pepper, and red pepper in a bowl. 2. Place the scallops in the air fry basket. 3. Transfer the basket to the 3rd rack position of Ninja Foodi XL Pro Air Oven and close the door. 4. Select the "Air Fry" Mode using FUNCTION +/- buttons and select Rack Level 3. 5. Set its cooking time to 8 minutes and temperature to 400°F/200°C, then press "START/STOP" to initiate cooking. 6. Enjoy.
Serving Suggestion: Serve the scallops with crispy onion rings on the side.
Variation Tip: Coat the scallops with breadcrumbs for a crispy texture.
Nutritional Information Per Serving: Calories 476 | Fat 17g | Sodium 1127mg | Carbs 4g | Fiber 1g | Sugar 3g | Protein 29g

Seafood Casserole

Prep Time: 15 minutes | Cook Time: 20 minutes | Serves: 8

Ingredients:

8 ounces haddock, skinned and diced
1 pound scallops
1 pound large shrimp, peeled and deveined
3-4 garlic cloves, minced
½ cup heavy cream

½ cup Swiss cheese, shredded
2 tablespoons Parmesan, grated
Paprika, to taste
Sea salt and black pepper, to taste

Preparation:

1. Toss shrimp, scallops, and haddock chunks in the sheet pan greased with cooking spray. 2. Drizzle salt, black pepper, and minced garlic over the seafood mix. 3. Top this seafood with cream, Swiss cheese, paprika, and Parmesan cheese. 4. Transfer the dish to Ninja Foodi XL Pro Air Oven and Close its lid. 5. Select the "Bake" Mode using FUNCTION +/- buttons and select Rack Level 2. 6. Set its cooking time to 20 minutes and temperature to 375°F/190°C, then press "START/STOP" to initiate cooking. 7. Serve warm.
Serving Suggestion: Serve the seafood casserole with fresh vegetable salad.
Variation Tip: Add alfredo sauce to the casserole for better taste.
Nutritional Information Per Serving: Calories 548 | Fat 13g | Sodium 353mg | Carbs 31g | Fiber 0.4g | Sugar 1g | Protein 29g

Buttered Crab Shells

Prep Time: 15 minutes | Cook Time: 20 minutes | Serves: 4

Ingredients:

4 soft crab shells, cleaned
1 cup buttermilk
3 eggs
2 cups panko breadcrumb

2 teaspoons seafood seasoning
1½ teaspoons lemon zest, grated
2 tablespoons butter, melted

Preparations:

1. In a shallow bowl, place the buttermilk. 2. In a second bowl, whisk the eggs. 3. In a third bowl, mix the breadcrumbs, seafood seasoning, and lemon zest together. 4. Soak the crab shells into the buttermilk for about 10 minutes. 5. Now, dip the crab shells into beaten eggs and then, coat with the breadcrumb mixture. 6. Press "Power" button of Ninja Foodi XL Pro Air Oven and select "Air Fry" function. 7. Press TEMP/SHADE +/- buttons to set the temperature at 375°F/190°C. 8. Now press TIME/SLICES +/- buttons to set the cooking time to 10 minutes. 9. Press "START/STOP" button to start. 10. When the unit beeps to show that it is preheated, open the lid and grease the air fry basket. 11. Place the crab shells into the prepared air fry basket and insert in the oven. 12. When cooking time is completed, open the lid and transfer the crab shells onto serving plates. 13. Drizzle crab shells with the melted butter and serve immediately.
Serving Suggestions: Serve alongside the lemon slices.
Variation Tip: Use seasoning of your choice.
Nutritional Information per Serving: Calories: 549 | Fat: 17.3g | Sat Fat: 7g | Carbohydrates: 11.5g | Fiber: 0.3g | Sugar: 3.3g | Protein: 53.5g

Nuts Crusted Salmon

Prep Time: 15 minutes | Cook Time: 15 minutes | Serves: 2

Ingredients:

2 (6-ounce) skinless salmon fillets
Salt and ground black pepper, as required
3 tablespoons walnuts, chopped finely

3 tablespoons quick-cooking oats, crushed
2 tablespoons olive oil

Preparation:

1. Rub the salmon fillets with salt and black pepper evenly. 2. In a bowl, mix the walnuts, oats and oil together. 3. Arrange the salmon fillets onto the greased sheet pan in a single layer. 4. Place the oat mixture over salmon fillets and gently, press down. 5. Press "Power" button of Ninja Foodi XL Pro Air Oven and select the "Bake" function. 6. Press TEMP/SHADE +/- buttons to set the temperature at 400°F/200°C. 7. Now press TIME/SLICES +/- buttons to set the cooking time to 15 minutes. 8. Press "START/STOP" button to start. 9. When the unit beeps to show that it is preheated, open the lid. 10. Insert the sheet pan in oven. 11. When cooking time is completed, open the lid and serve hot.
Serving Suggestions: Serve with steamed asparagus.
Variation Tip: Walnuts can be replaced with pecans.
Nutritional Information per Serving: Calories: 446 | Fat: 319g | Sat Fat: 4g | Carbohydrates: 6.4g | Fiber: 1.6g | Sugar: 0.2g | Protein: 36.8g

Scallops with Capers Sauce

Prep Time: 10 minutes | Cook Time: 6 minutes | Serves: 2

Ingredients:

- 10 (1-ounce) sea scallops, cleaned and patted very dry
- Salt and ground black pepper, as required
- ¼ cup extra-virgin olive oil
- 2 tablespoons fresh parsley, finely chopped
- 2 teaspoons capers, finely chopped
- 1 teaspoon fresh lemon zest, finely grated
- ½ teaspoon garlic, finely chopped

Preparation:

1. Season each scallop evenly with salt and black pepper. 2. Press "Power" button of Ninja Foodi XL Pro Air Oven and select "Air Fry" function. 3. Press TEMP/SHADE +/- buttons to set the temperature at 400°F/200°C. 4. Now press TIME/SLICES +/- buttons to set the cooking time to 6 minutes. 5. Press "START/STOP" button to start. 6. When the unit beeps to show that it is preheated, open the lid and grease the air fry basket. 7. Place the scallops into the prepared air fry basket and insert in the oven. 8. Meanwhile, for the sauce: in a bowl, mix the remaining ingredients. 9. When cooking time is completed, open the lid and transfer the scallops onto serving plates. 10. Top with the sauce and serve immediately.

Serving Suggestions: Serve with a garnishing of fresh herbs.
Variation Tip: Avoid shiny, wet or soft scallops.
Nutritional Information per Serving: Calories: 344 | Fat: 26.3g | Sat Fat: 3.7g | Carbohydrates: 4.2g | Fiber: 0.3g | Sugar: 0.1g | Protein: 24g

Buttered Trout

Prep Time: 10 minutes | Cook Time: 10 minutes | Serves: 2

Ingredients:

- 2 (6-ounces) trout fillets
- Salt and ground black pepper, as required
- 1 tablespoon butter, melted

Preparation:

1. Rinse the trout thoroughly. Season each trout fillet with salt and black pepper and then coat with the butter. 2. Arrange the trout fillets onto the greased sheet pan in a single layer. 3. Press "Power" button of Ninja Foodi XL Pro Air Oven and select "Air Fry" function. 4. Press TEMP/SHADE +/- buttons to set the temperature at 360°F/180°C. 5. Now press TIME/SLICES +/- buttons to set the cooking time to 10 minutes. 6. Press "START/STOP" button to start. 7. When the unit beeps to show that it is preheated, open the lid. 8. Insert the sheet pan in oven. 9. Flip the fillets once halfway through. 10. When cooking time is completed, open the lid and serve hot.

Serving Suggestions: Serve with your favorite salad.
Variation Tip: Feel free to add seasoning as you like.
Nutritional Information per Serving: Calories: 374 | Fat: 20.2g | Sat Fat: 6.2g | Carbohydrates: 0g | Fiber: 0g | Sugar: 0g | Protein: 45.4g

Cod Parcel

Prep Time: 10 minutes | Cook Time: 23 minutes | Serves: 4

Ingredients:

- 2 (4-ounce) cod fillets
- 6 asparagus stalks
- ¼ cup white sauce
- 1 teaspoon oil
- ¼ cup champagne
- Salt and ground black pepper, as required

Preparation:

1. In a bowl, mix all the ingredients together. 2. Divide the cod mixture over 2 pieces of foil evenly. 3. Seal the foil around the cod mixture to form the packet. 4. Press "Power" button of Ninja Foodi XL Pro Air Oven and select "Air Fry" function. 5. Press TEMP/SHADE +/- buttons to set the temperature at 355°F/180°C. 6. Now press TIME/SLICES +/- buttons to set the cooking time to 13 minutes. 7. Press "START/STOP" button to start. 8. When the unit beeps to show that it is preheated, open the lid. 9. Arrange the cod parcels in air fry basket and insert in the oven. 10. When cooking time is completed, open the lid and transfer the parcels onto serving plates. 11. The meat of cod should look translucent fairly. 12. Carefully unwrap the parcels and serve hot.

Serving Suggestions: Serve with mashed potatoes.
Variation Tip: Feel free to add seasoning of your choice.
Nutritional Information per Serving: Calories: 188 | Fat: 6.6g | Sat Fat: 1.2g | Carbohydrates: 5g | Fiber: 0.8g | Sugar: 2.2g | Protein: 22.2g

Scallops with Spinach

Prep Time: 15 minutes | Cook Time: 10 minutes | Serves: 2

Ingredients:

- ¾ cup heavy whipping cream
- 1 tablespoon tomato paste
- 1 teaspoon garlic, minced
- 1 tablespoon fresh basil, chopped
- Salt and ground black pepper, as required
- 8 jumbo sea scallops
- Olive oil cooking spray
- 1 (12-ounce) package frozen spinach, thawed and drained

Preparation:

1. In a bowl, place the cream, tomato paste, garlic, basil, salt, and black pepper and mix well. 2. Spray each scallop evenly with cooking spray and then, sprinkle with a little salt and black pepper. 3. In the bottom of a baking pan, place the spinach. 4. Arrange scallops on top of the spinach in a single layer and top with the cream mixture evenly. 5. Press "Power" button of Ninja Foodi XL Pro Air Oven and select "Air Fry" function. 6. Press TEMP/SHADE +/- buttons to set the temperature at 350°F/175°C. 7. Now press TIME/SLICES +/- buttons to set the cooking time to 10 minutes. 8. Press "START/STOP" button to start. 9. When the unit beeps to show that it is preheated, open the lid. 10. Place the pan into the prepared air fry basket and insert in the oven. 11. When cooking time is completed, open the lid and serve hot.

Serving Suggestions: Serve with crusty bread.
Variation Tip: Spinach can be replaced with kale.
Nutritional Information per Serving: Calories: 309 | Fat: 18.8g | Sat Fat: 10.6g | Carbohydrates: 12.3g | Fiber: 4.1g | Sugar: 1.7g | Protein: 26.4g

Cajun Salmon

Prep Time: 10 minutes | Cook Time: 7 minutes | Serves: 2

Ingredients:

- 2 (7-ounce) (¾-inch-thick) salmon fillets
- 1 tablespoon Cajun seasoning
- ½ teaspoon sugar
- 1 tablespoon fresh lemon juice

Preparation:

1. Sprinkle the salmon fillets with Cajun seasoning and sugar evenly. 2. Press "Power" button of Ninja Foodi XL Pro Air Oven and select "Air Fry" function. 3. Press TEMP/SHADE +/- buttons to set the temperature at 360°F/180°C. 4. Now press TIME/SLICES +/- buttons to set the cooking time to 7 minutes. 5. Press "START/STOP" button to start. 6. When the unit beeps to show that it is preheated, open the lid. 7. Arrange the salmon fillets, skin-side up in the greased air fry basket and insert in the oven. 8. When cooking time is completed, open the lid and transfer the salmon fillets onto a platter. 9. Drizzle with the lemon juice and serve hot.

Serving Suggestions: Serve with mashed cauliflower.
Variation Tip: Adjust the ratio of Cajun seasoning according to your taste.
Nutritional Information per Serving: Calories: 268 | Fat: 12.3g | Sat Fat: 1.8g | Carbohydrates: 1.2g | Fiber: 0g | Sugar: 1.2g | Protein: 36.8g

Crab Cakes

Prep Time: 15 minutes | Cook Time: 10 minutes | Serves: 4

Ingredients:

- ¼ cup red bell pepper, seeded and chopped finely
- 2 scallions, chopped finely
- 2 tablespoons mayonnaise
- 2 tablespoons breadcrumbs
- 1 tablespoon Dijon mustard
- 1 teaspoon old bay seasoning
- 8 ounces lump crabmeat, drained

Preparation:

1. In a large bowl, add all the ingredients except crabmeat and mix until well combined. 2. Gently fold in the crabmeat. 3. Make 4 equal-sized patties from the mixture. 4. Arrange the patties onto the lightly greased sheet pan. 5. Press "Power" button of Ninja Foodi XL Pro Air Oven and press FUNCTION +/- buttons to select the "Air Fry" function. 6. Press TEMP/SHADE +/- buttons to set the temperature at 370°F/185°C. 7. Now press TIME/SLICES +/- buttons to set the cooking time to 10 minutes. 8. Press "Start/Stop" button to start. 9. When the unit beeps to show that it is preheated, open the oven door and insert the sheet pan in oven. 10. When cooking time is completed, open the oven door and serve hot.

Serving Suggestions: Serve alongside the fresh salad.
Variation Tip: Make sure to remove any cartilage from crabmeat.
Nutritional Information per Serving: Calories: 91 | Fat: 7.4g | Sat Fat: 0.4g | Carbohydrates: 6.4g | Fiber: 0.6g | Sugar: 1.3g | Protein: 9.1g

Salmon & Asparagus Parcel

Prep Time: 15 minutes | Cook Time: 13 minutes | Serves: 2

Ingredients:

- 2 (4-ounce) salmon fillets
- 6 asparagus stalks
- ¼ cup white sauce
- 1 teaspoon oil
- ¼ cup champagne
- Salt and ground black pepper, as required

Preparation:

1. In a bowl, mix together all the ingredients. 2. Divide the salmon mixture over 2 pieces of foil evenly. 3. Seal the foil around the salmon mixture to form the packet. 4. Press "Power" button of Ninja Foodi XL Pro Air Oven and select "Air Fry" function. 5. Press TEMP/SHADE +/- buttons to set the temperature at 355°F/180°C. Select 2 LEVEL. 6. Now press TIME/SLICES +/- buttons to set the cooking time to 13 minutes. 7. Press "Start/Stop" button to start. 8. When the unit beeps to show that it is preheated, open the oven door. 9. Arrange the salmon parcels into the air fry basket on Level 4 and roast tray over wire rack on Level 2. 10. When cooking time is completed, open the oven door and serve hot.

Serving Suggestions: Serve with the garnishing of fresh herbs.
Variation Tip: Don't overcook the salmon.
Nutritional Information per Serving: Calories: 243 | Fat: 12.7g | Sat Fat: 2.2g | Carbohydrates: 9.4g | Fiber: 1.8g | Sugar: 6g | Protein: 25g

Rum-Glazed Shrimp

Prep Time: 10 minutes | Cook Time: 5 minutes | Serves: 4

Ingredients:

- 1½ pounds shrimp, peeled and deveined
- 3 tablespoons olive oil
- ⅓ cup sweet chili sauce
- ¼ cup soy sauce
- ¼ Captain Morgan Spiced Rum
- 2 garlic cloves, minced
- Juice of 1 lime
- ½ teaspoon crushed red pepper flakes
- 1 green onion, thinly sliced

Preparation:

1. Mix shrimp with all the ingredients in a bowl. 2. Cover and marinate the shrimp for 30 minutes. 3. Spread the glazed shrimp in a sheet pan. 4. Transfer the pan to the 2nd rack position of Ninja Foodi XL Pro Air Oven and close the door. 5. Select the "Bake" Mode using FUNCTION +/- buttons and select Rack Level 2. 6. Set its cooking time to 5 minutes and temperature to 375°F/190°C, then press "START/STOP" to initiate cooking. 7. Serve warm.

Serving Suggestion: Serve the shrimp with sautéed asparagus.
Variation Tip: Spread the shrimp on top of the lettuce leaves.
Nutritional Information Per Serving: Calories 378 | Fat 7g | Sodium 316mg | Carbs 6.2g | Fiber 0.3g | Sugar 0.3g | Protein 26g

Pesto Salmon

Prep Time: 15 minutes | Cook Time: 15 minutes | Serves: 4

Ingredients:

- 1¼ pound fresh salmon fillet, cut into 4 fillets
- 2 tablespoons white wine
- 1 tablespoon fresh lemon juice
- 2 tablespoons pesto

Preparation:

1. Arrange the salmon fillets onto a foil-lined baking pan, skin-side down. 2. Drizzle the salmon fillets with wine and lemon juice. 3. Set aside for about 15 minutes. 4. Spread pesto over each salmon fillet evenly. 5. Press "Power" button of Ninja Foodi XL Pro Air Oven and select the "Broil" function. 6. Press TIME/SLICES +/- buttons to set the cooking time to 15 minutes. 7. Press the TEMP/SLICES +/- buttons to select HI. 8. Press "START/STOP" button to start. 9. When the unit beeps to show that it is preheated, open the lid. 10. Insert the baking pan in oven. 11. When cooking time is completed, open the lid and serve hot.

Serving Suggestions: Serve with lemon slices.
Variation Tip: Feel free to add seasoning of your choice.
Nutritional Information per Serving: Calories: 228 | Fat: 12g | Sat Fat: 1.9g | Carbohydrates: 0.8g | Fiber: 0.2g | Sugar: 0.6g | Protein: 28.3g

Crispy Flounder

Prep Time: 15 minutes | Cook Time: 12 minutes | Serves: 3

Ingredients:

- 1 egg
- 1 cup dry Italian breadcrumb
- ¼ cup olive oil
- 3 (6-ounce) flounder fillets

Preparation:

1. In a shallow bowl, beat the egg. 2. In another bowl, add the breadcrumbs and oil and mix until a crumbly mixture is formed. 3. Dip the flounder fillets into the beaten egg and then coat with the breadcrumb mixture. 4. Press "Power" button of Ninja Foodi XL Pro Air Oven and select "Air Fry" function. 5. Press TEMP/SHADE +/- buttons to set the temperature at 355°F/180°C. 6. Now press TIME/SLICES +/- buttons to set the cooking time to 12 minutes. 7. Press "START/STOP" button to start. 8. When the unit beeps to show that it is preheated, open the lid and grease the air fry basket. 9. Place the flounder fillets into the prepared air fry basket and insert in the oven. 10. When cooking time is completed, open the lid and serve hot.

Serving Suggestions: Serve with potato chips.
Variation Tip: To avoid gluten, use crushed pork rinds instead of breadcrumbs.
Nutritional Information per Serving: Calories: 508 | Fat: 22.8g | Sat Fat: 3.9g | Carbohydrates: 26.5g | Fiber: 1.8g | Sugar: 2.5g | Protein: 47.8g

Lobster Tail Casserole

Prep Time: 15 minutes | Cook Time: 16 minutes | Serves: 6

Ingredients:

- 1 pound salmon fillets, cut into 8 equal pieces
- 16 large sea scallops
- 16 large prawns, peeled and deveined
- 8 East Coast lobster tails split in half
- ⅓ cup butter
- ¼ cup white wine
- ¼ cup lemon juice
- 2 tablespoons chopped fresh tarragon
- 2 medium garlic cloves, minced
- ½ teaspoon paprika
- ¼ teaspoon ground cayenne pepper

Preparation:

1. Whisk butter with lemon juice, wine, garlic, tarragon, paprika, salt, and cayenne pepper in a small saucepan. 2. Stir cook this mixture over medium heat for 1 minute. 3. Toss scallop, salmon fillet, and prawns in the sheet pan and pour the butter mixture on top. 4. Transfer the pan to the 2nd rack position of Ninja Foodi XL Pro Air Oven and close the door. 5. Select the "Bake" Mode using FUNCTION +/- buttons and select Rack Level 2. 6. Set its cooking time to 15 minutes and temperature to 450°F/230°C, then press "START/STOP" to initiate cooking. 7. Serve warm.

Serving Suggestion: Serve the casserole with fresh greens and chili sauce on the side.
Variation Tip: Add breadcrumbs on top for a crispy touch.
Nutritional Information Per Serving: Calories 457 | Fat 19g | Sodium 557mg | Carbs 9g | Fiber 1.8g | Sugar 1.2g | Protein 32.5g

Beer-Battered Fish

Prep Time: 15 minutes | Cook Time: 15 minutes | Serves: 4

Ingredients:

- 1½ cups all-purpose flour
- Kosher salt, to taste
- ½ teaspoon Old Bay seasoning
- 1 (12-ounce) bottle lager
- 1 large egg, beaten
- 2 pounds cod, cut into 12 pieces
- Freshly ground black pepper
- Vegetable oil for frying
- Lemon wedges, for serving

Preparation:

1. Mix flour with old bay, salt, egg, and beer in a bowl. 2. Rub the cod with black pepper and salt. 3. Coat the codfish with the beer batter and place it in the air fry basket. 4. Transfer the basket to the 3rd rack position of Ninja Foodi XL Pro Air Oven and close the door. 5. Select the "Air Fry" Mode using FUNCTION +/- buttons and select Rack Level 3. 6. Set its cooking time to 15 minutes and temperature to 350°F/175°C, then press "START/STOP" to initiate cooking. 7. Serve warm.

Serving Suggestion: Serve the fish with potato fries and tomato ketchup.
Variation Tip: Rub the fish with lemon juice before coating.
Nutritional Information Per Serving: Calories 428 | Fat 17g | Sodium 723mg | Carbs 21g | Fiber 2.5g | Sugar 2g | Protein 43g

Crispy Cod

Prep Time: 15 minutes | Cook Time: 15 minutes | Serves: 4

Ingredients:

- 4 (4-ounce) (¾-inch thick) cod fillets, with fish scale removed
- Salt, as required
- 2 tablespoons all-purpose flour
- 2 eggs
- ½ cup panko breadcrumbs
- 1 teaspoon fresh dill, minced
- ½ teaspoon dry mustard
- ½ teaspoon lemon zest, grated
- ½ teaspoon onion powder
- ½ teaspoon paprika
- Olive oil cooking spray

Preparation:

1. Season the cod fillets with salt generously. 2. In a shallow bowl, place the flour. 3. Crack the eggs in a second bowl and beat well. 4. In a third bowl, mix the panko, dill, lemon zest, mustard, and spices together. 5. Coat each cod fillet with the flour, then dip into beaten eggs and finally, coat with panko mixture. 6. Press "Power" button of Ninja Foodi XL Pro Air Oven and select "Air Fry" function. 7. Press TEMP/SHADE +/- buttons to set the temperature at 400°F/200°C. 8. Now press TIME/SLICES +/- buttons to set the cooking time to 15 minutes. 9. Press "START/STOP" button to start. 10. When the unit beeps to show that it is preheated, open the lid and grease the air fry basket. 11. Place the cod fillets into the prepared air fry basket and insert in the oven. 12. Flip the cod fillets once halfway through. 13. When cooking time is completed, open the lid and serve hot.

Serving Suggestions: Serve with steamed green beans.
Variation Tip: Feel free to add seasoning of your choice.
Nutritional Information per Serving: Calories: 190 | Fat: 4.3g | Sat Fat: 1.1g | Carbohydrates: 5.9g | Fiber: 0.4g | Sugar: 0.4g | Protein: 24g

Fish Newburg with Haddock

Prep Time: 15 minutes | Cook Time: 29 minutes | Serves: 4

Ingredients:

- 1½ pounds haddock fillets
- Salt and freshly ground black pepper
- 4 tablespoons butter
- 1 tablespoon 2 teaspoons flour
- ¼ teaspoon sweet paprika
- ¼ teaspoon ground nutmeg
- Dash cayenne pepper
- ¾ cup heavy cream
- ½ cup milk
- 3 tablespoons dry sherry
- 2 large egg yolks
- 4 pastry shells

Preparation:

1. Rub haddock with black pepper and salt, then place in a sheet pan. 2. Place the spiced haddock in the pastry shell and close it like a calzone. 3. Drizzle 1 tablespoon of melted butter on top. 4. Transfer the pan to the 2nd rack position of Ninja Foodi XL Pro Air Oven and close the door. 5. Select the "Bake" Mode using FUNCTION +/- buttons and select Rack Level 2. 6. Set its cooking time to 25 minutes and temperature to 350°F/175°C, then press "START/STOP" to initiate cooking. 7. Meanwhile, melt 3 tablespoons of butter in a suitable saucepan over low heat. 8. Stir in nutmeg, cayenne, paprika, and salt, then mix well. 9. Add flour to the spice butter and whisk well to avoid lumps. 10. Cook for 2 minutes, then add milk and cream. Mix well and cook until thickens. 11. Beat egg yolks with sherry in a bowl and stir in a ladle of cream mixture. 12. Mix well and return the mixture to its saucepan. 13. Cook the mixture on low heat for 2 minutes. 14. Add the baked wrapped haddock to its sauce and cook until warm. 15. Serve warm.

Serving Suggestion: Serve the haddock with fried rice.
Variation Tip: Drizzle parmesan cheese on top before cooking.
Nutritional Information Per Serving: Calories 421 | Fat 7.4g | Sodium 356mg | Carbs 9.3g | Fiber 2.4g | Sugar 5g | Protein 37.2g

Salmon Burgers

Prep Time: 15 minutes | Cook Time: 22 minutes | Serves: 6

Ingredients:

- 3 large russet potatoes, peeled and cubed
- 1 (6-ounce) cooked salmon fillet
- 1 egg
- ¾ cup frozen vegetables (of your choice), parboiled and drained
- 2 tablespoons fresh parsley, chopped
- 1 teaspoon fresh dill, chopped
- Salt and ground black pepper, as required
- 1 cup breadcrumbs
- ¼ cup olive oil

Preparation:

1. In a pan of boiling water, cook the potatoes for about 10 minutes. 2. Drain the potatoes well. 3. Transfer the potatoes into a bowl and mash with a potato masher. 4. Set aside to cool completely. 5. In another bowl, add the salmon and flake with a fork. 6. Add the cooked potatoes, egg, parboiled vegetables, parsley, dill, salt and black pepper and mix until well combined. 7. Make 6 equal-sized patties from the mixture. 8. Coat patties with breadcrumb evenly and then drizzle with the oil evenly. 9. Press "Power" button of Ninja Foodi XL Pro Air Oven and select "Air Fry" function. 10. Press TEMP/SHADE +/- buttons to set the temperature at 355°F/180°C. 11. Now press TIME/SLICES +/- buttons to set the cooking time to 12 minutes. 12. Press "START/STOP" button to start. 13. When the unit beeps to show that it is preheated, open the lid. 14. Arrange the patties in greased air fry basket and insert in the oven. 15. Flip the patties once halfway through. 16. When cooking time is completed, open the lid and serve hot.

Serving Suggestions: Serve your favorite dipping sauce.
Variation Tip: You can use herbs of your choice in this recipe.
Nutritional Information per Serving: Calories: 334 | Fat: 12.1g | Sat Fat: 2g | Carbohydrates: 45.2g | Fiber: 6.3g | Sugar: 4g | Protein: 12.5g

Prawns in Butter Sauce

Prep Time: 15 minutes | Cook Time: 6 minutes | Serves: 2

Ingredients:

- ½ pound large prawns, peeled and deveined
- 1 large garlic clove, minced
- 1 tablespoon butter, melted
- 1 teaspoon fresh lemon zest, grated

Preparation:

1. In a bowl, add all the ingredients and toss to coat well. 2. Set aside at room temperature for about 30 minutes. 3. Arrange the prawn mixture into a baking pan. 4. Press "Power" button of Ninja Foodi XL Pro Air Oven and select "Bake" function. 5. Press TEMP/SHADE +/- buttons to set the temperature at 450°F/230°C. 6. Now press TIME/SLICES +/- buttons to set the cooking time to 6 minutes. 7. Press "START/STOP" button to start. 8. When the unit beeps to show that it is preheated, open the lid. 9. Arrange the pan over the wire rack and insert in the oven. 10. When cooking time is completed, open the lid and serve immediately.

Serving Suggestions: Avoid shrimp from smelling like ammonia. Serve with fresh salad.
Variation Tip: Feel Free to add seasoning of your choice.
Nutritional Information per Serving: Calories: 189 | Fat: 7.7g | Sat Fat: 4.2g | Carbohydrates: 2.4g | Fiber: 0.1g | Sugar: 0.1g | Protein: 26g

Spicy Salmon

Prep Time: 10 minutes | Cook Time: 11 minutes | Serves: 2

Ingredients:

- 1 teaspoon smoked paprika
- 1 teaspoon cayenne pepper
- 1 teaspoon onion powder
- 1 teaspoon garlic powder
- Salt and ground black pepper, as required
- 2 (6-ounce) (1½-inch thick) salmon fillets
- 2 teaspoons olive oil

Preparation:

1. Add the spices in a bowl and mix well. 2. Drizzle the salmon fillets with oil and then rub with the spice mixture. 3. Press "Power" button of Ninja Foodi XL Pro Air Oven and select "Air Fry" function. 4. Press TEMP/SHADE +/- buttons to set the temperature at 390°F/200°C. 5. Now press TIME/SLICES +/- buttons to set the cooking time to 11 minutes. 6. Press "Start/Stop" button to start. 7. When the unit beeps to show that it is preheated, open the oven door. 8. Arrange the salmon fillets into the greased air fry basket on Level 3. 9. When cooking time is completed, open the oven door and serve hot.

Serving Suggestions: Serve with your favorite salad.
Variation Tip: Adjust the ratio of spices according to your taste.
Nutritional Information per Serving: Calories: 280 | Fat: 15.5g | Sat Fat: 2.2g | Carbohydrates: 3.1g | Fiber: 0.8g | Sugar: 1g | Protein: 33.6g

Fish in Yogurt Marinade

Prep Time: 15 minutes | Cook Time: 10 minutes | Serves: 2

Ingredients:

- 1 cup plain Greek yogurt
- Finely grated zest of 1 lemon
- 1 tablespoon lemon juice
- 1 tablespoon finely minced garlic
- 3 tablespoons fresh oregano leaves
- 1 teaspoon ground cumin
- ¼ teaspoon ground allspice
- ½ teaspoon salt
- ½ teaspoon freshly ground black pepper
- 1½ pounds perch filets

Preparation:

1. Mix lemon zest, yogurt, garlic, cumin, oregano, black pepper, salt, and allspices in a shallow pan. 2. Add fish to this marinade, mix well to coat then cover it with a plastic wrap. 3. Marinate for 15 minutes in the refrigerator, then uncover. 4. Transfer the fish pan to the 2nd rack position of Ninja Foodi XL Pro Air Oven and close the door. 5. Select the "Bake" Mode using FUNCTION +/- buttons and select Rack Level 2. 6. Set its cooking time to 10 minutes and temperature to 450°F/230°C, then press "START/STOP" to initiate cooking. 7. Serve warm.

Serving Suggestion: Serve the fish with lemon slices and fried rice.
Variation Tip: Use white pepper for seasoning for a change of flavor.
Nutritional Information Per Serving: Calories 438 | Fat 21g | Sodium 146mg | Carbs 7.1g | Fiber 0.1g | Sugar 0.4g | Protein 23g

Salmon with Broccoli

Prep Time: 15 minutes | Cook Time: 12 minutes | Serves: 2

Ingredients:

1½ cups small broccoli florets
2 tablespoons vegetable oil, divided
Salt and ground black pepper, as required
1 (½-inch) piece fresh ginger, grated
1 tablespoon soy sauce
1 teaspoon rice vinegar
1 teaspoon light brown sugar
¼ teaspoon cornstarch
2 (6-ounce) skin-on salmon fillets

Preparation:

1. In a bowl, mix together the broccoli, 1 tablespoon of oil, salt, and black pepper. 2. In another bowl, mix well the ginger, soy sauce, vinegar, sugar, and cornstarch. 3. Coat the salmon fillets with remaining oil and then with the ginger mixture. 4. Press "Power" button of Ninja Foodi XL Pro Air Oven and select "Air Fry" function. Select 2 LEVEL. 5. Press TEMP/SHADE +/- buttons to set the temperature at 375°F/190°C. 6. Now press TIME/SLICES +/- buttons to set the cooking time to 12 minutes. 7. Press "Start/Stop" button to start. 8. When the unit beeps to show that it is preheated, open the oven door. 9. Arrange the broccoli florets evenly into the greased air fry basket and roast tray top with the salmon fillets. 10. Insert the basket Level 3 and roast tray over wire rack on Level 1. 11. When cooking time is completed, remove basket and wire rack from oven and cool for 5 minutes before serving.
Serving Suggestions: Serve with the garnishing of lemon zest.
Variation Tip: Use low-sodium soy sauce.
Nutritional Information per Serving: Calories: 385 | Fat: 24.4g | Sat Fat: 4.2g | Carbohydrates: 7.8g | Fiber: 2.1g | Sugar: 3g | Protein: 35.6g

Baked Tilapia with Buttery Crumb Topping

Prep Time: 15 minutes | Cook Time: 16 minutes | Serves: 4

Ingredients:

4 tilapia fillets
Salt and pepper to taste
1 cup bread crumbs
3 tablespoons butter, melted
½ teaspoon dried basil

Preparation:

1. Rub the tilapia fillets with black pepper and salt, then place them in the sheet pan. 2. Mix butter, breadcrumbs, and seasonings in a bowl. 3. Sprinkle the breadcrumbs mixture on top of the tilapia. 4. Transfer the fish to the 2nd rack position of Ninja Foodi XL Pro Air Oven and close the door. 5. Select the "Bake" Mode using FUNCTION +/- buttons and select Rack Level 2. 6. Set its cooking time to 15 minutes and temperature to 375°F/190°C, then press "START/STOP" to initiate cooking. 7. Switch to Broil at HI and cook for 1 minute. 8. Serve warm.
Serving Suggestion: Serve the tilapia with vegetable rice.
Variation Tip: Add crushed corn flakes on top for more crispiness.
Nutritional Information Per Serving: Calories 558 | Fat 9g | Sodium 994mg | Carbs 1g | Fiber 0.4g | Sugar 3g | Protein 16g

Parmesan Flounder

Prep Time: 15 minutes | Cook Time: 20 minutes | Serves: 4

Ingredients:

¼ cup olive oil
4 fillets flounder
Kosher salt, to taste
Freshly ground black pepper
½ cup Parmesan, grated
¼ cup bread crumbs
4 garlic cloves, minced
Juice and zest of 1 lemon

Preparation:

1. Mix parmesan, breadcrumbs, and all the ingredients in a bowl and coat the flounder well. 2. Place the fish in a sheet pan. 3. Transfer the fish to the 2nd rack position of Ninja Foodi XL Pro Air Oven and close the door. 4. Select the "Bake" Mode using FUNCTION +/- buttons and select Rack Level 2. 5. Set its cooking time to 20 minutes and temperature to 425°F/220°C, then press "START/STOP" to initiate cooking. 6. Serve warm.
Serving Suggestion: Serve the flounder with fresh greens and yogurt dip.
Variation Tip: Drizzle cheddar cheese on top for a rich taste.
Nutritional Information Per Serving: Calories 351 | Fat 4g | Sodium 236mg | Carbs 9.1g | Fiber 0.3g | Sugar 0.1g | Protein 36g

Tangy Sea Bass

Prep Time: 10 minutes | Cook Time: 12 minutes | Serves: 2

Ingredients:

- 2 (5-ounce) sea bass fillets
- 1 garlic clove, minced
- 1 teaspoon fresh dill, minced
- 1 tablespoon olive oil
- 1 tablespoon balsamic vinegar
- Salt and ground black pepper, as required

Preparation:

1. In a large resealable bag, add all the ingredients. 2. Seal the bag and shake well to mix. 3. Refrigerate to marinate for at least 30 minutes. 4. Remove the fish fillets from bag and shake off the excess marinade. 5. Arrange the fish fillets onto the greased sheet pan in a single layer. 6. Press "Power" button of Ninja Foodi XL Pro Air Oven and select "Bake" function. 7. Press TEMP/SHADE +/- buttons to set the temperature at 450°F/230°C. 8. Now press TIME/SLICES +/- buttons to set the cooking time to 12 minutes. 9. Press "Start/Stop" button to start. 10. When the unit beeps to show that it is preheated, open the oven door and insert the sheet pan on Level 3. 11. Open the Flip the fish fillets once halfway through. 12. When cooking time is completed, open the oven door and serve hot.

Serving Suggestions: Serve with fresh salad.
Variation Tip: Rinse fish with cool, running water and pat it dry.
Nutritional Information per Serving: Calories: 241 | Fat: 10.7g | Sat Fat: 1.9g | Carbohydrates: 0.9g | Fiber: 0.1g | Sugar: 0.1g | Protein: 33.7g

Salmon with Prawns

Prep Time: 15 minutes | Cook Time: 18 minutes | Serves: 4

Ingredients:

- 4 (4-ounce) salmon fillets
- 2 tablespoons olive oil
- ½ pound cherry tomatoes, chopped
- 8 large prawns, peeled and deveined
- 2 tablespoons fresh lemon juice
- 2 tablespoons fresh thyme, chopped

Preparation:

1. In the bottom of a greased sheet pan, place salmon fillets and tomatoes in a greased baking dish in a single layer and drizzle with the oil. 2. Arrange the prawns on top in a single layer. 3. Drizzle with lemon juice and sprinkle with thyme. 4. Press "Power" button of Ninja Foodi XL Pro Air Oven and select "Air Fry" function. 5. Press TEMP/SHADE +/- buttons to set the temperature at 390°F/200°C. 6. Now press TIME/SLICES +/- buttons to set the cooking time to 8 minutes. 7. Press "Start/Stop" button to start. 8. When the unit beeps to show that it is preheated, open the oven door. 9. Arrange the baking pan over wire rake and insert into rails of Level 3. 10. When cooking time is completed, open the oven door and serve immediately.

Serving Suggestions: Serve with pasta of your choice.
Variation Tip: Make sure to use fresh salmon and prawns.
Nutritional Information per Serving: Calories: 239 | Fat: 14.5g | Sat Fat: 2.2g | Carbohydrates: 3.4g | Fiber: 1.2g | Sugar: 1.7g | Protein: 25.2g

Cod Burgers

Prep Time: 15 minutes | Cook Time: 7 minutes | Serves: 4

Ingredients:

- ½ pound cod fillets
- ½ teaspoon fresh lime zest, grated finely
- ½ egg
- ½ teaspoon red chili paste
- Salt, to taste
- ½ tablespoon fresh lime juice
- 3 tablespoons coconut, grated and divided
- 1 small scallion, chopped finely
- 1 tablespoon fresh parsley, chopped

Preparation:

1. In a food processor, add cod filets, lime zest, egg, chili paste, salt and lime juice and pulse until smooth. 2. Transfer the cod mixture into a bowl. 3. Add 1½ tablespoons of coconut, scallion and parsley and mix until well combined. 4. Make 4 equal-sized patties from the mixture. 5. In a shallow dish, place the remaining coconut. 6. Coat the patties in coconut evenly. 7. Press "Power" button of Ninja Foodi XL Pro Air Oven and select "Air Fry" function. 8. Press TEMP/SHADE +/- buttons to set the temperature at 375°F/190°C. 9. Now press TIME/SLICES +/- buttons to set the cooking time to 7 minutes. 10. Press "Start/Stop" button to start. 11. When the unit beeps to show that it is preheated, open the oven door. 12. Arrange the patties into the greased air fry basket on Level 3. 13. When cooking time is completed, open the oven door and serve hot.

Serving Suggestions: Serve alongside the dipping sauce.
Variation Tip: Use unsweetened coconut.
Nutritional Information per Serving: Calories: 70 | Fat: 2.4g | Sat Fat: 1.3g | Carbohydrates: 1.1g | Fiber: 0.4g | Sugar: 0.5g | Protein: 11g

Maple Bacon Salmon

Prep Time: 15 minutes | Cook Time: 29 minutes | Serves: 4

Ingredients:

- Salmon
- 1 lemon, sliced
- 1 (2¼ pounds) skin-on salmon fillet
- 2½ teaspoons salt, black pepper, and garlic seasoning
- 1 tablespoon Dijon mustard
- ⅓ cup olive oil
- 2 tablespoons lemon juice
- 2 tablespoons maple syrup
- Chopped chives for garnish
- Candied Bacon
- 3 tablespoons maple syrup
- 1 tablespoon packed brown sugar
- ¼ teaspoon salt, black pepper and garlic seasoning

Preparation:

1. Place lemon slices in a sheet pan and top them with salmon. 2. Drizzle salt, black pepper, and garlic seasoning on top. 3. Mix mustard, oil, maple syrup, lemon juice, salt, black pepper, and seasoning in a bowl. 4. Pour this sauce over the salmon. 5. Transfer the pan to the 2nd rack position of Ninja Foodi XL Pro Air Oven and close the door. 6. Select the "Air Fry" Mode using FUNCTION +/- buttons and select Rack Level 2. 7. Set its cooking time to 25 minutes and temperature to 350°F/175°C, then press "START/STOP" to initiate cooking. 8. Meanwhile, mix brown sugar, salt, black pepper, and garlic seasoning in a bowl. 9. Sauté bacon in a skillet until crispy and pour the sugar syrup on top. 10. Cook for 4 minutes until the liquid is absorbed. 11. Allow the bacon to cool and then crumble it. 12. Garnish the salmon with crumbled bacon. 13. Serve warm.

Serving Suggestion: Serve the salmon with roasted broccoli florets.
Variation Tip: Drizzle lemon butter on top before cooking.
Nutritional Information Per Serving: Calories 415 | Fat 15g | Sodium 634mg | Carbs 4.3g | Fiber 1.4g | Sugar 1g | Protein 23.3g

Spiced Shrimp

Prep Time: 15 minutes | Cook Time: 5 minutes | Serves: 3

Ingredients:

- 1 pound tiger shrimp
- 3 tablespoons olive oil
- 1 teaspoon old bay seasoning
- ½ teaspoon cayenne pepper
- ½ teaspoon smoked paprika
- Salt, as required

Preparation:

1. In a large bowl, add all the ingredients and stir to combine. 2. Press "Power" button of Ninja Foodi XL Pro Air Oven and select "Air Fry" function. 3. Press TEMP/SHADE +/- buttons to set the temperature at 390°F/200°C. 4. Now press TIME/SLICES +/- buttons to set the cooking time to 5 minutes. 5. Press "Start/Stop" button to start. 6. When the unit beeps to show that it is preheated, open the oven door. 7. Arrange the shrimp into the greased air fry basket on Level 3. 8. When cooking time is completed, open the oven door and serve hot.

Serving Suggestions: Serve with fresh greens.
Variation Tip: You can use seasoning of your choice.
Nutritional Information per Serving: Calories: 272 | Fat: 15.7g | Sat Fat: 2.5g | Carbohydrates: 0.4g | Fiber: 0.2g | Sugar: 0.1g | Protein: 31.7g

Crispy Catfish

Prep Time: 15 minutes | Cook Time: 15 minutes | Serves: 5

Ingredients:

- 5 (6-ounce) catfish fillets
- 1 cup milk
- 2 teaspoons fresh lemon juice
- ½ cup yellow mustard
- ½ cup cornmeal
- ¼ cup all-purpose flour
- 2 tablespoons dried parsley flakes
- ¼ teaspoon red chili powder
- ¼ teaspoon cayenne pepper
- ¼ teaspoon onion powder
- ¼ teaspoon garlic powder
- Salt and ground black pepper, as required
- Olive oil cooking spray

Preparation:

1. In a large bowl, place the catfish, milk, and lemon juice and refrigerate for about 15 minutes. 2. In a shallow bowl, add the mustard. 3. In another bowl, mix together the cornmeal, flour, parsley flakes and spices. 4. Remove the catfish fillets from milk mixture and with paper towels, pat them dry. 5. Coat each fish fillet with mustard and then roll into cornmeal mixture. 6. Then, spray each fillet with the cooking spray. 7. Arrange the 3 catfish fillets into the greased air fry basket and 2 into roast tray. Press "Power" button of Ninja Foodi XL Pro Air Oven and select "Air Fry" function. Select 2 LEVEL. 8. Press TEMP/SHADE +/- buttons to set the temperature at 400°F/200°C. 9. Now press TIME/SLICES +/- buttons to set the cooking time to 15 minutes. 10. Press "Start/Stop" button to start. 11. When the unit beeps to show that it is preheated, open the oven door. 12. Slide the basket on Level 3 and roast tray over wire rack on Level 1. 13. After 10 minutes of cooking, flip the fillets and spray with the cooking spray. 14. When cooking time is completed, open the oven door and serve hot.

Serving Suggestions: Serve with cheese sauce.
Variation Tip: Use freshly squeezed lemon juice.
Nutritional Information per Serving: Calories: 340 | Fat: 15.5g | Sat Fat: 3.1g | Carbohydrates: 18.3g | Fiber: 2g | Sugar: 2.7g | Protein: 30.9g

Baked Sardines with Garlic and Oregano

Prep Time: 15 minutes | Cook Time: 45 minutes | Serves: 4

Ingredients:

2 pounds fresh sardines
Salt and black pepper to taste
2 tablespoons Greek oregano
6 cloves garlic, thinly sliced
½ cup olive oil
½ cup freshly squeezed lemon juice
½ cup water

Preparation:

1. Mix salt, black pepper, oregano, garlic, olive oil, lemon juice, and water in a sheet pan. 2. Spread the sardines in the marinade and rub well. 3. Leave the sardines for 10 minutes to marinate. 4. Transfer the pan to the 3rd rack position of Ninja Foodi XL Pro Air Oven and close the door. 5. Select the "Air Fry" Mode using FUNCTION +/- buttons and select Rack Level 3. 6. Set its cooking time to 45 minutes and temperature to 355°F/180°C, then press "START/STOP" to initiate cooking. 7. Serve warm.

Serving Suggestion: Serve the sardines with crispy bread and sautéed veggies.
Variation Tip: Add chili flakes on top for more spice.
Nutritional Information Per Serving: Calories 392 | Fat 16g | Sodium 466mg | Carbs 3.9g | Fiber 0.9g | Sugar 0.6g | Protein 48g

Cod with Sauce

Prep Time: 15 minutes | Cook Time: 15 minutes | Serves: 2

Ingredients:

2 (7-ounce) cod fillets
Salt and ground black pepper, as required
¼ teaspoon sesame oil
1 cup water
5 little squares rock sugar
5 tablespoons light soy sauce
1 teaspoon dark soy sauce
2 scallions (green part), sliced
¼ cup fresh cilantro, chopped
3 tablespoons olive oil
5 ginger slices

Preparation:

1. Season each cod fillet evenly with salt, and black pepper and drizzle with sesame oil. 2. Set aside at room temperature for about 15-20 minutes. 3. Insert the wire rack on Level 1. Press "Power" button of Ninja Foodi XL Pro Air Oven and select "Air Fry" function. Select 2 LEVEL. 4. Press TEMP/SHADE +/- buttons to set the temperature at 355°F/180°C. 5. Now press TIME/SLICES +/- buttons to set the cooking time to 12 minutes. 6. Press "Start/Stop" button to start. 7. When the unit beeps to show that it is preheated, open the oven door. 8. Arrange the cod fillets into the greased air fry basket on Level 3 and greased sheet pan over wire rack on Level 1. 9. Meanwhile, in a small pan, add the water and bring it to a boil. 10. Add the rock sugar and both soy sauces and cook until sugar is dissolved, stirring continuously. 11. Remove from the heat and set aside. 12. In a small frying pan, heat the olive oil over medium heat and sauté the ginger slices for about 2-3 minutes. 13. Remove the frying pan from heat and discard the ginger slices. 14. When cooking time is completed, open the oven door and transfer the cod fillets onto serving plates. 15. Top each fillet with scallion and cilantro. 16. Carefully pour the hot oil evenly over cod fillets. 17. Top with the sauce mixture and serve.

Serving Suggestions: Serve with boiled rice.
Variation Tip: For best result, use toasted sesame oil.
Nutritional Information per Serving: Calories: 380 | Fat: 23.4g | Sat Fat: 3.1g | Carbohydrates: 5g | Fiber: 0.8g | Sugar: 1.1g | Protein: 38.3g

Garlic Shrimp with Lemon

Prep Time: 5 minutes | Cook Time: 12 minutes | Serves: 1

Ingredients:

½ pound raw shrimp
⅛ teaspoon garlic powder
Salt and black pepper, to taste
Vegetable oil, to coat shrimp
Chili flakes
Lemon wedges
Parsley

Preparation:

1. Take a bowl and coat the shrimp with vegetable oil. 2. Add garlic powder, pepper and salt and toss to coat well. 3. Now, transfer shrimp to a plate or air fry basket. 4. Turn on your Ninja Foodi XL Pro Air Oven and select "Air Fry". 5. Select the timer for about 12 minutes and temperature for 400°F/200°C. 6. When the unit beeps to signify it is preheated, open the oven and place the air fry basket on Level 3, Close the oven and let it cook. 7. Transfer shrimp to a bowl and add lemon wedges. 8. Sprinkle parsley and chili flakes evenly on top. 9. Serve and enjoy!

Serving Suggestions: Serve it with macaroni salad.
Variation Tip: Try not to cook for too long otherwise it can get dry.
Nutritional Information per Serving: Calories: 398 | Fat: 17.9g | Sat Fat: 2.2g | Carbohydrates: 4.7g | Fiber: 0.4g | Sugar: 0.4g | Protein: 51.9g

Garlic Butter Salmon Bites

Prep Time: 6 minutes | Cook Time: 10 minutes | Serves: 2

Ingredients:

- 1 tablespoon lemon juice
- 2 tablespoons butter
- ½ tablespoon garlic, minced
- ½ teaspoon pepper
- 4 ounces salmon
- ½ teaspoon salt
- ½ tablespoon apple cider or rice vinegar

Preparation:

1. Take a large bowl and add everything except salmon and whisk together until well combined. 2. Slice the salmon into small cubes and marinade them into the mixture. 3. Cover the bowl with plastic wrap and refrigerate it for about an hour. 4. Now, spread out the marinated salmon cubes into the air fry basket. 5. Turn on your Ninja Foodi XL Pro Air Oven and select "Air Fry". 6. Select the timer for 10 minutes and temperature for 350°F/175°C. 7. When the unit beeps to signify it has preheated, open the oven and slide the air fry basket into rail of Level 3, Close the oven and let it cook. 8. Wait till the salmon is finely cooked. 9. Serve and enjoy!

Serving Suggestions: Serve with cheese on top.
Variation Tip: You can also coat salmon using bread crumbs for a fine taste.
Nutritional Information per Serving: Calories: 159 | Fat: 12.2g | Sat Fat: 6g | Carbohydrates: 1.7g | Fiber: 0.2g | Sugar: 0.6g | Protein: 11.3g

Seafood Medley Mix

Prep Time: 5 minutes | Cook Time: 15 minutes | Serves: 1

Ingredients:

- ½ pound frozen seafood medley
- Oil or cooking spray
- Salt and black pepper, to taste

Preparation:

1. Take an air fry basket and evenly spray with a cooking spray. 2. Put frozen seafood medley in the air fry basket. 3. Turn on your Ninja Foodi XL Pro Air Oven and select "Air Fry". 4. Select the timer for 15 minutes and temperature for 400°F/200°C. 5. When the unit beeps to signify it is preheated, open the oven and place the air fry basket into rail of Level 3. 6. Season the seafood medley with salt and pepper. 7. Serve and enjoy!

Serving Suggestions: Serve it with crispy garlic bread.
Variation Tip: Drizzle little bit of butter and lemon on top.
Nutritional Information per Serving: Calories: 323 | Fat: 15.6g | Sat Fat: 3.8g | Carbohydrates: 5.1g | Fiber: 0g | Sugar: 0g | Protein: 32.4g

Tilapia with Herbs and Garlic

Prep Time: 4 minutes | Cook Time: 10 minutes | Serves: 1

Ingredients:

- 1 teaspoon olive oil
- 1 teaspoon fresh chives, chopped
- 1 fresh tilapia fillet
- ½ teaspoon garlic, minced
- 1 teaspoon fresh parsley, chopped
- Fresh ground pepper, to taste
- Salt, to taste

Preparation:

1. Take a small bowl and add everything except the tilapia fillets and stir together. 2. Dredge tilapia fillets in the prepared mixture. 3. Turn on your Ninja Foodi XL Pro Air Oven and select "Air Fry". 4. Select the timer for about 10 minutes and temperature for 400°F/200°C. 5. When the unit beeps to signify it is preheated, open the oven and place the air fry basket into rail of Level 3. 6. Grease the air fry basket using little olive oil and place the seasoned fillets. Close the oven. 7. Let it cook and then serve.

Serving Suggestions: Serve with tomato salad.
Variation Tip: Try to pat tilapia fillets dry using a paper towel.
Nutritional Information per Serving: Calories: 136 | Fat: 5.7g | Sat Fat: 1.1g | Carbohydrates: 0.6g | Fiber: 0.1g | Sugar: 0g | Protein: 21.2g

Shrimp Fajitas

Prep Time: 5 minutes | Cook Time: 10 minutes | Serves: 2

Ingredients:

- ½ pound raw shrimp
- ½ small onion, sliced
- ½ tablespoon vegetable oil, divided
- ½ tablespoon fajita seasoning
- 1 red bell pepper, sliced
- 1 green bell pepper, sliced

Preparation:

1. Take a bowl and season the vegetables. Add half of the oil and fajita seasoning. Place the vegetable mixture into an air fry basket. 2. Turn on your Ninja Foodi XL Pro Air Oven and select "Air Fry". 3. Select the timer for 3 minutes and temperature for 375°F/190°C. 4. When the unit beeps to signify it has preheated, open the oven and slide the air fry basket into rail of Level 3. Close the oven and let it cook. 5. Air fry the vegetables. 6. Now, meanwhile season the shrimp with rest of oil and fajita seasoning. 7. After 3 minutes add the seasoned shrimp to the side. 8. Now, air fry for another 6 minutes at the same temperature. 9. Serve and enjoy!

Serving Suggestions: Serve it with tortilla bread and fresh avocado slices.
Variation Tip: You can omit bell peppers if you like.
Nutritional Information per Serving: Calories: 195 | Fat: 5.3g | Sat Fat: 1.3g | Carbohydrates: 9.4g | Fiber: 0.4g | Sugar: 5.2g | Protein: 26g

Air Fried Fish Sticks

Prep Time: 6 minutes | Cook Time: 15 minutes | Serves: 1

Ingredients:

- ½ pound fish fillets
- ¼ teaspoon ground black pepper, divided
- 1 egg
- ¼ cup flour
- ½ teaspoon salt, divided
- ½ cup breadcrumbs, dried

Preparation:

1. Take a bowl and add flour, salt and pepper. 2. In a second bowl, whisk the egg. In another bowl, add breadcrumbs. 3. Dredge the fish in flour, then dip in egg and lastly coat with breadcrumbs. 4. Once they are done, put them in an air fry basket. 5. Turn on your Ninja Foodi XL Pro Air Oven and select "Air Fry". 6. Select the timer for about 10 to 15 minutes and temperature for 400°F/200°C. 7. When the unit beeps to signify it is preheated, open the oven and place the air fry basket into rail of Level 3. Close the oven and let it cook. 8. Serve and enjoy!

Serving Suggestions: Serve with fresh lemon juice.
Variation Tip: You can season fish with salt beforehand.
Nutritional Information per Serving: Calories: 918 | Fat: 35.4g | Sat Fat: 8.5g | Carbohydrates: 101.9g | Fiber: 4.5g | Sugar: 3.8g | Protein: 49.3g

Breaded Shrimp

Prep Time: 8 minutes | Cook Time: 7 minutes | Serves: 2

Ingredients:

- ¼ teaspoon garlic powder
- ¼ teaspoon onion powder
- ¼ teaspoon salt
- ½ pound raw shrimp
- 1 egg
- 2 teaspoons flour
- ½ teaspoon corn starch
- 1 tablespoon water
- 6 tablespoons fine breadcrumbs
- 6 tablespoons panko breadcrumbs

Preparation:

1. Take a small bowl, add flour, corn starch, garlic powder, onion powder, and salt. 2. Add shrimp in the bowl and toss to coat well. 3. In a second bowl, whisk in the egg. 4. Mix the panko breadcrumbs and fine breadcrumbs together in another bowl. 5. Now, take seasoned shrimp, dip in the egg and place in the breadcrumbs mixture. 6. Lightly grease the air fry basket. 7. Turn on your Ninja Foodi XL Pro Air Oven and select "Air Fry". 8. Select the timer for about 7 minutes and temperature for 370°F/185°C. 9. When the unit beeps to signify it is preheated, open the oven and place the air fry basket into rail of Level 3. 10. Place the coated shrimp to the air fry basket. Close the oven and let it cook. 11. Serve and enjoy!

Serving Suggestions: Serve it with tartar sauce or a dipping sauce of your choice.
Variation Tip: Try to rinse shrimp using cold water beforehand.
Nutritional Information per Serving: Calories: 1351 | Fat: 26.6g | Sat Fat: 10.3g | Carbohydrates: 54.3g | Fiber: 1.3g | Sugar: 1g | Protein: 37.7g

Air Fried Fish Cakes

Prep Time: 5 minutes | Cook Time: 10 minutes | Serves: 1

Ingredients:

- ½ pound white fish, finely chopped
- ⅓ cup panko breadcrumbs
- 2 tablespoons cilantro, chopped
- 1 tablespoon chili sauce
- Cooking spray
- ½ egg
- 1 tablespoon mayonnaise
- ⅛ teaspoon ground pepper
- 1 pinch of salt

Preparation:

1. Take a bowl and add all ingredients together until well combined. 2. Shape the mixture into cakes. 3. Grease the air fry basket using cooking spray. 4. Turn on your Ninja Foodi XL Pro Air Oven and select "Air Fry". 5. Select the timer for about 10 minutes and temperature for 400°F/200°C. 6. When the unit beeps to signify it is preheated, open the oven and place the air fry basket into rail of Level 3. 7. Let the fish cakes cook until they are golden brown. 8. Serve and enjoy!

Serving Suggestions: Serve with lemon wedges to enhance taste.
Variation Tip: Squeeze out any excess moisture before adding fish to the mixture.
Nutritional Information per Serving: Calories: 517 | Fat: 17g | Sat Fat: 4.3g | Carbohydrates: 9.7g | Fiber: 0.3g | Sugar: 1.4g | Protein: 57.6g

Lobster Tails with Lemon-Garlic Butter

Prep Time: 5 minutes | Cook Time: 10 minutes | Serves: 1

Ingredients:

- 2 tablespoons butter
- ½ teaspoon lemon zest
- 1 lobster tail
- ½ clove garlic, grated
- ½ teaspoon parsley, chopped
- Salt, to taste
- Fresh ground black pepper, to taste

Preparation:

1. Cut the lobster tail lengthwise through the center of the hard top shell. 2. Cut to the bottom of the shell and spread the tail halves apart. 3. Place the lobster tail in the roast tray. 4. Take a saucepan and melt butter on medium heat. 5. Add garlic and lemon zest and cook for 30 seconds. 6. Now, pour the butter mixture onto lobster tail. 7. Insert a wire rack on Level 3. Turn on your Ninja Foodi XL Pro Air Oven and select "Air Fry". 8. Select the timer for about 5 to 7 minutes and temperature for 380°F/195°C. 9. When the unit beeps to signify it is preheated, open the oven and place the roast tray on sheet pan onto the wire rack. Close the oven. 10. Let it cook and serve with parsley as topping.

Serving Suggestions: Serve with lemon wedges on side.
Variation Tip: You can use small piece of foil to hold in the butter mixture.
Nutritional Information per Serving: Calories: 337 | Fat: 24.3g | Sat Fat: 14.9g | Carbohydrates: 0.8g | Fiber: 0.1g | Sugar: 0.1g | Protein: 27.9g

Greek Baked Bonito with Herbs and Potatoes

Prep Time: 30 minutes | Cook Time: 1 hour 30 minutes | Serves: 6

Ingredients:

- 3 pounds whole bonito
- Sea salt, to taste
- Freshly ground black pepper, to taste
- 2 teaspoons Greek oregano
- 5 to 6 cloves garlic, sliced
- 2½ pounds potatoes
- Cooking spray
- ½ cup olive oil
- 6 tablespoons freshly squeezed lemon juice
- 1⅓ cups water

Preparation:

1. Insert a wire rack on Level 3 in the oven. Select the BAKE function, 355°F/180°C, for 1 hour, 30 minutes. While the oven is preheating, prepare the ingredients. 2. Remove and discard the fish's head and intestines. Cut along the back, remove the bloodline, and cut the fish in half lengthwise. 3. Rinse and pat the fish dry. Sprinkle with the salt, pepper, and 1 teaspoon of oregano. Then, insert the sliced garlic into the meatiest parts of the fish. 4. Next, peel the potatoes and cut them into equal-sized wedge-shaped pieces. Sprinkle salt, pepper, and the remaining oregano over the potatoes. 5. Use the cooking spray to lightly spray a large roasting pan (one that is oven-appropriate). Add the fish, skin side down, and put the potatoes around it. 6. Take a small bowl, and whisk together the lemon juice and oil. Pour the mixture over the fish and potatoes and add the water. 7. When the unit beeps to signify it has preheated, open the oven and insert the roasting pan on wire rack. 8. Bake the fillets for 1½ hours in the preheated oven.

Serving Suggestion: Garnish with some greens and serve it alongside the baked potatoes.
Variation Tip: You can combine chipotle chilies, Mexican oregano, crushed garlic, lime juice, salt, and olive oil to make a paste. Use this for a Mexican flavor.
Nutritional Information Per Serving: Calories: 1000 | Fat: 24g | Sodium: 16057mg | Carbs: 42g | Fiber: 4g | Sugar: 2g | Protein: 147g

Lemon Pepper Shrimp

Prep Time: 5 minutes | Cook Time: 8 minutes | Serves: 4

Ingredients:

- 2 lemons, juiced
- ½ tablespoon lemon pepper
- 2 tablespoons olive oil
- ½ teaspoon paprika
- ½ teaspoon garlic powder
- 1½ pounds shrimp

Preparation:

1. Take a bowl, add all the ingredients together and mix well. 2. Add shrimp and toss to coat well. 3. Turn on your Ninja Foodi XL Pro Air Oven and select "Air Fry". 4. Select the timer for about 6 to 8 minutes and temperature for 400°F/200°C. 5. When the unit beeps to signify it is preheated, open the oven and place the air fry basket on Level 3. 6. Place shrimp in the air fry basket and cook until pink. 7. Serve and enjoy!

Serving Suggestions: Serve with lemon slices.
Variation Tip: You can also add a couple drops of tabasco with olive oil.
Nutritional Information per Serving: Calories: 274 | Fat: 10g | Sat Fat: 1.9g | Carbohydrates: 6.2g | Fiber: 1.2g | Sugar: 0.9g | Protein: 39.3g

Brown Sugar and Garlic Air Fryer Salmon

Prep Time: 5 minutes | Cook Time: 10 minutes | Serves: 4

Ingredients:

- 1 pound salmon
- Salt and pepper, to taste
- 2 tablespoons brown sugar
- 1 teaspoon chili powder
- ½ teaspoon paprika
- 1 teaspoon Italian seasoning
- 1 teaspoon garlic powder

Preparation:

1. Select the AIR FRY function, 400°F/200°C, for 10 minutes. While the oven is preheating, prepare the ingredients. 2. Season the salmon with salt and pepper. 3. Take a small bowl and add the chili powder, Italian seasoning, brown sugar, paprika, and garlic powder. Rub the mixture on the salmon. 4. Put the salmon in the air fry basket, skin side down. 5. When the unit beeps to signify it has preheated, open the oven and insert the air fry basket into rail of Level 3. 6. Close the oven and cook for about 10 minutes. 7. When cooked, remove from the oven and serve.

Serving Suggestion: You can use cayenne pepper instead of paprika.
Variation Tip: You can add asparagus to the recipe.
Nutritional Information Per Serving: Calories: 190 | Fat: 7.7g | Sodium: 61mg | Carbs: 7g | Fiber: 1g | Sugar: 6g | Protein: 23g

Crispy Air Fryer Fish Tacos

Prep Time: 25 minutes | Cook Time: 10 minutes | Serves: 2 to 4

Ingredients:

- 1 cup panko breadcrumbs
- 1¼ teaspoons garlic powder
- 1½ teaspoons chili powder
- ½ teaspoon onion powder
- 1 teaspoon ground cumin
- ¾ teaspoon kosher salt

For the Salsa:
- 2 tablespoons lime juice
- 2 teaspoons honey
- 1 small garlic clove, grated
- ½ teaspoon kosher salt
- ½ teaspoon ground cumin
- ½ teaspoon chili powder
- ¼ teaspoon black pepper
- 24 ounces barramundi
- 1 large egg
- 2 tablespoons water
- 16 flour tortillas

- 2 tablespoons olive oil
- 5 cups cabbage, shredded
- Diced jalapeño, diced
- 1 cup pineapple, chopped
- ¼ cup fresh cilantro, chopped
- ¼ cup red onion, diced

Preparation:

1. Select the AIR FRY function, 380°F/195°C, for 10 minutes. Select 2 Level. While the oven is preheating, start preparing the ingredients. 2. Take a shallow bowl and mix the panko, chili powder, garlic powder, salt, onion powder, cumin, and black pepper. Stir to combine. 3. Take another shallow bowl and combine the egg and water. Pat the fish dry using paper towels and cut the fish into pieces. Then sprinkle it with salt and pepper. 4. First, dip the fish pieces into the egg mixture, then coat in the breadcrumb mixture. Make sure the breadcrumbs are pressed into the fish. 5. Add half of the fillets to the air fry basket and spray with olive oil spray. And another half to a sheet pan and spray with olive oil spray. 6. When the unit beeps to signify it has preheated, open the oven and insert the air fry basket into rail of Level 3 and the sheet pan into rail of Level 1. 7. Cook for about 4 minutes, turn over, spray with oil spray, and cook for another 2 minutes. Repeat for the next batch. 8. Meanwhile, whisk together the honey, cumin, garlic, lime juice, olive oil, and chili powder in a medium bowl. Then, add the jalapeño, cilantro, cabbage, pineapple, and red onion. Toss to combine, then season with salt and pepper. 9. Warm the tortillas in the microwave or over an open flame. Add a little slaw to the tortillas. Top with the cooked fish and cover with some more slaw.

Serving Suggestion: Serve with sour cream and a squeeze of lime juice.
Variation Tip: Try experimenting with the ingredients of salsa for added flavors.
Nutritional Information Per Serving: Calories: 82 | Fat: 3g | Sodium: 162mg | Carbs: 5g | Fiber: 1g | Sugar: 2g | Protein: 9g

Baked Sole with Mint and Ginger

Prep Time: 10 minutes | Cook Time: 15 minutes | Serves: 4

Ingredients:

- 2 pounds petrale sole fillets
- 1 bunch fresh mint
- 2 pieces ginger, peeled and chopped
- 1 tablespoon vegetable oil
- ½ teaspoon salt
- ¼ teaspoon freshly ground black pepper

Preparation:

1. Insert a wire rack on Level 3. Select the BAKE function, 375°F/190°C, for 15 minutes. While the oven is preheating, prepare the ingredients. 2. Rinse and pat dry the fillets, then arrange them on an air fryer-safe rimmed baking pan. 3. Place the ginger, salt, pepper, mint, and oil in a blender and blend to make a smooth paste. 4. Rub the fillets evenly with the mint-ginger paste. 5. When the unit beeps to signify it has preheated, open the oven and insert the oven-safe baking pan on wire rack. 6. Bake the fish for about 15 minutes.

Serving Suggestion: You can serve the fish with some roasted veggies.
Variation Tip: You can try using canola oil.
Nutritional Information Per Serving: Calories: 230 | Fat: 9g | Sodium: 1089mg | Carbs: 1g | Fiber: 1g | Sugar: 0g | Protein: 35g

Air Fryer Tuna Patties

Prep Time: 15 minutes | Cook Time: 10 minutes | Serves: 2 to 3

Ingredients:

- 1-pound fresh tuna
- 2 to 3 large eggs
- Zest of 1 medium lemon
- 1 tablespoon lemon juice
- ½ cup breadcrumbs
- 3 tablespoons parmesan cheese, grated
- 1 celery stalk, finely chopped
- 3 tablespoons onion, minced
- ½ teaspoon garlic powder
- ½ teaspoon dried herbs
- ¼ teaspoon kosher salt
- Fresh cracked black pepper, to taste

Preparation:

1. Take a medium bowl, and combine the lemon juice, lemon zest, eggs, garlic powder, celery, parmesan cheese, onion, dried herbs, salt, and pepper. Stir and combine well. 2. Prepare the air fry basket with perforated air fryer baking paper and lightly spray the sheet. 3. Scoop up ¼ cup of the mixture and shape it into patties. Try to keep the patties the same size. Chill them for about 1 hour. 4. Select the AIR FRY function. Select 2 LEVEL. 5. Place the patties in the prepared air fry basket and sheet pan, spray with some cooking oil. 6. When the unit beeps to signify it has preheated, open the oven and insert air fry basket into rail of Level 3 and sheet pan on Level 1. 7. Close the oven and cook them for about 10 minutes at 360°F/180°C, flipping halfway through. Respray the tops after flipping them.

Serving Suggestion: Serve with tartar sauce and some lemon slices.
Variation Tip: You can try adding any combo of dried herbs like oregano, dill, basil, or thyme.
Nutritional Information Per Serving: Calories: 85k | Fat: 3g | Sodium: 282mg | Carbs: 1g | Fiber: 1g | Sugar: 1g | Protein: 13g

Scallops with Chanterelles

Prep Time: 10 minutes | Cook Time: 15 minutes | Serves: 3

Ingredients:

- 1 tablespoon balsamic vinegar
- ½ pound scallops
- 3 tablespoons butter
- ½ tomato, peeled, seeded, and chopped
- 1 tablespoon butter
- ¼ pound chanterelle mushrooms

Preparation:

1. Take a pan and add half tablespoon butter over medium heat. 2. Stir in chanterelles and cook for 5 to 8 minutes. 3. Transfer to a bowl. 4. Add remaining butter in the same pan over low heat and cook for 5 minutes. 5. Stir in tomato and balsamic vinegar and cook for 2 minutes. 6. Stir the tomato mixture into mushrooms. 7. Place the mixture into a roast tray. 8. Turn on your Ninja Foodi XL Pro Air Oven and select "Broil". 9. Select the timer for about 2 minutes per side and temperature for HI. 10. Slide the roast tray on sheet pan on Level 3. 11. Serve warm and enjoy!

Serving Suggestions: Serve with mashed potatoes and green onions.
Variation Tip: Use extra chanterelles on top.
Nutritional Information per Serving: Calories: 361 | Fat: 16.7g | Sat Fat: 9.1g | Carbohydrates: 22.2g | Fiber: 9.9g | Sugar: 0.8g | Protein: 23.7g

Chapter 6 Vegetables and Sides Recipes

99	Sweet & Spicy Parsnips	106	Brussels Sprouts Gratin
99	Fried Tortellini	106	Cheesy Kale
99	Roast Cauliflower and Broccoli	107	Cheesy Green Bean Casserole
100	Stuffed Eggplants	107	Beans & Veggie Burgers
100	Vegan Cakes	107	Tofu in Sweet & Sour Sauce
100	Caramelized Baby Carrots	108	Spicy Potato
101	Blue Cheese Soufflés	108	Veggies Stuffed Bell Peppers
101	Wine Braised Mushrooms	108	Pita Bread Pizza
101	Fajitas	109	Baked Potato
102	Tofu with Broccoli	109	Asparagus with Garlic and Parmesan
102	Quinoa Burgers	109	Stuffed Zucchini
102	Broccoli with Cauliflower	110	Broiled Broccoli
103	Veggie Rice	110	Stuffed Peppers
103	Soy Sauce Green Beans	110	Green Tomatoes
103	Cauliflower in Buffalo Sauce	111	Parmesan Carrot
104	Vinegar Green Beans	111	Roasted Green Beans
104	Herbed Bell Peppers	111	Garlic Parmesan Roasted Potatoes
104	Sweet Potato Casserole	112	Broccoli Cheese Casserole
105	Roasted Vegetables	112	Creamy Roast Mushrooms
105	Parmesan Broccoli	112	Garlic Parmesan Roasted Asparagus
105	Broccoli Casserole	113	Air Fryer Sweet and Roasted Carrots
106	Vegetable Casserole		

Sweet & Spicy Parsnips

Prep Time: 15 minutes | Cook Time: 44 minutes | Serves: 5

Ingredients:

1½ pounds parsnip, peeled and cut into 1-inch chunks
1 tablespoon butter, melted
2 tablespoons honey
1 tablespoon dried parsley flakes, crushed
¼ teaspoon red pepper flakes, crushed
Salt and ground black pepper, as required

Preparation:

1. In a large bowl, mix together the parsnips and butter. 2. Press "Power" button of Ninja Foodi XL Pro Air Oven and select "Air Fry" function. Select 2 LEVEL. 3. Press TEMP/SHADE +/- buttons to set the temperature at 355°F/180°C. 4. Now press TIME/SLICES +/- buttons to set the cooking time to 44 minutes. 5. Press "Start/Stop" button to start. 6. When the unit beeps to show that it is preheated, open the oven door. 7. Separate the parsnip chunks into the greased air fry basket on Level 3 and roast tray over sheet pan on Level 1. 8. Meanwhile, in another large bowl, mix together the remaining ingredients. 9. After 40 minutes of cooking, press "Start/Stop" button to pause the unit. 10. Transfer the parsnip chunks into the bowl of honey mixture and toss to coat well. 11. Again, arrange the parsnip chunks into the air fry basket on Level 3 and roast tray on Level 1. 12. When cooking time is completed, open the oven door and serve hot.

Serving Suggestions: Serve with garlic bread.
Variation Tip: Make sure to cut the parsnip into uniform-sized chunks.
Nutritional Information per Serving: Calories: 149 | Fat: 2.7g | Sat Fat: 1.5g | Carbohydrates: 31.5g | Fiber: 6.7g | Sugar: 13.5g | Protein: 1.7g

Fried Tortellini

Prep Time: 15 minutes | Cook Time: 10 minutes | Serves: 8

Ingredients:

1 (9-ounce) package cheese tortellini
1 cup Panko breadcrumbs
⅓ cup Parmesan, grated
1 teaspoon dried oregano
½ teaspoon garlic powder
½ teaspoon crushed red pepper flakes
Kosher salt, to taste
Freshly ground black pepper, to taste
1 cup all-purpose flour
2 large eggs

Preparation:

1. Boil tortellini according to salted boiling water according to package's instructions, then drain. 2. Mix panko with garlic powder, black pepper, salt, red pepper flakes, oregano, Parmesan in a small bowl. 3. Beat eggs in one bowl and spread flour on a plate. 4. Coat the tortellini with the flour, dip into the eggs and then coat with the panko mixture. 5. Spread the tortellini in the air fry basket and spray them with cooking oil. 6. Transfer the basket to the 3rd rack position of Ninja Foodi XL Pro Air Oven and close the door. 7. Select the "Air Fry" Mode using FUNCTION +/- buttons and select Rack Level 3. 8. Set its cooking time to 10 minutes and temperature to 400°F/200°C, then press "START/STOP" to initiate cooking. 9. Serve warm.

Serving Suggestion: Serve the tortellini with tomato sauce on the side.
Variation Tip: Use crushed cornflakes to coat the tortellini.
Nutritional Information Per Serving: Calories 151 | Fat 19g | Sodium 412mg | Carbs 23g | Fiber 0.3g | Sugar 1g | Protein 3g

Roast Cauliflower and Broccoli

Prep Time: 15 minutes | Cook Time: 10 minutes | Serves: 4

Ingredients:

½ pound broccoli, florets
½ pound cauliflower, florets
1 tablespoon olive oil
Black pepper, to taste
Salt, to taste
⅓ cup water

Preparation:

1. Toss all the veggies with seasoning in a large bowl. 2. Spread these vegetables in the air fry basket. 3. Transfer the basket to the 3rd rack position of Ninja Foodi XL Pro Air Oven and close the door. 4. Select the "Air Fry" Mode using FUNCTION +/- buttons and select Rack Level 3. 5. Set its cooking time to 10 minutes and temperature to 400°F/200°C, then press "START/STOP" to initiate cooking. 6. Serve warm.

Serving Suggestion: Serve the roasted cauliflower with white rice.
Variation Tip: Add green beans to the mixture before baking.
Nutritional Information Per Serving: Calories 318 | Fat 15.7g | Sodium 124mg | Carbs 7g | Fiber 0.1g | Sugar 0.3g | Protein 4.9g

Stuffed Eggplants

Prep Time: 20 minutes | Cook Time: 11 minutes | Serves: 4

Ingredients:

4 small eggplants, halved lengthwise
1 teaspoon fresh lime juice
1 teaspoon vegetable oil
1 small onion, chopped
¼ teaspoon garlic, chopped
½ of small tomato, chopped
Salt and ground black pepper, as required
1 tablespoon cottage cheese, chopped
¼ of green bell pepper, seeded and chopped
1 tablespoon tomato paste
1 tablespoon fresh cilantro, chopped

Preparation:

1. Carefully cut a slice from one side of each eggplant lengthwise. 2. With a small spoon, scoop out the flesh from each eggplant, leaving a thick shell. 3. Transfer the eggplant flesh into a bowl. 4. Drizzle the eggplants with lime juice evenly. 5. Press "Power" button of Ninja Foodi XL Pro Air Oven and select "Air Fry" function. 6. Press TEMP/SHADE +/- buttons to set the temperature at 320°F/160°C. 7. Now press TIME/SLICES +/- buttons to set the cooking time to 3 minutes. 8. Press "Start/Stop" button to start. 9. When the unit beeps to show that it is preheated, open the oven door. 10. Arrange the hollowed eggplants into the greased air fry basket on Level 3. 11. Meanwhile, in a skillet, heat the oil over medium heat and sauté the onion and garlic for about 2 minutes. 12. Add the eggplant flesh, tomato, salt, and black pepper and sauté for about 2 minutes. 13. Stir in the cheese, bell pepper, tomato paste, and cilantro and cook for about 1 minute. 14. Remove the pan of the veggie mixture from heat. 15. When the cooking time is completed, open the oven door and arrange the cooked eggplants onto a plate. 16. Stuff each eggplant with the veggie mixture. 17. Close each with its cut part. 18. Again, arrange the eggplants shells into the greased air fry basket on Level 3. 19. Press "Power" button of Ninja Foodi XL Pro Air Oven and select "Air Fry" function. 20. Press TEMP/SHADE +/- buttons to set the temperature at 320°F/160°C. 21. Now press TIME/SLICES +/- buttons to set the cooking time to 8 minutes. 22. Press "Start/Stop" button to start. 23. When cooking time is completed, open the oven door and transfer the eggplants onto serving plates. 24. Serve hot.

Serving Suggestions: Serve with the topping feta cheese.
Variation Tip: Clean the eggplant by running under cold running water.
Nutritional Information per Serving: Calories: 131 | Fat: 2g | Sat Fat: 0.3g | Carbohydrates: 27.8g | Fiber: 5.3g | Sugar: 4.3g | Protein: 5.1g

Vegan Cakes

Prep Time: 15 minutes | Cook Time: 15 minutes | Serves:8

Ingredients:

4 potatoes, diced and boiled
1 bunch green onions
1 lime, zest, and juice
1½ inch knob of fresh ginger
1 tablespoon tamari
4 tablespoons red curry paste
4 sheets nori
1 (398 grams) can heart of palm, drained
¾ cup canned artichoke hearts, drained
Black pepper, to taste
Salt, to taste

Preparation:

1. Add potatoes, green onions, lime zest, juice, and the rest of the ingredients to a food processor. 2. Press the pulse button and blend until smooth. 3. Make 8 small patties out of this mixture. 4. Place the patties in the air fry basket. 5. Transfer the basket to the 3rd rack position of Ninja Foodi XL Pro Air Oven and close the door. 6. Select the "Air Fry" Mode using FUNCTION +/- buttons and select Rack Level 3. 7. Set its cooking time to 15 minutes and temperature to 400°F/200°C, then press "START/STOP" to initiate cooking. 8. Serve warm.

Serving Suggestion: Serve the vegan cakes with roasted asparagus.
Variation Tip: Add boiled quinoa to the cake mixture.
Nutritional Information Per Serving: Calories 324 | Fat 5g | Sodium 432mg | Carbs 13.1g | Fiber 0.3g | Sugar 1g | Protein 5.7g

Caramelized Baby Carrots

Prep Time: 10 minutes | Cook Time: 15 minutes | Serves: 4

Ingredients:

½ cup butter, melted
½ cup brown sugar
1 pound bag baby carrots

Preparation:

1. In a bowl, mix the butter, brown sugar and carrots together. 2. Press "Power" button of Ninja Foodi XL Pro Air Oven and select "Air Fry" function. 3. Press TEMP/SHADE +/- buttons to set the temperature at 400°F/200°C. 4. Now press TIME/SLICES +/- buttons to set the cooking time to 15 minutes. 5. Press "START/STOP" button to start. 6. When the unit beeps to show that it is preheated, open the lid. 7. Arrange the carrots in a greased air fry basket and insert in the oven. 8. When cooking time is completed, open the lid and serve warm.

Serving Suggestions: Serve with favorite greens.
Variation Tip: Make sure to pat dry the carrots before cooking.
Nutritional Information per Serving: Calories: 312 | Fat: 23.2g | Sat Fat: 14.5g | Carbohydrates: 27.1g | Fiber: 3.3g | Sugar: 23g | Protein: 1g

Blue Cheese Soufflés

Prep Time: 15 minutes | Cook Time: 17 minutes | Serves: 4

Ingredients:

- 2 ounces unsalted butter
- 1-ounce breadcrumbs
- 1-ounce plain flour
- Pinch English mustard powder
- Pinch cayenne pepper
- 10 ounces semi-skimmed milk
- 3 ounces blue murder cheese
- 1 fresh thyme sprig, chopped
- 4 medium eggs, separated

Preparation:

1. Grease four ramekins with butter and sprinkle with breadcrumbs. 2. Melt butter in a suitable saucepan, stir in flour, cayenne, and mustard powder. 3. Then mix well and cook for 1 minute, then slowly pour in the milk. 4. Mix well until smooth, then boil its sauce. Cook for 2 minutes. 5. Stir in cheese, and mix well until melted. 6. Add black pepper, salt, and egg yolks. 7. Beat egg whites in a bowl with a mixer until they make stiff peaks. 8. Add egg whites to the cheese sauce, then mix well. 9. Divide the mixture into the ramekins and transfer to Ninja Foodi XL Pro Air Oven, then close its door. 10. Select the "Air Fry" Mode using FUNCTION +/- buttons and select Rack Level 2. 11. Set its cooking time to 14 minutes and temperature to 350°F/175°C, then press "START/STOP" to initiate cooking. 12. Serve warm.

Serving Suggestion: Serve the soufflé with sautéed asparagus and toasted bread slices.
Variation Tip: Add crumbled bacon to the soufflé.
Nutritional Information Per Serving: Calories 236 | Fat 10g | Sodium 249mg | Carbs 8g | Fiber 2g | Sugar 3g | Protein 4g

Wine Braised Mushrooms

Prep Time: 10 minutes | Cook Time: 32 minutes | Serves: 6

Ingredients:

- 1 tablespoon butter
- 2 teaspoons Herbs de Provence
- ½ teaspoon garlic powder
- 2 pounds fresh mushrooms, quartered
- 2 tablespoons white wine

Preparation:

1. In a frying pan, mix together the butter, Herbs de Provence, and garlic powder over medium-low heat and stir fry for about 2 minutes. 2. Stir in the mushrooms and remove from the heat. 3. Transfer the mushroom mixture into a baking pan. 4. Press "Power" button of Ninja Foodi XL Pro Air Oven and select "Air Fry" function. 5. Press TEMP/SHADE +/- buttons to set the temperature at 320°F/160°C. 6. Now press TIME/SLICES +/- buttons to set the cooking time to 30 minutes. 7. Press "START/STOP" button to start. 8. When the unit beeps to show that it is preheated, open the lid. 9. Arrange the pan over the wire rack and insert in the oven. 10. After 25 minutes of cooking, stir the wine into mushroom mixture. 11. When cooking time is completed, open the lid and serve hot.

Serving Suggestions: Serve with a garnishing of fresh herbs.
Variation Tip: White wine can be replaced with broth.
Nutritional Information per Serving: Calories: 54 | Fat: 2.4g | Sat Fat: 1.2g | Carbohydrates: 5.3g | Fiber: 1.5g | Sugar: 2.7g | Protein: 4.8g

Fajitas

Prep Time: 15 minutes | Cook Time: 15 minutes | Serves: 4

Ingredients:

- 3 bell peppers, sliced
- 1 large yellow onion, sliced
- 1 (15-ounce) can pinto beans, drained, rinsed
- 1 tablespoon olive oil
- ¼ teaspoon paprika
- ¼ teaspoon garlic powder
- ¼ teaspoon cumin
- ¼ teaspoon salt
- ¼ cup cheddar cheese, shredded
- Tortillas for serving

Preparation:

1. Spread the pinto beans in the Ninja Sheet pan, lined with parchment paper. 2. Top the beans with bell peppers, yellow onion, olive oil, paprika, garlic powder, cumin, salt, and cheese. 3. Transfer the pan to the 2nd rack position of Ninja Foodi XL Pro Air Oven and close the door. 4. Select the "Bake" Mode using FUNCTION +/- buttons and select Rack Level 2. 5. Set its cooking time to 15 minutes and temperature to 350°F/175°C, then press "START/STOP" to initiate cooking. 6. Serve in tortillas.

Serving Suggestion: Serve the fajitas in warmed tortillas, avocado slices, tomato sauce or guacamole.
Variation Tip: Add crushed tortillas on top before baking.
Nutritional Information Per Serving: Calories 391 | Fat 2.2g | Sodium 276mg | Carbs 7.7g | Fiber 0.9g | Sugar 1.4g | Protein 8.8g

Tofu with Broccoli

Prep Time: 15 minutes | Cook Time: 15 minutes | Serves: 3

Ingredients:

- 8 ounces firm tofu, completely drained, pressed, and cubed
- 1 head broccoli, cut into florets
- 1 tablespoon butter, melted
- 1 teaspoon ground turmeric
- ¼ teaspoon paprika
- Salt and ground black pepper, as required

Preparation:

1. In a bowl, mix all ingredients together. 2. Place the tofu mixture in the greased cooking pan. 3. Press "Power" button of Ninja Foodi XL Pro Air Oven and select "Air Fry" function. 4. Press TEMP/SHADE +/- buttons to set the temperature at 390°F/200°C. 5. Now press TIME/SLICES +/- buttons to set the cooking time to 15 minutes. 6. Press "START/STOP" button to start. 7. When the unit beeps to show that it is preheated, open the lid. 8. Insert the baking pan in oven. 9. Toss the tofu mixture once halfway through. 10. When cooking time is completed, open the lid and serve hot.

Serving Suggestions: Serve with cooked pasta.
Variation Tip: Add some seasoning as you like.
Nutritional Information per Serving: Calories: 119 | Fat: 7.4g | Sat Fat: 3.1g | Carbohydrates: 7.5g | Fiber: 3.1g | Sugar: 1.9g | Protein: 8.7g

Quinoa Burgers

Prep Time: 10 minutes | Cook Time: 10 minutes | Serves: 4

Ingredients:

- ½ cup cooked and cooled quinoa
- 1 cup rolled oats
- 2 eggs, lightly beaten
- ¼ cup white onion, minced
- ¼ cup feta cheese, crumbled
- Salt and ground black pepper, as required
- Olive oil cooking spray

Preparation:

1. In a large bowl, add all ingredients and mix until well combined. 2. Make 4 equal-sized patties from the mixture. 3. Lightly spray the patties with cooking spray. 4. Press "Power" button of Ninja Foodi XL Pro Air Oven and select "Air Fry" function. 5. Press TEMP/SHADE +/- buttons to set the temperature at 400°F/200°C. 6. Now press TIME/SLICES +/- buttons to set the cooking time to 10 minutes. 7. Press "Start/Stop" button to start. 8. When the unit beeps to show that it is preheated, open the oven door. 9. Arrange the patties into the greased air fry basket on Level 3. 10. Flip the patties once halfway through. 11. When cooking time is completed, open the oven door and transfer the patties onto a platter. 12. Serve warm.

Serving Suggestions: Serve with green sauce.
Variation Tip: For crispy texture, refrigerate the patties for at least 15 minutes before cooking.
Nutritional Information per Serving: Calories: 215 | Fat: 6.6g | Sat Fat: 2.5g | Carbohydrates: 28.7g | Fiber: 3.7g | Sugar: 1.1g | Protein: 9.9g

Broccoli with Cauliflower

Prep Time: 15 minutes | Cook Time: 20 minutes | Serves: 4

Ingredients:

- 1½ cups broccoli, cut into 1-inch pieces
- 1½ cups cauliflower, cut into 1-inch pieces
- 1 tablespoon olive oil
- Salt, as required

Preparation:

1. In a bowl, add the vegetables, oil, and salt and toss to coat well. 2. Press "Power" button of Ninja Foodi XL Pro Air Oven and select "Air Fry" function. 3. Press TEMP/SHADE +/- buttons to set the temperature at 375°F/190°C. 4. Now press TIME/SLICES +/- buttons to set the cooking time to 20 minutes. 5. Press "Start/Stop" button to start. 6. When the unit beeps to show that it is preheated, open the oven door. 7. Arrange the veggie mixture into the greased air fry basket and slide the basket on Level 3. 8. When cooking time is completed, open the oven door and serve hot.

Serving Suggestions: Serve with the drizzling of lemon juice.
Variation Tip: You can add spices according to your taste.
Nutritional Information per Serving: Calories: 51 | Fat: 3.7g | Sat Fat: 0.5g | Carbohydrates: 4.3g | Fiber: 1.8g | Sugar: 1.5g | Protein: 1.7g

Veggie Rice

Prep Time: 15 minutes | Cook Time: 18 minutes | Serves: 2

Ingredients:

- 2 cups cooked white rice
- 1 tablespoon vegetable oil
- 2 teaspoons sesame oil, toasted and divided
- 1 tablespoon water
- Salt and ground white pepper, as required
- 1 large egg, lightly beaten
- ½ cup frozen peas, thawed
- ½ cup frozen carrots, thawed
- 1 teaspoon soy sauce
- 1 teaspoon Sriracha sauce
- ½ teaspoon sesame seeds, toasted

Preparation:

1. In a large bowl, add the rice, vegetable oil, one teaspoon of sesame oil, water, salt, and white pepper and mix well. 2. Transfer rice mixture into a lightly greased baking pan. 3. Press "Power" button of Ninja Foodi XL Pro Air Oven and select "Air Fry" function. 4. Press TEMP/SHADE +/- buttons to set the temperature at 380°F/195°C. 5. Now press TIME/SLICES +/- buttons to set the cooking time to 18 minutes. 6. Press "START/STOP" button to start. 7. When the unit beeps to show that it is preheated, open the lid. 8. Place the pan over the wire rack and insert in the oven. 9. While cooking, stir the mixture once after 12 minutes. 10. After 12 minutes of cooking, place the beaten egg over rice. 11. After 16 minutes of cooking, stir in the peas and carrots into rice mixture. 12. Meanwhile, in a bowl, mix the soy sauce, Sriracha sauce, sesame seeds and the remaining sesame oil together. 13. When cooking time is completed, open the lid and transfer the rice mixture into a serving bowl. 14. Drizzle with the sauce mixture and serve.

Serving Suggestions: Serve with yogurt sauce.
Variation Tip: Thaw the vegetables completely before cooking.
Nutritional Information per Serving: Calories: 443 | Fat: 16.4g | Sat Fat: 3.2g | Carbohydrates: 62.3g | Fiber: 3.6g | Sugar: 3.6g | Protein: 10.1g

Soy Sauce Green Beans

Prep Time: 10 minutes | Cook Time: 10 minutes | Serves: 2

Ingredients:

- 8 ounces fresh green beans, trimmed and cut in half
- 1 tablespoon soy sauce
- 1 teaspoon sesame oil

Preparation:

1. In a bowl, mix the green beans, soy sauce and sesame oil together. 2. Press "Power" button of Ninja Foodi XL Pro Air Oven and select "Air Fry" function. 3. Press TEMP/SHADE +/- buttons to set the temperature at 390°F/200°C. 4. Now press TIME/SLICES +/- buttons to set the cooking time to 10 minutes. 5. Press "START/STOP" button to start. 6. When the unit beeps to show that it is preheated, open the lid. 7. Arrange the green beans in air fry basket and insert in the oven. 8. When cooking time is completed, open the lid and serve hot.

Serving Suggestions: Serve with the garnishing of sesame seeds.
Variation Tip: You can add seasoning of your choice.
Nutritional Information per Serving: Calories: 62 | Fat: 2.6g | Sat Fat: 0.4g | Carbohydrates: 8.8g | Fiber: 4g | Sugar: 1.7g | Protein: 2.6g

Cauliflower in Buffalo Sauce

Prep Time: 10 minutes | Cook Time: 12 minutes | Serves: 4

Ingredients:

- 1 large head cauliflower, cut into bite-size florets
- 1 tablespoon olive oil
- 2 teaspoons garlic powder
- Salt and ground black pepper, as required
- ⅔ cup warm buffalo sauce

Preparation:

1. In a large bowl, add cauliflower florets, olive oil, garlic powder, salt and pepper and toss to coat. 2. Press "Power" button of Ninja Foodi XL Pro Air Oven and select "Air Fry" function. Select 2 LEVEL. 3. Press TEMP/SHADE +/- buttons to set the temperature at 375°F/190°C. 4. Now press TIME/SLICES +/- buttons to set the cooking time to 12 minutes. 5. Press "Start/Stop" button to start. 6. When the unit beeps to show that it is preheated, open the oven door. 7. Arrange the cauliflower florets in the air fry basket on Level 1 and roast tray over wire rack on Level 3. 8. After 7 minutes of cooking, coat the cauliflower florets with buffalo sauce. 9. When cooking time is completed, open the oven door and serve hot.

Serving Suggestions: Serve with the garnishing of scallions.
Variation Tip: Use best quality buffalo sauce.
Nutritional Information per Serving: Calories: 183 | Fat: 17.1g | Sat Fat: 4.3g | Carbohydrates: 5.9g | Fiber: 1.8g | Sugar: 1.0g | Protein: 1.6g

Vinegar Green Beans

Prep Time: 10 minutes | Cook Time: 20 minutes | Serves: 2

Ingredients:

- 1 (10-ounce) bag frozen cut green beans
- ¼ cup nutritional yeast
- 3 tablespoons balsamic vinegar
- Salt and ground black pepper, as required

Preparation:

1. In a bowl, add the green beans, nutritional yeast, vinegar, salt, and black pepper and toss to coat well. 2. Press "Power" button of Ninja Foodi XL Pro Air Oven and select "Air Fry" function. Select 2 LEVEL. 3. Press TEMP/SHADE +/- buttons to set the temperature at 400°F/200°C. 4. Now press TIME/SLICES +/- buttons to set the cooking time to 20 minutes. 5. Press "Start/Stop" button to start. 6. When the unit beeps to show that it is preheated, open the oven door. 7. Separate the green beans into the greased air fry basket on Level 3 and roast tray over wire rack on Level 1. 8. When cooking time is completed, open the oven door and serve hot.

Serving Suggestions: Serve with the garnishing of sesame seeds.
Variation Tip: Balsamic vinegar can be replaced with lemon juice.
Nutritional Information per Serving: Calories: 115 | Fat: 1.3g | Sat Fat: 0.2g | Carbohydrates: 18.5g | Fiber: 9.3g | Sugar: 1.8g | Protein: 11.3g

Herbed Bell Peppers

Prep Time: 10 minutes | Cook Time: 8 minutes | Serves: 4

Ingredients:

- 1½ pounds mixed bell peppers, seeded and sliced
- 1 small onion, sliced
- ½ teaspoon dried thyme, crushed
- ½ teaspoon dried savory, crushed
- Salt and ground black pepper, as required
- 2 tablespoon butter, melted

Preparation:

1. In a bowl, add the bell peppers, onion, herbs, salt and black pepper and toss to coat well. 2. Press "Power" button of Ninja Foodi XL Pro Air Oven and select "Air Fry" function. 3. Press TEMP/SHADE +/- buttons to set the temperature at 360°F/180°C. 4. Now press TIME/SLICES +/- buttons to set the cooking time to 8 minutes. 5. Press "Start/Stop" button to start. 6. When the unit beeps to show that it is preheated, open the oven door. 7. Arrange the bell peppers into the air fry basket on Level 3. 8. When cooking time is completed, open the oven door and transfer the bell peppers into a bowl. 9. Drizzle with butter and serve immediately.

Serving Suggestions: Serve with boiled rice.
Variation Tip: Feel free to use herbs of your choice.
Nutritional Information per Serving: Calories: 73 | Fat: 5.9g | Sat Fat: 3.7g | Carbohydrates: 5.2g | Fiber: 1.1g | Sugar: 3g | Protein: 0.7g

Sweet Potato Casserole

Prep Time: 15 minutes | Cook Time: 35 minutes | Serves: 6

Ingredients:

- 3 cups sweet potatoes, mashed and cooled
- 1½ cups brown sugar, packed
- 2 large eggs, beaten
- 1 teaspoon vanilla extract
- ½ cup milk
- ¾ cup butter, melted
- ⅓ cup flour
- 4 ounces pecans, chopped

Preparation:

1. Mix the sweet potato mash with vanilla extract, milk, eggs, 1 cup of brown sugar, and ½ cup of melted butter in a large bowl. 2. Spread this sweet potato mixture in a casserole dish. 3. Now whisk remaining sugar and butter with flour in a separate bowl. 4. Fold in pecan, then top the sweet potatoes mixed with this pecan mixture. 5. Transfer the dish to the 2nd rack position of Ninja Foodi XL Pro Air Oven and close the door. 6. Select the "Bake" Mode using FUNCTION +/- buttons and select Rack Level 2. 7. Set its cooking time to 35 minutes and temperature to 350°F/175°C, then press "START/STOP" to initiate cooking. 8. Slice and serve!

Serving Suggestion: Serve the sweet potato casserole with roasted pecans.
Variation Tip: Add breadcrumbs on top before baking for a crispy texture.
Nutritional Information Per Serving: Calories 353 | Fat 3g | Sodium 510mg | Carbs 32g | Fiber 3g | Sugar 4g | Protein 4g

Roasted Vegetables

Prep Time: 15 minutes | Cook Time: 15 minutes | Serves: 6

Ingredients:

- 2 medium bell peppers cored, chopped
- 2 medium carrots, peeled and sliced
- 1 small zucchini, ends trimmed, sliced
- 1 medium broccoli, florets
- ½ red onion, peeled and diced
- 2 tablespoons olive oil
- 1½ teaspoons Italian seasoning
- 2 garlic cloves, minced
- Salt and freshly ground black pepper
- 1 cup grape tomatoes
- 1 tablespoon fresh lemon juice

Preparation:

1. Toss all the veggies with olive oil, Italian seasoning, salt, black pepper, and garlic in a large salad bowl. 2. Spread this broccoli-zucchini mixture in the sheet pan. 3. Transfer the pan to the 2nd rack position of Ninja Foodi XL Pro Air Oven and close the door. 4. Select the "Bake" Mode using FUNCTION +/- buttons and select Rack Level 2. 5. Set its cooking time to 15 minutes and temperature to 400°F/200°C, then press "START/STOP" to initiate cooking. 6. Serve warm with lemon juice on top. 7. Enjoy.

Serving Suggestion: Serve the roasted vegetables with guacamole on the side.
Variation Tip: Add olives or sliced mushrooms to the vegetable mixture.
Nutritional Information Per Serving: Calories 346 | Fat 15g | Sodium 220mg | Carbs 4.3g | Fiber 2.4g | Sugar 1.2g | Protein 12.4g

Parmesan Broccoli

Prep Time: 10 minutes | Cook Time: 15 minutes | Serves: 8

Ingredients:

- 2 pounds broccoli, cut into 1-inch florets
- 2 tablespoons butter
- Salt and ground black pepper, as required
- ¼ cup Parmesan cheese, grated

Preparation:

1. In a pan of boiling water, add the broccoli and cook for about 3-4 minutes. 2. Drain the broccoli well. 3. In a bowl, place the broccoli, cauliflower, oil, salt, and black pepper and toss to coat well. 4. Press "Power" button of Ninja Foodi XL Pro Air Oven and select "Air Fry" function. 5. Press TEMP/SHADE +/- buttons to set the temperature at 400°F/200°C. 6. Now press TIME/SLICES +/- buttons to set the cooking time to 15 minutes. 7. Press "START/STOP" button to start. 8. When the unit beeps to show that it is preheated, open the lid. 9. Arrange the broccoli mixture in air fry basket and insert in the oven. 10. Toss the broccoli mixture once halfway through. 11. When cooking time is completed, open the lid and transfer the veggie mixture into a large bowl. 12. Immediately stir in the cheese and serve immediately.

Serving Suggestions: Serve with a drizzling of lemon juice.
Variation Tip: Choose broccoli heads with tight, green florets and firm stalks.
Nutritional Information per Serving: Calories: 73 | Fat: 3.9g | Sat Fat: 2.1g | Carbohydrates: 7.5g | Fiber: 3g | Sugar: 1.9g | Protein: 4.2g

Broccoli Casserole

Prep Time: 15 minutes | Cook Time: 45 minutes | Serves: 6

Ingredients:

- 1 cup mayonnaise
- 10 ½ ounces cream of celery soup
- 2 large eggs, beaten
- 20 ounces chopped broccoli
- 2 tablespoons onion, minced
- 1 cup Cheddar cheese, grated
- 1 tablespoon Worcestershire sauce
- 1 teaspoon seasoned salt
- Black pepper, to taste
- 2 tablespoons butter

Preparation:

1. Whisk mayonnaise with eggs, condensed soup in a large bowl. 2. Stir in salt, black pepper, Worcestershire sauce, and cheddar cheese. 3. Spread broccoli and onion in a greased casserole dish. 4. Top the veggies with the mayonnaise mixture. 5. Transfer this broccoli casserole to Ninja Foodi XL Pro Air Oven and Close its lid. 6. Select the "Bake" Mode using FUNCTION +/- buttons and select Rack Level 2. 7. Set its cooking time to 45 minutes and temperature to 350°F/175°C, then press "START/STOP" to initiate cooking. 8. Slice and serve warm.

Serving Suggestion: Serve the broccoli casserole with spaghetti or any other pasta.
Variation Tip: Top the casserole with a pepperoni slice before cooking.
Nutritional Information Per Serving: Calories 341 | Fat 24g | Sodium 547mg | Carbs 26.4g | Fiber 1.2g | Sugar 1g | Protein 10.3g

Vegetable Casserole

Prep Time: 15 minutes | Cook Time: 42 minutes | Serves: 6

Ingredients:

- 2 cups peas
- 8 ounces mushrooms, sliced
- 4 tablespoons all-purpose flour
- 1½ cups celery, sliced
- 1½ cups carrots, sliced
- ½ teaspoon mustard powder
- 2 cups of milk
- Salt and black pepper, to taste
- 7 tablespoons butter
- 1 cup breadcrumbs
- ½ cup Parmesan cheese, grated

Preparation:

1. Grease and rub a casserole dish with butter and keep it aside. 2. Add carrots, onion, and celery to a saucepan, then fill it with water. 3. Cover this pot and cook for 10 minutes, then stir in peas. 4. Cook for 4 minutes, then strain the vegetables. 5. Now melt 1 tablespoon of butter in the same saucepan and toss in mushrooms to sauté. 6. Once the mushrooms are soft, transfer them to the vegetables. 7. Prepare its sauce by melting 4 tablespoons of butter in a suitable saucepan. 8. Stir in mustard and flour, then stir cook for 2 minutes. 9. Gradually pour in the milk and stir cook until thickened, then add salt and black pepper. 10. Add vegetables and mushrooms to the flour milk mixture and mix well. 11. Spread this vegetable blend in the casserole dish evenly. 12. Toss the breadcrumbs with the remaining butter and spread it on top of vegetables. 13. Top this casserole dish with cheese. 14. Transfer the dish to the 2nd rack position of Ninja Foodi XL Pro Air Oven and close the door. 15. Select the "Air Fry" Mode using FUNCTION +/- buttons and select Rack Level 2. 16. Set its cooking time to 25 minutes and temperature to 350°F/175°C, then press "START/STOP" to initiate cooking. 17. Serve warm.

Serving Suggestion: Serve the vegetable casserole with a tortilla.
Variation Tip: Add broccoli florets to the mixture and then cook.
Nutritional Information Per Serving: Calories 338 | Fat 24g | Sodium 620mg | Carbs 18.3g | Fiber 2.4g | Sugar 1.2g | Protein 5.4g

Brussels Sprouts Gratin

Prep Time: 15 minutes | Cook Time: 35 minutes | Serves: 6

Ingredients:

- 1 pound Brussels sprouts
- 1 garlic clove, cut in half
- 3 tablespoons butter, divided
- 2 tablespoons shallots, minced
- 2 tablespoons all-purpose flour
- Kosher salt, to taste
- Freshly ground black pepper
- 1 dash ground nutmeg
- 1 cup milk
- ½ cup fontina cheese, shredded
- 1 strip of bacon, cooked and crumbled
- ½ cup fine bread crumbs

Preparation:

1. Trim the Brussels sprouts and remove their outer leaves. 2. Slice the sprouts into quarters, then rinse them under cold water. 3. Grease a gratin dish with cooking spray and rub it with garlic halves. 4. Boil salted water in a suitable pan, then add Brussels sprouts. 5. Cook the sprouts for 3 minutes, then immediately drain. 6. Place a suitable saucepan over medium-low heat and melt 2 tablespoons of butter in it. 7. Toss in shallots and sauté until soft, then stir in flour, nutmeg, ½ teaspoon of salt, and black pepper. 8. Stir cook for 2 minutes, then gradually add milk and a half and half cream. 9. Mix well and add bacon along with shredded cheese. 10. Fold in Brussels sprouts and transfer this mixture to the casserole dish. 11. Toss breadcrumbs with 1 tablespoon of butter and spread over the casserole. 12. Transfer the gratin to the 2nd rack position of Ninja Foodi XL Pro Air Oven and close the door. 13. Select the "Bake" Mode using FUNCTION +/- buttons and select Rack Level 2. 14. Set its cooking time to 25 minutes and temperature to 350°F/175°C, then press "START/STOP" to initiate cooking. 15. Enjoy!

Serving Suggestion: Serve the gratin with mashed potatoes.
Variation Tip: Add crushed crackers on top for a crunchy taste.
Nutritional Information Per Serving: Calories 378 | Fat 3.8g | Sodium 620mg | Carbs 33.3g | Fiber 2.4g | Sugar 1.2g | Protein 14g

Cheesy Kale

Prep Time: 10 minutes | Cook Time: 15 minutes | Serves: 3

Ingredients:

- 1 pound fresh kale, tough ribs removed and chopped
- 3 tablespoons olive oil
- Salt and ground black pepper, as required
- 1 cup goat cheese, crumbled
- 1 teaspoon fresh lemon juice

Preparation:

1. In a bowl, add the kale, oil, salt and black pepper and mix well. 2. Press "Power" button of Ninja Foodi XL Pro Air Oven and select "Air Fry" function. 3. Press TEMP/SHADE +/- buttons to set the temperature at 340°F/170°C. 4. Now press TIME/SLICES +/- buttons to set the cooking time to 15 minutes. 5. Press "START/STOP" button to start. 6. When the unit beeps to show that it is preheated, open the lid and grease the air fry basket. 7. Arrange the kale into air fry basket and insert in the oven. 8. When cooking time is completed, open the lid and immediately transfer the kale mixture into a bowl. 9. Stir in the cheese and lemon juice and serve hot.

Serving Suggestions: Serve with a garnishing of lemon zest.
Variation Tip: Goat cheese can be replaced with feta.
Nutritional Information per Serving: Calories: 327 | Fat: 24.7g | Sat Fat: 9.5g | Carbohydrates: 17.9g | Fiber: 2.3g | Sugar: 2g | Protein: 11.6g

Cheesy Green Bean Casserole

Prep Time: 15 minutes | Cook Time: 35 minutes | Serves: 6

Ingredients:

- 4 cups green beans, cooked and chopped
- 3 tablespoons butter
- 8 ounces mushrooms, sliced
- ¼ cup onion, chopped
- 2 tablespoons flour
- 1 teaspoon salt
- ¼ teaspoon ground black pepper
- 1½ cups milk
- 2 cups cheddar cheese, shredded
- 2 tablespoons sour cream
- 1 cup soft breadcrumbs
- 2 tablespoons butter, melted
- ¼ cup Parmesan cheese, grated
- 1 cup French fried onions

Preparation:

1. Add butter to a suitable saucepan and melt it over medium-low heat. 2. Toss in onion and mushrooms, then sauté until soft. 3. Stir in flour, salt, and black pepper. Mix well, then slowly pour in the milk. 4. Stir in sour cream, green beans, and cheddar cheese, then cook until it thickens. 5. Transfer this green bean mixture to a casserole dish and spread it evenly. 6. Toss breadcrumbs with fried onion and butter. 7. Top the casserole with this bread crumbs mixture. 8. Transfer the dish to the 2nd rack position of Ninja Foodi XL Pro Air Oven and close the door. 9. Select the "Bake" Mode using FUNCTION +/- buttons and select Rack Level 2. 10. Set its cooking time to 25 minutes and temperature to 350°F/175°C, then press "START/STOP" to initiate cooking. 11. Serve and enjoy!

Serving Suggestion: Serve the casserole with mashed cauliflower.
Variation Tip: Add crispy dried onion for better taste.
Nutritional Information Per Serving: Calories 304 | Fat 31g | Sodium 834mg | Carbs 21.4g | Fiber 0.2g | Sugar 0.3g | Protein 4.6g

Beans & Veggie Burgers

Prep Time: 15 minutes | Cook Time: 22 minutes | Serves: 4

Ingredients:

- 1 cup cooked black beans
- 2 cups boiled potatoes, peeled and mashed
- 1 cup fresh spinach, chopped
- 1 cup fresh mushrooms, chopped
- 2 teaspoons Chile lime seasoning
- Olive oil cooking spray

Preparation:

1. In a large bowl, add the beans, potatoes, spinach, mushrooms, and seasoning and with your hands, mix until well combined. 2. Make 4 equal-sized patties from the mixture. 3. Spray the patties with cooking spray evenly. 4. Press "Power" button of Ninja Foodi XL Pro Air Oven and select "Air Fry" function. 5. Press TEMP/SHADE +/- buttons to set the temperature at 370°F/185°C. 6. Now press TIME/SLICES +/- buttons to set the cooking time to 22 minutes. 7. Press "START/STOP" button to start. 8. When the unit beeps to show that it is preheated, open the lid. 9. Arrange the patties in the greased air fry basket and insert in the oven. 10. Flip the patties once after 12 minutes. 11. When cooking time is completed, open the lid and transfer the patties onto a serving platter. 12. Serve warm.

Serving Suggestions: Serve with avocado and tomato salad.
Variation Tip: Feel free to add seasoning of your choice.
Nutritional Information per Serving: Calories: 113 | Fat: 0.4g | Sat Fat: 0g | Carbohydrates:23.1g | Fiber: 6.2g | Sugar: 1.7g | Protein: 6g

Tofu in Sweet & Sour Sauce

Prep Time: 20 minutes | Cook Time: 20 minutes | Serves: 4

Ingredients:

For Tofu:
- 1 (14-ounce) block firm tofu, pressed and cubed
- ½ cup arrowroot flour

For Sauce:
- 4 tablespoons low-sodium soy sauce
- 1½ tablespoons rice vinegar
- 1½ tablespoons chili sauce
- 1 tablespoon agave nectar
- ½ teaspoon sesame oil
- 2 large garlic cloves, minced
- 1 teaspoon fresh ginger, peeled and grated
- 2 scallions (green part), chopped

Preparation:

1. In a bowl, mix the tofu, arrowroot flour, and sesame oil together. 2. Press "Power" button of Ninja Foodi XL Pro Air Oven and select "Air Fry" function. 3. Press TEMP/SHADE +/- buttons to set the temperature at 360°F/180°C. 4. Now press TIME/SLICES +/- buttons to set the cooking time to 20 minutes. 5. Press "START/STOP" button to start. 6. When the unit beeps to show that it is preheated, open the lid. 7. Arrange the tofu cubes in greased air fry basket and insert in the oven. 8. Flip the tofu cubes once halfway through. 9. Meanwhile, for the sauce: in a bowl, add all the ingredients except scallions and beat until well combined. 10. When cooking time is completed, open the lid and remove the tofu. 11. Transfer the tofu into a skillet with sauce over medium heat and cook for about 3 minutes, stirring occasionally. 12. Garnish with scallions and serve hot.

Serving Suggestions: Serve with plain boiled rice.
Variation Tip: Add pineapple for a savory choice.
Nutritional Information per Serving: Calories: 115 | Fat: 4.8g | Sat Fat: 1g | Carbohydrates: 10.2g | Fiber: 1.7g | Sugar: 5.6g | Protein: 0.1g

Spicy Potato

Prep Time: 15 minutes | Cook Time: 25 minutes | Serves: 4

Ingredients:

- 2 cups water
- 6 russet potatoes, peeled and cubed
- ½ tablespoon extra-virgin olive oil
- ½ of onion, chopped
- 1 tablespoon fresh rosemary, chopped
- 1 garlic clove, minced
- 1 jalapeño pepper, chopped
- ½ teaspoon garam masala powder
- ¼ teaspoon ground cumin
- ¼ teaspoon red chili powder
- Salt and ground black pepper, as required

Preparation:

1. In a large bowl, add the water and potatoes and set aside for about 30 minutes. 2. Drain well and pat dry with the paper towels. 3. In a bowl, add the potatoes and oil and toss to coat well. 4. Press "Power" button of Ninja Foodi XL Pro Air Oven and select "Air Fry" function. 5. Now press TIME/SLICES +/- buttons to set the cooking time to 5 minutes. 6. Press TEMP/SHADE +/- buttons to set the temperature at 330°F/165°C. 7. Press "START/STOP" button to start. 8. When the unit beeps to show that it is preheated, open the lid. 9. Arrange the potato cubes in air fry basket and insert in the oven. 10. Remove from oven and transfer the potatoes into a bowl. 11. Add the remaining ingredients and toss to coat well. 12. Press "Power" button of Ninja Foodi XL Pro Air Oven and select "Air Fry" function. 13. Press TEMP/SHADE +/- buttons to set the temperature at 390°F/200°C. 14. Now press TIME/SLICES +/- buttons to set the cooking time to 20 minutes. 15. Press "START/STOP" button to start. 16. When the unit beeps to show that it is preheated, open the lid. 17. Arrange the potato mixture in air fry basket and insert in the oven. 18. When cooking time is completed, open the lid and serve hot.

Serving Suggestions: Serve with plain bread.
Variation Tip: Adjust the ratio of spices.
Nutritional Information per Serving: Calories: 274 | Fat: 2.3g | Sat Fat: 0.4g | Carbohydrates: 52.6g | Fiber: 8.5g | Sugar: 4.4g | Protein: 5.7g

Veggies Stuffed Bell Peppers

Prep Time: 20 minutes | Cook Time: 25 minutes | Serves: 6

Ingredients:

- 6 large bell peppers
- 1 bread roll, finely chopped
- 1 carrot, peeled and finely chopped
- 1 onion, finely chopped
- 1 potato, peeled and finely chopped
- ½ cup fresh peas, shelled
- 2 garlic cloves, minced
- 2 teaspoons fresh parsley, chopped
- Salt and ground black pepper, as required
- ⅓ cup cheddar cheese, grated

Preparation:

1. Remove the tops of each bell pepper and discard the seeds. 2. Chop the bell pepper tops finely. 3. In a bowl, place bell pepper tops, bread loaf, vegetables, garlic, parsley, salt and black pepper and mix well. 4. Stuff each bell pepper with the vegetable mixture. 5. Press "Power" button of Ninja Foodi XL Pro Air Oven and select "Air Fry" function. Select 2 LEVEL. 6. Press TEMP/SHADE +/- buttons to set the temperature at 330°F/165°C. 7. Now press TIME/SLICES +/- buttons to set the cooking time to 25 minutes. 8. Press "Start/Stop" button to start. 9. When the unit beeps to show that it is preheated, open the oven door. 10. Separate the bell peppers into the greased air fry basket on Level 3 and sheet pan over wire rack on Level 1. 11. After 20 minutes, sprinkle each bell pepper with cheddar cheese. 12. When cooking time is completed, open the oven door and transfer the bell peppers onto serving plates. 13. Serve hot.

Serving Suggestions: Serve with fresh salad.
Variation Tip: For best result, remove the seeds from bell peppers completely.
Nutritional Information per Serving: Calories: 123 | Fat: 2.7g | Sat Fat: 1.2g | Carbohydrates: 21.7g | Fiber: 3.7g | Sugar: 8g | Protein: 4.8g

Pita Bread Pizza

Prep Time: 10 minutes | Cook Time: 5 minutes | Serves: 1

Ingredients:

- 2 tablespoons marinara sauce
- 1 whole-wheat pita bread
- ½ cup fresh baby spinach leaves
- ½ of small plum tomato, cut into 4 slices
- ½ of garlic clove, sliced thinly
- ½ ounce part-skim mozzarella cheese, shredded
- ½ tablespoon Parmigiano-Reggiano cheese, shredded

Preparation:

1. Arrange the pita bread onto a plate. 2. Spread marinara sauce over 1 side of each pita bread evenly. 3. Top with the spinach leaves, followed by tomato slices, garlic and cheeses. 4. Press "Power" button of Ninja Foodi XL Pro Air Oven and select "Air Fry" function. 5. Press TEMP/SHADE +/- buttons to set the temperature at 350°F/175°C. 6. Now press TIME/SLICES +/- buttons to set the cooking time to 5 minutes. 7. Press "Start/Stop" button to start. 8. When the unit beeps to show that it is preheated, open the oven door. 9. Arrange the pita bread into the greased air fry basket on Level 3. 10. When cooking time is completed, open the oven door and transfer the pizza onto a serving plate. 11. Set aside to cool slightly. 12. Serve warm.

Serving Suggestions: Serve alongside the greens.
Variation Tip: You can replace pizza sauce with marinara sauce.
Nutritional Information per Serving: Calories: 266 | Fat: 6.2g | Sat Fat: 2.6g | Carbohydrates: 43.1g | Fiber: 6.5g | Sugar: 4.6g | Protein: 13g

Baked Potato

Prep Time: 5 minutes | Cook Time: 45 minutes | Serves: 4

Ingredients:

- 4 russet potatoes
- 1½ tablespoons olive oil
- 1½ tablespoons sea salt

Preparation:

1. Poke each potato, massage it all over with olive oil and sea salt. 2. Place the potato in the sheet pan. 3. Insert a wire rack on Level 3. Turn on Ninja Foodi XL Pro Air Oven and select "Bake". 4. Select the timer for 40 minutes and the temperature for 350°F/175°C. 5. When the unit beeps to signify it has preheated, open the oven and place the sheet pan onto wire rack. Close the oven and let it cook. 6. Remove the baked potatoes from the Ninja Foodi, split them in half, and top them with chosen toppings!

Serving Suggestions: Top with chopped green onions.
Variation Tip: You can also add cheese on top.
Nutritional Information per Serving: Calories: 213 | Fat: 5g | Sat Fat: 1g | Carbohydrates: 37g | Fiber: 4g | Sugar: 2g | Protein: 5g

Asparagus with Garlic and Parmesan

Prep Time: 5 minutes | Cook Time: 10 minutes | Serves: 4

Ingredients:

- 1 bundle asparagus
- 1 teaspoon olive oil
- ⅛ teaspoon garlic salt
- 1 tablespoon parmesan cheese
- Pepper to taste

Preparation:

1. Clean the asparagus and dry it. To remove the woody stalks, cut 1 inch off the bottom. 2. In a sheet pan, arrange asparagus in a single layer and spray with oil. 3. On top of the asparagus, evenly sprinkle garlic salt. Season with salt and pepper, then sprinkle with Parmesan cheese. 4. Turn on Ninja Foodi XL Pro Air Oven and select "Air Fry". 5. Select the timer for 10 minutes and the temperature for 350°F/175°C. 6. When the unit beeps to signify it has preheated, open the oven and place the sheet pan onto Level 3 in oven. Close the oven and let it cook. 7. Enjoy right away.

Serving Suggestions: Sprinkle more parmesan cheese before serving.
Variation Tip: You can also sprinkle some paprika.
Nutritional Information per Serving: Calories: 18 | Fat: 2g | Sat Fat: 1g | Carbohydrates: 1g | Fiber: 0g | Sugar: 0g | Protein: 1g

Stuffed Zucchini

Prep Time: 20 minutes | Cook Time: 35 minutes | Serves: 4

Ingredients:

- 2 zucchinis, cut in half lengthwise
- ½ teaspoon garlic powder
- Salt, as required
- 1 teaspoon olive oil
- 4 ounces fresh mushrooms, chopped
- 4 ounces carrots, peeled and shredded
- 3 ounces onion, chopped
- 4 ounces goat cheese, crumbled
- 12 fresh basil leaves
- ½ teaspoon onion powder

Preparation:

1. Carefully, scoop the flesh from the middle of each zucchini half. 2. Season each zucchini half with a little garlic powder and salt. 3. Arrange the zucchini halves into the greased baking pan. 4. Place the oat mixture over salmon fillets and gently, press down. 5. Press "Power" button of Ninja Foodi XL Pro Air Oven and select the "Bake" function. 6. Now press TIME/SLICES +/- buttons to set the cooking time to 20 minutes. 7. Press TEMP/SHADE +/- buttons to set the temperature at 450°F/230°C. 8. Press "START/STOP" button to start. 9. When the unit beeps to show that it is preheated, open the lid. 10. Insert the baking pan in oven. 11. Meanwhile, in a skillet, heat the oil over medium heat and cook the mushrooms, carrots, onions, onion powder and salt and cook for about 5-6 minutes. 12. Remove from the heat and set aside. 13. Remove the baking pan from oven and set aside. 14. Stuff each zucchini half with veggie mixture and top with basil leaves, followed by the cheese. 15. Press "Power" button of Ninja Foodi XL Pro Air Oven and select the "Bake" function. 16. Press TEMP/SHADE +/- buttons to set the temperature at 450°F/230°C. 17. Now press TIME/SLICES +/- buttons to set the cooking time to 15 minutes. 18. Press "START/STOP" button to start. 19. When the unit beeps to show that it is preheated, open the lid. 20. Insert the baking pan in oven. 21. When cooking time is completed, open the lid and transfer the zucchini halves onto a platter. 22. Serve warm.

Serving Suggestions: Serve alongside fresh greens.
Variation Tip: Any kind of cheese can be used in this recipe.
Nutritional Information per Serving: Calories: 181 | Fat: 11.6g | Sat Fat: 7.2g | Carbohydrates: 10.1g | Fiber: 2.6g | Sugar: 5.3g | Protein: 11.3g

Broiled Broccoli

Prep Time: 5 minutes | Cook Time: 20 minutes | Serves: 4

Ingredients:

2 heads of broccoli, diced into large chunks
1½ teaspoons olive oil

Salt and pepper, to taste

Preparation:

1. Slice your broccoli into large chunks. Left the stems long to make sure they would not break apart. 2. Sprinkle the broccoli with 1 tablespoon of olive oil in a large mixing bowl and season to taste with salt and pepper. Toss everything together to make sure the broccoli is well-coated. 3. Place the broccoli on the sheet pan in a single layer. 4. Insert a wire rack on Level 3. Turn on Ninja Foodi XL Pro Air Oven and select "Broil". 5. Select the timer for 15 minutes and temperature to LO. 6. When the unit beeps to signify it is preheated, open the oven and place the sheet pan onto wire rack. Close the oven and let it cook. 7. Serve and enjoy.

Serving Suggestions: Top with some garlic sauce.
Variation Tip: You can also serve with steam rice.
Nutritional Information per Serving: Calories: 20 | Fat: 1g | Sat Fat: 0.3g | Carbohydrates: 0g | Fiber: 0g | Sugar: 0g | Protein: 0g

Stuffed Peppers

Prep Time: 15 minutes | Cook Time: 15 minutes | Serves: 6

Ingredients:

6 green bell peppers
1 pound lean ground beef
1 tablespoon olive oil
¼ cup green onion, diced
¼ cup fresh parsley

½ teaspoon ground sage
½ teaspoon garlic salt
1 cup rice, cooked
1 cup marinara sauce to taste
¼ cup mozzarella cheese, shredded

Preparation:

1. Cook the ground beef in a medium sized skillet until it is well done. 2. Return the beef to the pan after draining it. 3. Combine the olive oil, green onion, parsley, sage, and salt in a large mixing bowl and add to the skillet with beef. 4. Add the cooked rice and marinara sauce in the skillet and stir this rice-beef mixture thoroughly. 5. Remove the tops off each pepper and discard the seeds. 6. Scoop the mixture into each pepper and place it in the air fry basket. 7. Turn on Ninja Foodi XL Pro Air Oven and select "Air Fry". 8. Select the timer for 10 minutes and temperature for 355°F/180°C. 9. When the unit beeps to signify it is preheated, open the oven and place the air fry basket into the rail of Level 3. Close the oven and let it cook. 10. Dish out to serve and enjoy.

Serving Suggestions: Top with some fresh parsley.
Variation Tip: You can use any cheese.
Nutritional Information per Serving: Calories: 296 | Fat: 13g | Sat Fat: 4g | Carbohydrates: 19g | Fiber: 2g | Sugar: 6g | Protein: 25g

Green Tomatoes

Prep Time: 15 minutes | Cook Time: 7 minutes | Serves: 4

Ingredients:

3 green tomatoes
½ teaspoon salt
½ cup flour
2 eggs

⅓ cup cornmeal
⅓ cup breadcrumbs
⅛ teaspoon paprika

Preparation:

1. Slice the green tomatoes into ¼-inch slices and generously coat with salt. Allow for at least 5 minutes of resting time. 2. Put the flour in one bowl, the egg (whisked) in the second, and the cornmeal, breadcrumbs, and paprika in the third bowl to make a breading station. 3. Using a paper towel, pat green tomato slices dry. 4. Dip each tomato slice into the flour, then the egg, and finally the cornmeal mixture, making sure the tomato slices are completely covered. 5. Place them in air fry basket in a single layer. 6. Turn on Ninja Foodi XL Pro Air Oven and select "Air Fry". 7. Select the timer for 9 minutes and the temperature for 380°F/195°C. 8. When the unit beeps to signify it is preheated, open the oven and place the air fry basket into rail of Level 3. 9. Cook for 7-9 minutes, flipping and spritzing with oil halfway through.

Serving Suggestions: Sprinkle more parmesan cheese before serving.
Variation Tip: You can also add a pinch of cayenne pepper.
Nutritional Information per Serving: Calories: 186 | Fat: 4g | Sat Fat: 1g | Carbohydrates: 31g | Fiber: 3g | Sugar: 4g | Protein: 8g

Parmesan Carrot

Prep Time: 10 minutes | Cook Time: 20 minutes | Serves: 2

Ingredients:

- 3 carrots
- 1 tablespoon olive oil
- 1 clove garlic, crushed
- 2 tablespoons parmesan cheese, grated
- ¼ teaspoon red pepper, crushed

Preparation:

1. Stir in the crushed garlic with olive oil. 2. Carrots should be washed and dried. Cut the tops in half and remove the tops. Then, to make flat surfaces, cut each half in half. 3. Toss the carrot fries with the garlic and olive oil mixture. 4. Combine the parmesan, red pepper, and black pepper in a mixing bowl. Half of the mixture should be sprinkled over the carrot fries that have been coated. 5. Toss in the remaining parmesan mixture and repeat. 6. Arrange evenly the carrot fries in an air fry basket and on a roast tray. 7. Turn on Ninja Foodi XL Pro Air Oven and select "Air Fry". Select 2 LEVEL. 8. Select the timer for 20 minutes and the temperature for 350°F/175°C. 9. When the unit beeps to signify it is preheated, open the oven and place the air fry basket into the rail of Level 4 and the roast tray on a sheet pan on Level 2. 10. Remove from Ninja Foodi XL Pro Air Oven to serve.

Serving Suggestions: Sprinkle more parmesan cheese before serving.
Variation Tip: You can also add a pinch of cayenne pepper.
Nutritional Information per Serving: Calories: 106 | Fat: 7g | Sat Fat: 1.1g | Carbohydrates: 10g | Fiber: 3g | Sugar: 5g | Protein: 1.2g

Roasted Green Beans

Prep Time: 5 minutes | Cook Time: 15 minutes | Serves: 4

Ingredients:

- 2 tablespoons lard
- 290g whole green beans
- 1 tablespoon minced garlic
- 2 tablespoons pimentos, diced
- Garlic powder, to taste
- Onion powder, to taste
- Salt, to taste

Preparation:

1. In a stovetop pot, melt the lard. 2. Sauté until the green beans are bright green and glossy, then add the additional ingredients. 3. Using parchment paper, line the air fry basket. 4. Arrange the greens in a single layer on the air fry basket. 5. Turn on Ninja Foodi XL Pro Air Oven and select "Air Fry". 6. Select the timer for 15 minutes and the temperature at 390°F/200°C. 7. When the unit beeps to signify it is preheated, open the oven and place the air fry basket into rail of Level 3 in oven. Close the oven and let it cook. 8. Remove from Ninja Foodi XL Pro Air Oven to serve.

Serving Suggestions: Sprinkle some sesame seeds on top.
Variation Tip: You can also add pinch of black pepper.
Nutritional Information per Serving: Calories: 91 | Fat: 7g | Sat Fat: 3g | Carbohydrates: 6g | Fiber: 2g | Sugar: 3g | Protein: 2g

Garlic Parmesan Roasted Potatoes

Prep Time: 10 minutes | Cook Time: 30 minutes | Serves: 6

Ingredients:

- 3 pounds red potatoes, quartered
- 2 tablespoons olive oil
- 5 cloves garlic, minced
- 1 teaspoon dried thyme
- ½ teaspoon dried oregano
- ½ teaspoon dried basil
- ⅓ cup parmesan, freshly grated
- Kosher salt, to taste
- Freshly ground black pepper, to taste
- 2 tablespoons unsalted butter
- 2 tablespoons parsley leaves, chopped

Preparation:

1. Select the AIR ROAST function, 400°F/200°C, for 35 minutes. Allow the oven to preheat. 2. Grease the roast tray and place the potatoes onto it. Then, add the garlic, basil, olive oil, thyme, parmesan, and oregano. Season with salt and pepper and gently toss to combine. 3. When the unit beeps to signify it has preheated, open the oven. Insert the roast tray on sheet pan into rail of Level 3 and cook for about 25 to 35 minutes. 4. When done, stir in the butter and let it melt. You may need to cook in batches.

Serving Suggestion: Garnish with the parsley before serving.
Variation Tip: You can experiment with different types of herbs and cheese.
Nutritional Information Per Serving: Calories: 259 | Fat: 10g | Sodium: 98.9mg | Carbs: 36.5g | Fiber: 4.5g | Sugar: 2.3g | Protein: 6.6g

Broccoli Cheese Casserole

Prep Time: 15 minutes | Cook Time: 30 minutes | Serves: 10

Ingredients:

- 2 bunches broccoli
- ¼ cup water
- 1 large egg, lightly beaten
- 10½ ounces cream of chicken soup
- ½ cup mayonnaise
- ½ cup sour cream
- 8 ounces sharp cheddar cheese, shredded
- ½ small onion, chopped
- 1 teaspoon salt

For the topping:
- 1 cup Ritz crackers, crushed
- 2 tablespoons butter, melted

Preparation:

1. Insert a wire rack on Level 3. Select the BAKE function, 350°F/175°C, for 30 minutes. While the oven is preheating, prepare an air fryer-safe casserole dish with non-stick spray. 2. Wash and dry the broccoli before cutting it into florets. Place the florets into a large microwave-safe bowl with the water. Tightly cover the bowl with plastic wrap and microwave for about 5 minutes, then let it stand for 2 minutes before draining. 3. Take a large bowl, and combine the rest of the ingredients except the butter and crackers. Next, add the broccoli to the bowl and mix to coat. Place the broccoli in the prepared baking dish. 4. When the unit beeps to signify it has preheated, open the oven and insert the oven-safe casserole dish on the wire rack Bake for 20 minutes. 5. Meanwhile, in a small bowl, mix the crackers and butter. Take the casserole out of the oven and sprinkle with the topping. Cook for another 10 minutes.

Serving Suggestion: Sprinkle with some cheese and serve with a green salad.

Variation Tip: You can use cheddar cheese substitutes like Colby cheese or gouda.

Nutritional Information Per Serving: Calories: 287 | Fat: 24g | Sodium: 722mg | Carbs: 11.41g | Fiber: 3.26g | Sugar: 3.26g | Protein: 11g

Creamy Roast Mushrooms

Prep Time: 5 minutes | Cook Time: 20 minutes | Serves: 4

Ingredients:

- 35 ounces button mushrooms
- 2 tablespoons olive oil
- 4 tablespoons creme fraiche
- Salt and pepper, to taste

Preparation:

1. Select the AIR ROAST function, 395°F/200°C, for 20 minutes. While the oven is preheating, prepare the ingredients. 2. Pour the olive oil into the roast tray, then add the mushrooms and toss to combine. 3. Top the mushrooms with the crème fraiche. 4. When the unit beeps to signify it has preheated, open your oven and insert the roast tray on sheet pan on Level 3. Cook for about 20 minutes. 5. Lastly, stir the mushrooms to coat them in the creamy sauce evenly.

Serving Suggestion: Garnish with fresh parsley before serving.

Variation Tip: You can replace creme fraiche with sour cream.

Nutritional Information Per Serving: Calories: 108k | Fat: 10g | Sodium: 20mg | Carbs: 4g | Fiber: 1g | Sugar: 2g | Protein: 3g

Garlic Parmesan Roasted Asparagus

Prep Time: 5 minutes | Cook Time: 8 minutes | Serves: 4

Ingredients:

- ½ pound fresh asparagus
- ½ teaspoon salt
- ½ teaspoon fresh ground black pepper
- 3 cloves garlic, minced
- 2 to 3 tablespoons parmesan cheese, grated
- Olive oil spray

Preparation:

1. Insert a wire rack on Level 3. Select the AIR ROAST function, 425°F/220°C, for 8 minutes. While the oven is preheating, prepare the ingredients. 2. Line an air fryer-appropriate rimmed baking sheet with aluminum foil. Set it aside. 3. Rinse the asparagus and trim off their woody ends. Lay them out on the prepared baking sheet. 4. Lightly coat the asparagus with the olive oil spray. Sprinkle them with the garlic, salt, pepper, and parmesan cheese. Mix well with your hands, and spread them in a single layer again. Give them one more coat of olive oil. 5. When the unit beeps to signify it has preheated, open your oven and insert the baking sheet on wire rack. 6. Cook the asparagus for about 8 minutes.

Serving Suggestion: Sprinkle with salt, pepper, and more cheese before serving.

Variation Tip: Try using vegetable oil instead of olive oil.

Nutritional Information Per Serving: Calories: 24 | Fat: 1g | Sodium: 332mg | Carbs: 3g | Fiber: 1g | Sugar: 1g | Protein: 2g

Air Fryer Sweet and Roasted Carrots

Prep Time: 5 minutes | Cook Time: 20 minutes | Serves: 2

Ingredients:

Cooking spray
1 tablespoon melted butter
1 tablespoon hot honey
1 teaspoon orange zest, grated
½ teaspoon ground cardamom
½ pound baby carrots, sliced
1 tablespoon freshly squeezed orange juice
Pinch of salt
Ground black pepper, to taste

Preparation:

1. Select the AIR FRY function, 400°F/200°C, for 20 minutes. While the oven preheats, grease the air fry basket with cooking spray and prepare the ingredients. 2. Take a mixing bowl and combine the honey, cardamom, orange zest, and butter. Take out 1 tablespoon of the sauce and keep it aside in a separate bowl. 3. Add the sliced carrots to the remaining sauce and toss well to coat. Transfer the carrots to the air fry basket. 4. When the unit beeps to signify it has preheated, open your oven and insert the air fry basket on Level 3. 5. Close the oven and cook the carrots for 15 to 20 minutes, tossing them every 7 minutes. 6. Mix the orange juice with the sauce kept aside, then toss the carrots to combine.

Serving Suggestion: Season with salt and pepper and serve.
Variation Tip: You can try using almond cream instead of orange juice.
Nutritional Information Per Serving: Calories: 129k | Fat: 6g | Sodium: 206.4mg | Carbs: 19.3g | Fiber: 3.5g | Sugar: 14.6g | Protein: 1g

Chapter 7 Dessert Recipes

115	Air Fried Churros	121	Fried Oreo
115	Nutella Banana Pastries	122	Strawberry Cupcakes
115	Peanut Brittle Bars	122	Carrot Mug Cake
116	Air Fried Doughnuts	122	Shortbread Fingers
116	Fudge Brownies	123	Apple Pastries
116	Cannoli	123	Honeyed Banana
117	Cranberry-Apple Pie	123	Chocolate Chip Cookie
117	Brownie Bars	124	Blueberry Cobbler
118	Caramel Apple Pie	124	Butter Cake
118	Brownie Muffins	124	Raisin Bread Pudding
118	Cherry Jam tarts	125	Cookie Cake
119	Blueberry Hand Pies	125	Cinnamon Rolls
119	Chocolate Bites	125	Chocolate Chip Cookies
119	Cherry Clafoutis	126	Banana Pancakes Dippers
120	Vanilla Soufflé	126	Mini Crumb Cake Bites
120	Nutella Banana Muffins	126	Air Fryer Churros
120	Blueberry Muffins	127	Apple Chips
121	Walnut Brownies	127	Air Fryer Fried Oreos
121	Chocolate Soufflé	127	Fudgy Brownies

Air Fried Churros

Prep Time: 15 minutes | Cook Time: 12 minutes | Serves: 8

Ingredients:

1 cup of water
⅓ cup butter, cut into cubes
2 tablespoons granulated sugar
¼ teaspoons salt
Cinnamon Coating:
½ cup granulated sugar

1 cup all-purpose flour
2 large eggs
1 teaspoon vanilla extract
oil spray

¾ teaspoons ground cinnamon

Preparation:

1. Grease the sheet pan with cooking spray. 2. Warm water with butter, salt, and sugar in a suitable saucepan until it boils. 3. Now reduce its heat, then slowly stir in flour and mix well until smooth. 4. Remove the mixture from the heat and leave it for 4 minutes to cool. 5. Add vanilla extract and eggs, then beat the mixture until it comes together as a batter. 6. Transfer this churro mixture to a piping bag with star-shaped tips and pipe the batter on the prepared pan to get 4-inch churros using this batter. 7. Refrigerate these churros for 1 hour, then transfer them to the air fry basket. 8. Transfer the basket to the 3rd rack position of Ninja Foodi XL Pro Air Oven and close the door. 9. Select the "Air Fry" Mode using FUNCTION +/- buttons and select Rack Level 3. 10. Set its cooking time to 12 minutes and temperature to 375°F/190°C, then press "START/STOP" to initiate cooking. 11. Meanwhile, mix granulated sugar with cinnamon in a bowl. 12. Drizzle this mixture over the air fried churros. 13. Serve.

Serving Suggestion: Serve the churros with chocolate dip.
Variation Tip: Add powdered cinnamon to the churros batter.
Nutritional Information Per Serving: Calories 278 | Fat 10g | Sodium 218mg | Carbs 26g | Fiber 10g | Sugar 30g | Protein 4g

Nutella Banana Pastries

Prep Time: 15 minutes | Cook Time: 12 minutes | Serves: 4

Ingredients:

1 puff pastry sheet
½ cup Nutella

2 bananas, peeled and sliced

Preparation:

1. Cut the pastry sheet into 4 equal-sized squares. 2. Spread the Nutella on each square of pastry evenly. 3. Divide the banana slices over Nutella. 4. Fold each square into a triangle and with wet fingers, slightly press the edges. 5. Then with a fork, press the edges firmly. 6. Press "Power" button of Ninja Foodi XL Pro Air Oven and select "Air Fry" function. 7. Press TEMP/SHADE +/- buttons to set the temperature at 375°F/190°C. 8. Now press TIME/SLICES +/- buttons to set the cooking time to 12 minutes. 9. Press "Start/Stop" button to start. 10. When the unit beeps to show that it is preheated, open the oven door. 11. Arrange the pastries into the greased air fry basket and insert into rail of Level 3. 12. When cooking time is completed, open the oven door and serve warm.

Serving Suggestions: Serve with the sprinkling of cinnamon.
Variation Tip: You can use the fruit of your choice.
Nutritional Information per Serving: Calories: 221 | Fat: 10g | Sat Fat: 2.7g | Carbohydrates: 31.6g | Fiber: 2.6g | Sugar: 14.4g | Protein: 3.4g

Peanut Brittle Bars

Prep Time: 15 minutes | Cook Time: 28 minutes | Serves: 6

Ingredients:

1½ cups all-purpose flour
½ cup whole wheat flour
1 cup packed brown sugar
Topping
1 cup milk chocolate chips
2 cups salted peanuts

1 teaspoon baking soda
¼ teaspoon salt
1 cup butter

12¼ ounces caramel ice cream topping
3 tablespoons all-purpose flour

Preparation:

1. Mix flours with salt, baking soda, and brown sugar in a large bowl. 2. Spread the batter in a greased sheet pan. 3. Transfer the pan to the 2nd rack position of Ninja Foodi XL Pro Air Oven and close the door. 4. Select the "Air Fry" Mode using FUNCTION +/- buttons and select Rack Level 2. 5. Set its cooking time to 12 minutes and temperature to 350°F/175°C, then press "START/STOP" to initiate cooking. 6. Spread chocolate chips and peanuts on top. 7. Mix flour with caramels topping in a bowl and spread on top, 8. Bake again for 16 minutes. 9. Serve.

Serving Suggestion: Serve the bars with sweet cream cheese dip.
Variation Tip: Add crushed oats to bars for crumbly texture.
Nutritional Information Per Serving: Calories 153 | Fat 1g | Sodium 8mg | Carbs 26g | Fiber 0.8g | Sugar 56g | Protein 11g

Air Fried Doughnuts

Prep Time: 15 minutes | Cook Time: 6 minutes | Serves: 8

Ingredients:

Cooking spray
½ cup milk
¼ cup & 1 teaspoon granulated sugar
2¼ teaspoons active dry yeast
2 cup all-purpose flour
½ teaspoons kosher salt
4 tablespoons melted butter
1 large egg
1 teaspoon pure vanilla extract

Preparation:

1. Warm up the milk in a suitable saucepan, then add yeast and 1 teaspoon of sugar. 2. Mix well and leave this milk for 8 minutes. 3. Add flour, salt, butter, egg, vanilla, and ¼ cup of sugar to the warm milk. 4. Mix well and knead over a floured surface until smooth. 5. Place this dough in a lightly greased bowl and brush it with cooking oil. 6. Cover the prepared dough and leave it in a warm place for 1 hour. 7. Punch the raised dough, then roll into ½-inch-thick rectangle. 8. Cut 3" circles out of this dough sheet using a biscuit cutter. 9. Now cut the rounds from the center to make a hole. 10. Place the doughnuts in the air fry basket. 11. Transfer the basket to the 2nd rack position of Ninja Foodi XL Pro Air Oven and close the door. 12. Select the "Air Fry" Mode using FUNCTION +/- buttons and select Rack Level 2. 13. Set its cooking time to 6 minutes and temperature to 375°F/190°C, then press "START/STOP" to initiate cooking. 14. Cook the doughnuts in batches to avoid overcrowding. 15. Serve fresh.
Serving Suggestion: Serve the doughnuts with strawberry jam.
Variation Tip: Roll the doughnuts in the powder sugar to coat.
Nutritional Information Per Serving: Calories 128 | Fat 20g | Sodium 192mg | Carbs 27g | Fiber 0.9g | Sugar 19g | Protein 5.2g-

Fudge Brownies

Prep Time: 15 minutes | Cook Time: 20 minutes | Serves: 8

Ingredients:

1 cup sugar
½ cup butter, melted
½ cup flour
⅓ cup cocoa powder
1 teaspoon baking powder
2 eggs
1 teaspoon vanilla extract

Preparation:

1. Grease a baking pan. 2. In a large bowl, add the sugar and butter and whisk until light and fluffy. 3. Add the remaining ingredients and mix until well combined. 4. Place mixture into the prepared pan and with the back of a spatula, smooth the top surface. 5. Press "Power" button of Ninja Foodi XL Pro Air Oven and select "Air Fry" function. 6. Press TEMP/SHADE +/- buttons to set the temperature at 350°F/175°C. 7. Now press TIME/SLICES +/- buttons to set the cooking time to 20 minutes. 8. Press "START/STOP" button to start. 9. When the unit beeps to show that it is preheated, open the lid. 10. Arrange the pan in air fry basket and insert in the oven. 11. When cooking time is completed, open the lid and place the baking pan onto a wire rack to cool completely. 12. Cut into 8 equal-sized squares and serve.
Serving Suggestions: Serve with a drizzling of melted chocolate.
Variation Tip: Drizzle with some coconut flakes for a crispy taste.
Nutritional Information per Serving: Calories: 250 | Fat: 13.2g | Sat Fat: 7.9g | Carbohydrates: 33.4g | Fiber: 1.3g | Sugar: 25.2g | Protein: 3g

Cannoli

Prep Time: 15 minutes | Cook Time: 12 minutes | Serves: 4

Ingredients:

Filling
1 (16-ounce) container ricotta
½ cup mascarpone cheese
½ cup powdered sugar, divided
¾ cup heavy cream
Shells:
2 cups all-purpose flour
¼ cup granulated sugar
1 teaspoon kosher salt
½ teaspoon cinnamon
4 tablespoons cold butter, cut into cubes

1 teaspoon vanilla extract
1 teaspoon orange zest
¼ teaspoon kosher salt
½ cup mini chocolate chips, for garnish

6 tablespoons white wine
1 large egg
1 egg white for brushing
Vegetable oil for frying

Preparation:

1. For the filling, beat all the ingredients in a mixer and fold in whipped cream. 2. Cover and refrigerate this filling for 1 hour. 3. Mix all the shell ingredients in a bowl until smooth. 4. Cover this dough and refrigerate for 1 hour. 5. Roll the prepared dough into a ⅛-inch-thick sheet. 6. Cut 4 small circles out of the prepared dough and wrap it around the cannoli molds. 7. Brush the prepared dough with egg whites to seal the edges. 8. Place the shells in the air fry basket. 9. Transfer the basket to the 2nd rack position of Ninja Foodi XL Pro Air Oven and close the door. 10. Select the "Air Fry" Mode using FUNCTION +/- buttons and select Rack Level 2. 11. Set its cooking time to 12 minutes and temperature to 350°F/175°C, then press "START/STOP" to initiate cooking. 12. Place filling in a pastry bag fitted with an open star tip. Pipe filling into shells, then dip ends in mini chocolate chips. 13. Transfer the prepared filling to a piping bag. 14. Pipe the filling into the cannoli shells. 15. Serve.
Serving Suggestion: Serve the cannoli with chocolate chips and chocolate syrup.
Variation Tip: Coat the cannoli shells with coconut shreds.
Nutritional Information Per Serving: Calories 348 | Fat 16g | Sodium 95mg | Carbs 38.4g | Fiber 0.3g | Sugar 10g | Protein 14g

Cranberry-Apple Pie

Prep Time: 15 minutes | Cook Time: 45 minutes | Serves: 8

Ingredients:

2½ cups all-purpose flour
1 tablespoon sugar
¾ teaspoon salt
Filling
½ cup dried currants or raisins
2 tablespoons dark rum
1 cup fresh cranberries, divided
¾ cup sugar, divided
6 baking apples, peeled and cut into slices
Egg Wash
2 teaspoons sugar
Dash ground cinnamon

½ cup cold unsalted butter, cubed
⅓ cup cold shortening
7 tablespoons ice water

2 tablespoons tapioca
1 tablespoon lemon juice
2 teaspoons grated lemon zest
½ teaspoon ground cinnamon

1 large egg
1 tablespoon milk

Preparation:

1. Mix flour with butter, salt, and sugar in a bowl. 2. Stir in water and mix well until smooth. 3. Divide the prepared dough into two halves and spread each into a ⅛-inch-thick round. 4. Blend cranberries with sugar in a food processor. 5. Transfer to a bowl and stir in remaining filling ingredients. 6. Spread one dough round on a 9-inch pie plate. 7. Spread the prepared filling in the crust. 8. Slice the other dough round into strips and make a criss-cross pattern on top. 9. Brush the pie with egg and milk mixture, then drizzle sugar and cinnamon top. 10. Transfer the pan to the 2nd rack position of Ninja Foodi XL Pro Air Oven and close the door. 11. Select the "Bake" Mode using FUNCTION +/- buttons and select Rack Level 2. 12. Set its cooking time to 45 minutes and temperature to 325°F/160°C, then press "START/STOP" to initiate cooking. 13. Cool on a wire rack for 30 minutes. 14. Serve.
Serving Suggestion: Serve the pie with whipped cream on top.
Variation Tip: Add a tablespoon of apple sauce to the filling for sweeter taste.
Nutritional Information Per Serving: Calories 145 | Fat 3g | Sodium 355mg | Carbs 20g | Fiber 1g | Sugar 25g | Protein 1g

Brownie Bars

Prep Time: 15 minutes | Cook Time: 28 minutes | Serves: 8

Ingredients:

Brownie:
½ cup butter, cubed
1-ounce unsweetened chocolate
2 large eggs, beaten
1 teaspoon vanilla extract
Filling
6 ounces cream cheese softened
½ cup sugar
¼ cup butter, softened
Topping
1 cup (6-ounce) chocolate chips
1 cup walnuts, chopped
Frosting
¼ cup butter
¼ cup milk
2 ounces cream cheese

1 cup of sugar
1 cup all-purpose flour
1 teaspoon baking powder
1 cup walnuts, chopped

2 tablespoons all-purpose flour
1 large egg, beaten
½ teaspoon vanilla extract

2 cups mini marshmallows

1 ounce unsweetened chocolate
3 cups confectioners' sugar
1 teaspoon vanilla extract

Preparation:

1. In a small bowl, add and whisk all the ingredients for filling until smooth. 2. Melt butter with chocolate in a large saucepan over medium heat. 3. Mix well, then remove the melted chocolate from the heat. 4. Now stir in vanilla, eggs, baking powder, flour, sugar, and nuts then mix well. 5. Spread this chocolate batter in the sheet pan. 6. Drizzle nuts, marshmallows, and chocolate chips over the batter. 7. Transfer the pan to the 2nd rack position of Ninja Foodi XL Pro Air Oven and close the door. 8. Select the "Air Fry" Mode using FUNCTION +/- buttons and select Rack Level 2. 9. Set its cooking time to 28 minutes and temperature to 350°F/175°C, then press "START/STOP" to initiate cooking. 10. Meanwhile, prepare the frosting by heating butter with cream cheese, chocolate and milk in a suitable saucepan over medium heat. 11. Mix well, then remove it from the heat. 12. Stir in vanilla and sugar, then mix well. 13. Pour this frosting over the brownie. 14. Allow the brownie to cool then slice into bars. 15. Serve.
Serving Suggestion: Serve the bars with whipped cream and chocolate syrup on top.
Variation Tip: Add crushed pecans or peanuts to the filling.
Nutritional Information Per Serving: Calories 298 | Fat 14g | Sodium 272mg | Carbs 34g | Fiber 1g | Sugar 9.3g | Protein 13g

Caramel Apple Pie

Prep Time: 15 minutes | Cook Time: 48 minutes | Serves: 6

Ingredients:

Topping
- ¼ cup all-purpose flour
- ⅓ cup packed brown sugar
- 2 tablespoons butter, softened
- ½ teaspoon ground cinnamon

Pie
- 6 cups sliced peeled tart apples
- 1 tablespoon lemon juice
- ½ cup sugar
- 3 tablespoons all-purpose flour
- ½ teaspoon ground cinnamon
- 1 unbaked pastry shell (9 inches)
- 28 caramels
- 1 can (5 ounces) evaporated milk

Preparation:

1. Mix flour with cinnamon, butter, and brown sugar. 2. Spread this mixture in an 8-inch baking pan. 3. Transfer the pan to the 2nd rack position of Ninja Foodi XL Pro Air Oven and close the door. 4. Select the "Bake" Mode using FUNCTION +/- buttons and select Rack Level 2. 5. Set its cooking time to 8 minutes and temperature to 350°F/175°C, then press "START/STOP" to initiate cooking. 6. Meanwhile, mix apple with lemon juice, cinnamon, flour, and sugar. 7. Spread the filling in the baked crust and return to the oven. 8. Bake again for 35 minutes in Ninja Foodi XL Pro Air Oven. 9. Mix caramels with milk in a pan and cook until melted. 10. Spread the caramel on top of the pie and bake for 5 minutes. 11. Serve.

Serving Suggestion: Serve the pie with apple sauce on top.
Variation Tip: Crushed apple chips on top of the apple filling.
Nutritional Information Per Serving: Calories 203 | Fat 8.9g | Sodium 340mg | Carbs 24.7g | Fiber 1.2g | Sugar 11.3g | Protein 5.3g

Brownie Muffins

Prep Time: 10 minutes | Cook Time: 10 minutes | Serves: 12

Ingredients:

- 1 package Betty Crocker fudge brownie mix
- ¼ cup walnuts, chopped
- 1 egg
- ⅓ cup vegetable oil
- 2 teaspoons water

Preparation:

1. Grease 12 muffin molds. Set aside. 2. In a bowl, mix together all the ingredients. 3. Place the mixture into the prepared muffin molds. 4. Press "Power" button of Ninja Foodi XL Pro Air Oven and select "Air Fry" function. 5. Press TEMP/SHADE +/- buttons to set the temperature at 300°F/150°C. 6. Now press TIME/SLICES +/- buttons to set the cooking time to 10 minutes. 7. Press "Start/Stop" button to start. 8. When the unit beeps to show that it is preheated, open the oven door. 9. Arrange the muffin molds into the air fry basket and insert the basket into rail of Level 3. 10. When cooking time is completed, open the oven door and place the muffin molds onto a wire rack to cool for about 10 minutes. 11. Carefully invert the muffins onto the wire rack to completely cool before serving.

Serving Suggestions: Serve with the topping of coconut.
Variation Tip: You can use oil of your choice.
Nutritional Information per Serving: Calories: 168 | Fat: 8.9g | Sat Fat: 1.4g | Carbohydrates: 20.8g | Fiber: 1.1g | Sugar: 14g | Protein: 2g

Cherry Jam tarts

Prep Time: 15 minutes | Cook Time: 40 minutes | Serves: 6

Ingredients:

- 2 sheets short crust pastry

For the Frangipane
- 4 ounces butter softened
- 4 ounces golden caster sugar
- 1 egg
- 1 tablespoon plain flour
- 4 ounces ground almonds
- 3 ounces cherry jam

For the Icing
- 1 cup icing sugar
- 12 glacé cherries

Preparation:

1. Grease the 12 cups of the muffin tray with butter. 2. Roll the puff pastry into a 10 cm sheet, then cut 12 rounds out of it. 3. Place these rounds into each muffin cup and press them into these cups. 4. Transfer the muffin tray to the refrigerator and leave it for 20 minutes. 5. Add dried beans or pulses into each tart crust to add weight. 6. Transfer the muffin tray to the 2nd rack position of Ninja Foodi XL Pro Air Oven and close the door. 7. Select the "Bake" Mode using FUNCTION +/- buttons and select Rack Level 2. 8. Set its cooking time to 10 minutes and temperature to 350°F/175°C, then press "START/STOP" to initiate cooking. 9. Meanwhile, prepare the filling beat, beat butter with sugar and egg until fluffy. 10. Stir in flour and almonds ground, then mix well. 11. Divide this filling in the baked crusts and top them with a tablespoon of cherry jam. 12. Now again, place the muffin tray in Ninja Foodi XL Pro Air Oven. 13. Continue cooking on the "Bake" mode for 20 minutes at 350°F/175°C. 14. Whisk the icing sugar with 2 tablespoons of water and top the baked tarts with sugar mixture. 15. Serve.

Serving Suggestion: Serve the tarts with cherries on top.
Variation Tip: Add rum-soaked raisins to the tart filling.
Nutritional Information Per Serving: Calories 193 | Fat 3g | Sodium 277mg | Carbs 21g | Fiber 1g | Sugar 9g | Protein 2g

Blueberry Hand Pies

Prep Time: 15 minutes | Cook Time: 25 minutes | Serves: 6

Ingredients:

- 1 cup blueberries
- 2½ tablespoons caster sugar
- 1 teaspoon lemon juice
- 1 pinch salt
- 14 ounces refrigerated pie crust
- water
- Vanilla sugar to sprinkle on top

Preparation:

1. Toss the blueberries with salt, lemon juice, and sugar in a medium bowl. 2. Spread the pie crust into a round sheet and cut 6-4-inch circles out of it. 3. Add a tablespoon of blueberry filling at the center of each circle. 4. Moisten the edges of these circles and fold them in half, then pinch their edges together. 5. Press the edges using a fork to crimp its edges. 6. Place the hand pieces in the air fry basket and spray them with cooking oil. 7. Drizzle the vanilla sugar over the hand pies. 8. Transfer the sandwich to the 2nd rack position of Ninja Foodi XL Pro Air Oven and close the door. 9. Select the "Air Fry" Mode using FUNCTION +/- buttons and select Rack Level 2. 10. Set its cooking time to 25 minutes and temperature to 400°F/200°C, then press "START/STOP" to initiate cooking. 11. Serve fresh.

Serving Suggestion: Serve the pies with cream frosting and blueberry sauce on top.
Variation Tip: Add vanilla extract to the blueberry filling.
Nutritional Information Per Serving: Calories 253 | Fat 14g | Sodium 122mg | Carbs 36g | Fiber 1.2g | Sugar 12g | Protein 12g

Chocolate Bites

Prep Time: 15 minutes | Cook Time: 13 minutes | Serves: 8

Ingredients:

- 2 cups plain flour
- 2 tablespoons cocoa powder
- ½ cup icing sugar
- Pinch of ground cinnamon
- 1 teaspoon vanilla extract
- ¾ cup chilled butter
- ¼ cup chocolate, chopped into 8 chunks

Preparation:

1. In a bowl, mix the flour, icing sugar, cocoa powder, cinnamon and vanilla extract together. 2. With a pastry cutter, cut the butter and mix till a smooth dough forms. 3. Divide the dough into 8 equal-sized balls. 4. Press 1 chocolate chunk in the center of each ball and cover with the dough completely. 5. Place the balls into the baking pan. 6. Press "Power" button of Ninja Foodi XL Pro Air Oven and select the "Air Fry" function. 7. Press TEMP/SHADE +/- buttons to set the temperature at 355°F/180°C. 8. Now press TIME/SLICES +/- buttons to set the cooking time to 8 minutes. 9. Press "START/STOP" button to start. 10. When the unit beeps to show that it is preheated, open the lid. 11. Arrange the pan in air fry basket and insert in the oven. 12. After 8 minutes of cooking, set the temperature at 320°F/160°C for 5 minutes. 13. When cooking time is completed, open the lid and place the baking pan onto the wire rack to cool completely before serving.

Serving Suggestions: Serve with a sprinkling of coconut shreds.
Variation Tip: Add some mix-ins as you like.
Nutritional Information per Serving: Calories: 328 | Fat: 19.3g | Sat Fat: 12.2g | Carbohydrates: 35.3g | Fiber: 1.4g | Sugar: 10.2g | Protein: 4.1g

Cherry Clafoutis

Prep Time: 15 minutes | Cook Time: 25 minutes | Serves: 4

Ingredients:

- 1½ cups fresh cherries, pitted
- 3 tablespoons vodka
- ¼ cup flour
- 2 tablespoons sugar
- Pinch of salt
- ½ cup sour cream
- 1 egg
- 1 tablespoon butter
- ¼ cup powdered sugar

Preparation:

1. In a bowl, mix the cherries and vodka together. 2. In another bowl, mix the flour, sugar, and salt together. 3. Add the sour cream, and egg and mix until a smooth dough forms. 4. Grease a cake pan. 5. Place flour mixture evenly into the prepared cake pan. 6. Spread cherry mixture over the dough. 7. Place butter on top in the form of dots. 8. Press "Power" button of Ninja Foodi XL Pro Air Oven and select "Air Fry" function. 9. Press TEMP/SHADE +/- buttons to set the temperature at 355°F/180°C. 10. Now press TIME/SLICES +/- buttons to set the cooking time to 25 minutes. 11. Press "START/STOP" button to start. 12. When the unit beeps to show that it is preheated, open the lid. 13. Arrange the pan in air fry basket and insert in the oven. 14. When cooking time is completed, open the lid and place the pan onto a wire rack to cool for about 10-15 minutes before serving. 15. Now, invert the Clafoutis onto a platter and sprinkle with powdered sugar. 16. Cut the Clafoutis into desired sized slices and serve warm.

Serving Suggestions: Serve with a topping of whipped cream.
Variation Tip: Replace vodka with kirsch.
Nutritional Information per Serving: Calories: 241 | Fat: 10.1g | Sat Fat: 5.9g | Carbohydrates: 29g | Fiber: 1.3g | Sugar: 20.6g | Protein: 3.9g

Vanilla Soufflé

Prep Time: 15 minutes | Cook Time: 23 minutes | Serves: 6

Ingredients:

- ¼ cup butter, softened
- ¼ cup all-purpose flour
- ½ cup plus 2 tablespoons sugar, divided
- 1 cup milk
- 3 teaspoons vanilla extract, divided
- 4 egg yolks
- 5 egg whites
- 1 teaspoon cream of tartar
- 2 tablespoons powdered sugar plus extra for dusting

Preparation:

1. In a bowl, add the butter, and flour and mix until a smooth paste forms. 2. In a medium pan, mix ½ cup of sugar and milk over medium-low heat and cook for about 3 minutes or until the sugar is dissolved, stirring continuously together. 3. Add the flour mixture, whisking continuously and simmer for about 3-4 minutes or until mixture becomes thick. 4. Remove from the heat and stir in 1 teaspoon of vanilla extract. 5. Set aside for about 10 minutes to cool. 6. In a bowl, add the egg yolks and 1 teaspoon of vanilla extract and mix well. 7. Add the egg yolk mixture into milk mixture and mix until well combined. 8. In another bowl, add the egg whites, cream of tartar, remaining sugar, and vanilla extract and with a wire whisk, beat until stiff peaks form. 9. Fold the egg whites mixture into milk mixture. 10. Grease 6 ramekins and sprinkle each with a pinch of sugar. 11. Place mixture into the prepared ramekins and with the back of a spoon, smooth the top surface. 12. Press "Power" button of Ninja Foodi XL Pro Air Oven and select "Air Fry" function. 13. Press TEMP/SHADE +/- buttons to set the temperature at 330°F/165°C. 14. Now press TIME/SLICES +/- buttons to set the cooking time to 16 minutes. 15. Press "START/STOP" button to start. 16. When the unit beeps to show that it is preheated, open the lid. 17. Arrange the ramekins in air fry basket and insert in the oven. 18. When cooking time is completed, open the lid and place the ramekins onto a wire rack to cool slightly. 19. Sprinkle with the powdered sugar and serve warm.

Serving Suggestions: Room temperature eggs will get the best results. Serve with caramel sauce.
Variation Tip: Add some berries as you like.
Nutritional Information per Serving: Calories: 250 | Fat: 11.6g | Sat Fat: 6.5g | Carbohydrates: 29.8g | Fiber: 0.1g | Sugar: 25g | Protein: 6.8g

Nutella Banana Muffins

Prep Time: 15 minutes | Cook Time: 25 minutes | Serves: 12

Ingredients:

- 1⅔ cups plain flour
- 1 teaspoon baking soda
- 1 teaspoon baking powder
- 1 teaspoon ground cinnamon
- ¼ teaspoon salt
- 4 ripe bananas, peeled and mashed
- 2 eggs
- ½ cup brown sugar
- 1 teaspoon vanilla essence
- 3 tablespoons milk
- 1 tablespoon Nutella
- ¼ cup walnuts

Preparation:

1. Grease 12 muffin molds. Set aside. 2. In a large bowl, sift together the flour, baking soda, baking powder, cinnamon, and salt. 3. In another bowl, mix the remaining ingredients except walnuts together. 4. Add the banana mixture into flour mixture and mix until just combined. 5. Fold in the walnuts. 6. Place the mixture into the prepared muffin molds. 7. Press "Power" button of Ninja Foodi XL Pro Air Oven and select "Air Fry" function. 8. Press TEMP/SHADE +/- buttons to set the temperature at 250°F/120°C. 9. Now press TIME/SLICES +/- buttons to set the cooking time to 25 minutes. 10. Press "START/STOP" button to start. 11. When the unit beeps to show that it is preheated, open the lid. 12. Arrange the muffin molds in air fry basket and insert in the oven. 13. When cooking time is completed, open the lid and place the muffin molds onto a wire rack to cool for about 10 minutes. 14. Carefully, invert the muffins onto the wire rack to completely cool before serving.

Serving Suggestions: Have all ingredients at room temperature before you start making the batter. Enjoy with a glass of milk.
Variation Tip: Add some nuts for a crispy choice.
Nutritional Information per Serving: Calories: 227 | Fat: 6.6g | Sat Fat: 1.5g | Carbohydrates: 38.1g | Fiber: 2.4g | Sugar: 15.8g | Protein: 5.2g

Blueberry Muffins

Prep Time: 15 minutes | Cook Time: 20 minutes | Serves: 6

Ingredients:

- 1 egg, beaten
- 1 ripe banana, peeled and mashed
- 1¼ cups almond flour
- 2 tablespoons granulated sugar
- ½ teaspoon baking powder
- 1 tablespoon coconut oil, melted
- ⅛ cup maple syrup
- 1 teaspoon apple cider vinegar
- 1 teaspoon vanilla extract
- 1 teaspoon lemon zest, grated
- Pinch of ground cinnamon
- ½ cup fresh blueberries, ripened

Preparation:

1. In a large bowl, add all the ingredients except for blueberries and mix until well combined. 2. Gently fold in the blueberries. 3. Grease a 6 cups muffin pan. 4. Place the mixture into prepared muffin cups about ¾ full. 5. Press "Power" button of Ninja Foodi XL Pro Air Oven and select "Bake" function. 6. Press TEMP/SHADE +/- buttons to set the temperature at 375°F/190°C. 7. Now press TIME/SLICES +/- buttons to set the cooking time to 12 minutes. 8. Press "START/STOP" button to start. 9. When the unit beeps to show that it is preheated, open the lid. 10. Arrange the muffin pan over the wire rack and insert in the oven. 11. When cooking time is completed, open the lid and place the muffin molds onto a wire rack to cool for about 10 minutes. 12. Carefully invert the muffins onto the wire rack to completely cool before serving.

Serving Suggestions: Serve with a hot cup of coffee.
Variation Tip: Replace the blueberries with raspberries as you like.
Nutritional Information per Serving: Calories: 223 | Fat: 14.8g | Sat Fat: 3g | Carbohydrates: 20.1g | Fiber: 3.4g | Sugar: 12.5g | Protein: 6.2g

Walnut Brownies

Prep Time: 15 minutes | Cook Time: 22 minutes | Serves: 4

Ingredients:

- ½ cup chocolate, roughly chopped
- ⅓ cup butter
- 5 tablespoons sugar
- 1 egg, beaten
- 1 teaspoon vanilla extract
- Pinch of salt
- 5 tablespoons self-rising flour
- ¼ cup walnuts, chopped

Preparation:

1. In a microwave-safe bowl, add the chocolate and butter. Microwave on high heat for about 2 minutes, stirring after every 30 seconds. 2. Remove from microwave and set aside to cool. 3. In another bowl, add the sugar, egg, vanilla extract, and salt and whisk until creamy and light. 4. Add the chocolate mixture and whisk until well combined. 5. Add the flour, and walnuts and mix until well combined. 6. Line a sheet pan with a greased parchment paper. 7. Place mixture into the prepared pan and with the back of spatula, smooth the top surface. 8. Press "Power" button of Ninja Foodi XL Pro Air Oven and select "Air Fry" function. 9. Press TEMP/SHADE +/- buttons to set the temperature at 355°F/180°C. 10. Now press TIME/SLICES +/- buttons to set the cooking time to 20 minutes. 11. Press "Start/Stop" button to start. 12. When the unit beeps to show that it is preheated, open the oven door. 13. Arrange the pan over wire rack and insert into rail of Level 3. 14. When cooking time is completed, open the oven door and place the sheet pan onto a wire rack to cool completely. 15. Cut into 4 equal-sized squares and serve.

Serving Suggestions: Serve with the dusting of powdered sugar.
Variation Tip: You can also use almond extract in the recipe.
Nutritional Information per Serving: Calories: 407 | Fat: 27.4g | Sat Fat: 14.7g | Carbohydrates: 35.9g | Fiber: 1.5g | Sugar: 26.2g | Protein: 6g

Chocolate Soufflé

Prep Time: 15 minutes | Cook Time: 16 minutes | Serves: 2

Ingredients:

- 3 ounces semi-sweet chocolate, chopped
- ¼ cup butter
- 2 eggs, yolks and whites separated
- 3 tablespoons sugar
- ½ teaspoon pure vanilla extract
- 2 tablespoons all-purpose flour
- 1 teaspoon powdered sugar plus extra for dusting

Preparation:

1. In a microwave-safe bowl, place the butter and chocolate. Microwave on high heat for about 2 minutes or until melted completely, stirring after every 30 seconds. 2. Remove from the microwave and stir the mixture until smooth. 3. In another bowl, add the egg yolks and whisk well. 4. Add the sugar and vanilla extract and whisk well. 5. Add the chocolate mixture and mix until well combined. 6. Add the flour and mix well. 7. In a clean glass bowl, add the egg whites and whisk until soft peaks form. 8. Fold the whipped egg whites in 3 portions into the chocolate mixture. 9. Grease 2 ramekins and sprinkle each with a pinch of sugar. 10. Place mixture into the prepared ramekins and with the back of a spoon, smooth the top surface. 11. Insert wire rack on Level 3. Press "Power" button of Ninja Foodi XL Pro Air Oven and select "Air Fry" function. 12. Press TEMP/SHADE +/- buttons to set the temperature at 330°F/165°C. 13. Now press TIME/SLICES +/- buttons to set the cooking time to 14 minutes. 14. Press "Start/Stop" button to start. 15. When the unit beeps to show that it is preheated, open the oven door. 16. Arrange the ramekins over wire rack on Level 3. 17. When cooking time is completed, open the oven door and place the ramekins onto a wire rack to cool slightly. 18. Sprinkle with the powdered sugar and serve warm.

Serving Suggestions: Serve with the garnishing of berries.
Variation Tip: Use high-quality chocolate.
Nutritional Information per Serving: Calories: 591 | Fat: 87.3g | Sat Fat: 23g | Carbohydrates: 52.6g | Fiber: 0.2g | Sugar: 41.1g | Protein: 9.4g

Fried Oreo

Prep Time: 5 minutes | Cook Time: 5 minutes | Serves: 8

Ingredients:

- 8 Oreo cookies
- 1 package of Pillsbury crescents rolls

Preparation:

1. On a cutting board or counter, spread out the crescent dough. 2. Press down into each perforated line with your finger to make one large sheet. 3. Cut the dough into eighths. 4. In the center of each crescent roll square, place one Oreo cookie and roll each corner up. 5. Bunch up the remaining crescent roll to completely cover the Oreo cookie. 6. Place the Oreos in an even row in the sheet pan. 7. Insert a wire rack on Level 3. Turn on Ninja Foodi XL Pro Air Oven and select "Bake". 8. Select the timer for 5 minutes and the temperature for 320°F/160°C. 9. When the unit beeps to signify it has preheated, open the oven and place the sheet pan on the wire rack. 10. Close the oven and let it cook. 11. Allow cooling for two minutes before serving.

Serving Suggestions: Serve with chocolate sauce.
Variation Tip: Dust some powdered sugar on top.
Nutritional Information per Serving: Calories: 172 | Fat: 4g | Sat Fat: 1g | Carbohydrates: 32g | Fiber: 1g | Sugar: 21g | Protein: 2g

Strawberry Cupcakes

Prep Time: 20 minutes | Cook Time: 8 minutes | Serves: 10

Ingredients:

For Cupcakes:
- ½ cup caster sugar
- 7 tablespoons butter
- 2 eggs
- ½ teaspoon vanilla essence
- ⅞ cup self-rising flour

For Frosting:
- 1 cup icing sugar
- 3½ tablespoons butter
- 1 tablespoon whipped cream
- ¼ cup fresh strawberries, pureed
- ½ teaspoon pink food color

Preparation:

1. In a bowl, add the butter and sugar and beat until fluffy and light. 2. Add the eggs, one at a time and beat until well combined. 3. Stir in the vanilla extract. 4. Gradually, add the flour, beating continuously until well combined. 5. Place the mixture into 10 silicone cups. 6. Press "Power" button of Ninja Foodi XL Pro Air Oven and select "Air Fry" function. 7. Press TEMP/SHADE +/- buttons to set the temperature at 340°F/170°C. 8. Now press TIME/SLICES +/- buttons to set the cooking time to 8 minutes. 9. Press "Start/Stop" button to start. 10. When the unit beeps to show that it is preheated, open the oven door. 11. Arrange the silicone cups into the air fry basket and insert into rail of Level 3. 12. When cooking time is completed, open the oven door and place the silicon cups onto a wire rack to cool for about 10 minutes. 13. Carefully invert the muffins onto the wire rack to completely cool before frosting. 14. For frosting: in a bowl, add the icing sugar and butter and whisk until fluffy and light. 15. Add the whipped cream, strawberry puree, and color. Mix until well combined. 16. Fill the pastry bag with frosting and decorate the cupcakes.

Serving Suggestions: Serve with the garnishing of fresh strawberries.
Variation Tip: Use room temperature eggs.
Nutritional Information per Serving: Calories: 250 | Fat: 13.6g | Sat Fat: 8.2g | Carbohydrates: 30.7g | Fiber: 0.4g | Sugar: 22.1g | Protein: 2.4g

Carrot Mug Cake

Prep Time: 10 minutes | Cook Time: 20 minutes | Serves: 1

Ingredients:

- ¼ cup whole-wheat pastry flour
- 1 tablespoon coconut sugar
- ¼ teaspoon baking powder
- ⅛ teaspoon ground cinnamon
- ⅛ teaspoon ground ginger
- Pinch of ground cloves
- Pinch of ground allspice
- Pinch of salt
- 2 tablespoons plus 2 teaspoons unsweetened almond milk
- 2 tablespoons carrot, peeled and grated
- 2 tablespoons walnuts, chopped
- 1 tablespoon raisins
- 2 teaspoons applesauce

Preparation:

1. In a bowl, mix together the flour, sugar, baking powder, spices and salt. 2. Add the remaining ingredients and mix until well combined. 3. Place the mixture into a lightly greased ramekin. 4. Press "Power" button of Ninja Foodi XL Pro Air Oven and select the "Bake" function. 5. Press TEMP/SHADE +/- buttons to set the temperature at 350°F/175°C. 6. Now press TIME/SLICES +/- buttons to set the cooking time to 20 minutes. 7. Press "Start/Stop" button to start. 8. When the unit beeps to show that it is preheated, open the oven door. 9. Arrange the ramekin over the wire rack and insert into rail of Level 3. 10. When cooking time is completed, open the oven door and place the ramekin onto a wire rack to cool slightly before serving.

Serving Suggestions: Serve with the topping of whipped cream.
Variation Tip: Applesauce can be replaced with honey.
Nutritional Information per Serving: Calories: 301 | Fat: 10.1g | Sat Fat: 0.7g | Carbohydrates: 48.6g | Fiber: 3.2g | Sugar: 19.4g | Protein: 7.6g

Shortbread Fingers

Prep Time: 15 minutes | Cook Time: 12 minutes | Serves: 10

Ingredients:

- ⅓ cup caster sugar
- 1⅔ cups plain flour
- ¾ cup butter

Preparation:

1. In a large bowl, mix the sugar and flour together. 2. Add the butter and mix until a smooth dough forms. 3. Cut the dough into 10 equal-sized fingers. 4. With a fork, lightly prick the fingers. 5. Place the fingers into the lightly greased baking pan. 6. Press "Power" button of Ninja Foodi XL Pro Air Oven and select "Air Fry" function. 7. Press TEMP/SHADE +/- buttons to set the temperature at 355°F/180°C. 8. Now press TIME/SLICES +/- buttons to set the cooking time to 12 minutes. 9. Press "START/STOP" button to start. 10. When the unit beeps to show that it is preheated, open the lid. 11. Arrange the pan in air fry basket and insert in the oven. 12. When cooking time is completed, open the lid and place the baking pan onto a wire rack to cool for about 5-10 minutes. 13. Now, invert the shortbread fingers onto the wire rack to completely cool before serving.

Serving Suggestions: For best result, chill the dough in the refrigerator for 30 minutes before cooking. Serve with a dusting of powdered sugar.
Variation Tip: Replace the plain flour with some other flour of your choice.
Nutritional Information per Serving: Calories: 223 | Fat: 14g | Sat Fat: 8.8g | Carbohydrates: 22.6g | Fiber: 0.6g | Sugar: 0.7g | Protein: 2.3g

Apple Pastries

Prep Time: 15 minutes | Cook Time: 10 minutes | Serves: 6

Ingredients:

½ of large apple, peeled, cored and chopped
1 teaspoon fresh orange zest, grated finely
½ tablespoon white sugar
½ teaspoon ground cinnamon
7.05 ounces prepared frozen puff pastry

Preparation:

1. In a bowl, mix all ingredients except puff pastry together. 2. Cut the pastry in 16 squares. 3. Place about a teaspoon of the apple mixture in the center of each square. 4. Fold each square into a triangle and press the edges slightly with wet fingers. 5. Then with a fork, press the edges firmly. 6. Press "Power" button of Ninja Foodi XL Pro Air Oven and select "Air Fry" function. 7. Press TEMP/SHADE +/- buttons to set the temperature at 390°F/200°C. 8. Now press TIME/SLICES +/- buttons to set the cooking time to 10 minutes. 9. Press "START/STOP" button to start. 10. When the unit beeps to show that it is preheated, open the lid. 11. Arrange the pastries in the greased air fry basket and insert in the oven. 12. When cooking time is completed, open the lid and transfer the pastries onto a platter. 13. Serve warm.

Serving Suggestions: Serve with a dusting of powdered sugar.
Variation Tip: Use sweet apple.
Nutritional Information per Serving: Calories: 198 | Fat: 12.7g | Sat Fat: 3.2g | Carbohydrates: 18.8g | Fiber: 1.1g | Sugar: 3.2g | Protein: 2.5g

Honeyed Banana

Prep Time: 10 minutes | Cook Time: 10 minutes | Serves: 2

Ingredients:

1 ripe banana, peeled and sliced lengthwise
½ teaspoon fresh lemon juice
2 teaspoons honey
⅛ teaspoon ground cinnamon

Preparation:

1. Coat each banana half with lemon juice. 2. Arrange the banana halves onto the greased sheet pan cut sides up. 3. Drizzle the banana halves with honey and sprinkle with cinnamon. 4. Press "Power" button of Ninja Foodi XL Pro Air Oven and select "Air Fry" function. 5. Press TEMP/SHADE +/- buttons to set the temperature at 350°F/175°C. 6. Now press TIME/SLICES +/- buttons to set the cooking time to 10 minutes. 7. Press "START/STOP" button to start. 8. When the unit beeps to show that it is preheated, open the lid. 9. Insert the sheet pan in oven. 10. When cooking time is completed, open the lid and transfer the banana slices onto a platter. 11. Serve immediately.

Serving Suggestions: Serve with garnishing of almonds.
Variation Tip: Honey can be replaced with maple syrup.
Nutritional Information per Serving: Calories: 74 | Fat: 0.2g | Sat Fat: 0.1g | Carbohydrates: 19.4g | Fiber: 1.6g | Sugar: 13g | Protein: 0.7g

Chocolate Chip Cookie

Prep Time: 15 minutes | Cook Time: 12 minutes | Serves: 6

Ingredients:

½ cup butter, softened
½ cup sugar
½ cup brown sugar
1 egg
1 teaspoon vanilla
½ teaspoons baking soda
¼ teaspoons salt
1½ cups all-purpose flour
1 cup of chocolate chips

Preparation:

1. Grease the sheet pan with cooking spray. 2. Beat butter with sugar and brown sugar in a mixing bowl. 3. Stir in vanilla, egg, salt, flour, and baking soda, then mix well. 4. Fold in chocolate chips, then knead this dough a bit. 5. Spread the prepared dough in the prepared sheet pan evenly. 6. Transfer the pan to the 2nd rack position of Ninja Foodi XL Pro Air Oven and close the door. 7. Select the "Bake" Mode using FUNCTION +/- buttons and select Rack Level 2. 8. Set its cooking time to 12 minutes and temperature to 400°F/200°C, then press "START/STOP" to initiate cooking. 9. Serve oven fresh.

Serving Suggestion: Serve the cookies with warm milk.
Variation Tip: Dip the cookies in chocolate syrup to coat well.
Nutritional Information Per Serving: Calories 173 | Fat 12g | Sodium 79mg | Carbs 24.8g | Fiber 1.1g | Sugar 18g | Protein 15g

Blueberry Cobbler

Prep Time: 15 minutes | Cook Time: 20 minutes | Serves: 6

Ingredients:

For Filling:
- 2½ cups fresh blueberries
- 1 teaspoon vanilla extract
- 1 teaspoon fresh lemon juice
- 1 cup sugar
- 1 teaspoon flour
- 1 tablespoon butter, melted

For Topping:
- 1¾ cups all-purpose flour
- 6 tablespoons sugar
- 4 teaspoons baking powder
- 1 cup milk
- 5 tablespoons butter

For Sprinkling:
- 2 teaspoons sugar
- ¼ teaspoon ground cinnamon

Preparation:

1. For filling: in a bowl, add all the filling ingredients and mix until well combined. 2. For topping: in another large bowl, mix together the flour, baking powder, and sugar. 3. Add the milk and butter and mix until a crumply mixture forms. 4. For sprinkling: in a small bowl, mix together the sugar and cinnamon. 5. In the bottom of a greased pan, place the blueberries mixture and top with the flour mixture evenly. 6. Sprinkle the cinnamon sugar on top evenly. 7. Press "Power" button of Ninja Foodi XL Pro Air Oven and select "Air Fry" function. 8. Press TEMP/SHADE +/- buttons to set the temperature at 320°F/160°C. 9. Now press TIME/SLICES +/- buttons to set the cooking time to 20 minutes. 10. Press "Start/Stop" button to start. 11. When the unit beeps to show that it is preheated, open the oven door. 12. Arrange the pan in air fry basket and insert into the rail of Level 3. 13. When cooking time is complete, open the oven door and place the pan onto a wire rack to cool for about 10 minutes before serving.

Serving Suggestions: Serve with the topping of vanilla ice cream.
Variation Tip: If You want to use frozen blueberries, then thaw them completely.
Nutritional Information per Serving: Calories: 459 | Fat: 12.6g | Sat Fat: 7.8g | Carbohydrates: 84g | Fiber: 2.7g | Sugar: 53.6g | Protein: 5.5g

Butter Cake

Prep Time: 15 minutes | Cook Time: 15 minutes | Serves: 6

Ingredients:

- 3 ounces butter, softened
- ½ cup caster sugar
- 1 egg
- 1⅓ cups plain flour, sifted
- Pinch of salt
- ½ cup milk
- 1 tablespoon icing sugar

Preparation:

1. In a bowl, add the butter and sugar and whisk until light and creamy. 2. Add the egg and whisk until smooth and fluffy. 3. Add the flour and salt and mix well alternately with the milk. 4. Grease a small Bundt cake pan. 5. Place mixture evenly into the prepared cake pan. 6. Press "Power" button of Ninja Foodi XL Pro Air Oven and select "Air Fry" function. 7. Press TEMP/SHADE +/- buttons to set the temperature at 350°F/175°C. 8. Now press TIME/SLICES +/- buttons to set the cooking time to 15 minutes. 9. Press "Start/Stop" button to start. 10. When the unit beeps to show that it is preheated, open the oven door. 11. Arrange the pan over wire rack and insert into rail of Level 3. 12. When cooking time is completed, open the oven door and place the cake pan onto a wire rack to cool for about 10 minutes. 13. Carefully invert the cake onto the wire rack to completely cool before slicing. 14. Dust the cake with icing sugar and cut into desired-size slices.

Serving Suggestions: Serve with the sprinkling of cocoa powder.
Variation Tip: Use unsalted butter.
Nutritional Information per Serving: Calories: 291 | Fat: 12.9g | Sat Fat: 7.8g | Carbohydrates: 40.3g | Fiber: 0.8g | Sugar: 19g | Protein: 4.6g

Raisin Bread Pudding

Prep Time: 15 minutes | Cook Time: 12 minutes | Serves: 3

Ingredients:

- 1 cup milk
- 1 egg
- 1 tablespoon brown sugar
- ½ teaspoon ground cinnamon
- ¼ teaspoon vanilla extract
- 2 tablespoons raisins, soaked in hot water for 15 minutes
- 2 bread slices, cut into small cubes
- 1 tablespoon chocolate chips
- 1 tablespoon sugar

Preparation:

1. In a bowl, mix together the milk, egg, brown sugar, cinnamon, and vanilla extract. 2. Stir in the raisins. 3. In a sheet pan, spread the bread cubes and top evenly with the milk mixture. 4. Refrigerate for about 15-20 minutes. 5. Insert the wire rack on Level 3. Press "Power" button of Ninja Foodi XL Pro Air Oven and select "Air Fry" function. 6. Press TEMP/SHADE +/- buttons to set the temperature at 375°F/190°C. 7. Now press TIME/SLICES +/- buttons to set the cooking time to 12 minutes. 8. Press "Start/Stop" button to start. 9. When the unit beeps to show that it is preheated, open the oven door. 10. Arrange the pan over the wire rack on Level 3. 11. When cooking time is completed, open the oven door and place the sheet pan aside to cool slightly. 12. Serve warm.

Serving Suggestions: Serve with the drizzling of vanilla syrup.
Variation Tip: Use ode day-old bread.
Nutritional Information per Serving: Calories: 143 | Fat: 4.4g | Sat Fat: 2.2g | Carbohydrates: 21.3g | Fiber: 6.7g | Sugar: 16.4g | Protein: 5.5g

Cookie Cake

Prep Time: 10 minutes | Cook Time: 10 minutes | Serves: 2

Ingredients:

- 1 stick butter, softened
- ½ cup brown sugar, packed
- ¼ cup sugar
- 1 egg
- 1 teaspoon vanilla extract
- 1½ cups all-purpose flour
- ½ teaspoon baking soda
- 1 cup semi-sweet chocolate chips

Preparation:

1. Mix the cream, butter, brown sugar, and sugar in a large mixing bowl. 2. Mix in the vanilla and eggs until everything is well mixed. 3. Slowly stir in the flour, baking soda, and salt until combined, then stir in the chocolate chips. 4. Spray a 6-inch pan with oil, pour half of the batter into the pan, and press it down to evenly fill it. Refrigerate the other half for later use. 5. Place it on sheet pan on Level 3 inside the oven. 6. Turn on Ninja Foodi XL Pro Air Oven and select "Air Fry". 7. Select the timer for 5 minutes and the temperature for 370°F/185°C. 8. Remove it from the oven and set it aside for 5 minutes to cool.

Serving Suggestions: Serve some vanilla ice cream.
Variation Tip: You can also use almond butter.
Nutritional Information per Serving: Calories: 673 | Fat: 38g | Sat Fat: 23g | Carbohydrates: 82g | Fiber: 4g | Sugar: 2g | Protein: 8g

Cinnamon Rolls

Prep Time: 5 minutes | Cook Time: 30 minutes | Serves: 6

Ingredients:

- 2 tablespoons butter, melted
- ⅓ cup packed brown sugar
- ½ teaspoon ground cinnamon
- Salt, to taste
- All-purpose flour for surface
- 1 tube refrigerated crescent rolls
- 56g cream cheese, softened
- ½ cup powdered sugar
- 1 tablespoon whole milk

Preparation:

1. Combine butter, brown sugar, cinnamon, and a large pinch of salt in a medium mixing bowl until smooth and fluffy. 2. Roll out crescent rolls in one piece on a lightly floured surface. Fold in half by pinching the seams together. Make a medium rectangle out of the dough. 3. Cover the dough with butter mixture, leaving a ¼-inch border. Roll the dough, starting at one edge and cutting crosswise into 6 pieces. 4. Line bottom of basket with parchment paper and brush with butter. 5. Place the pieces cut-side up in the prepared air fry basket, equally spaced. 6. Turn on Ninja Foodi XL Pro Air Oven and select "Broil". 7. Select the timer for 15 minutes and the temperature for LO. 8. When the unit beeps to signify it has preheated, open the oven and place the air fry basket on Level 3 in oven. 9. Close the oven and let it cook. 10. Allow cooling for two minutes before serving.

Serving Suggestions: Top with almond butter.
Variation Tip: You can also use almond milk.
Nutritional Information per Serving: Calories: 183 | Fat: 8g | Sat Fat: 4g | Carbohydrates: 26g | Fiber: 0.4g | Sugar: 16g | Protein: 2.2g

Chocolate Chip Cookies

Prep Time: 10 minutes | Cook Time: 45 minutes | Serves: 4

Ingredients:

- ½ cup butter, melted
- ¼ cup packed brown sugar
- ¼ cup granulated sugar
- 1 large egg
- 1 teaspoon pure vanilla extract
- 1½ cups all-purpose flour
- ½ teaspoon baking soda
- ½ teaspoon kosher salt
- ½ teaspoon chocolate chips

Preparation:

1. Insert a wire rack on Level 3. Turn on Ninja Foodi XL Pro Air Oven and select "Air Fry". 2. Select the timer for 8 minutes and the temperature for 350°F/175°C. 3. Meanwhile, whisk together melted butter and sugars in a medium mixing bowl. Whisk in the egg and vanilla extract until fully combined. 4. Combine the flour, baking soda, and salt. 5. Scoop dough onto the sheet pan with a large cookie scoop (approximately 3 tablespoons), leaving 2 inches between each cookie, and press to flatten slightly. 6. When the unit beeps to signify it has preheated, open the oven and place the sheet pan onto the wire rack. 7. Close the oven and let it cook. 8. Allow cooling for two minutes before serving.

Serving Suggestions: Top some more chocolate chips.
Variation Tip: You can also add chopped walnuts.
Nutritional Information per Serving: Calories: 319 | Fat: 16.6g | Sat Fat: 10.1g | Carbohydrates: 38.4g | Fiber: 0.9g | Sugar: 14.6g | Protein: 4.5g

Banana Pancakes Dippers

Prep Time: 10 minutes | Cook Time: 15 minutes | Serves: 2

Ingredients:

1½ cups all-purpose flour
3 bananas, halved and sliced lengthwise
1 tablespoon baking powder
1 tablespoon packed brown sugar
1 teaspoon salt
¾ cup whole milk
½ cup sour cream
2 large eggs
1 teaspoon vanilla extract

Preparation:

1. Combine flour, baking powder, brown sugar, and salt in bowl. 2. Mix the milk and sour cream in a separate bowl, then add the eggs one at a time. Pour in the vanilla extract. 3. Combine the wet and dry ingredients until just mixed. 4. Grease the sheet pan with cooking spray and line it with parchment paper. 5. Place bananas in a single layer on parchment paper after dipping them in pancake batter. 6. Insert a wire rack on Level 3. Turn on Ninja Foodi XL Pro Air Oven and select "Air Roast". 7. Select the timer for 16 minutes and the temperature to 375°F/190°C. 8. When the unit beeps to signify it has preheated, open the oven and place the sheet pan on the wire rack. 9. Allow cooling for two minutes before serving.

Serving Suggestions: Serve with melted chocolate for dipping.
Variation Tip: You can also use almond milk.
Nutritional Information per Serving: Calories: 670 | Fat: 18.6g | Sat Fat: 10g | Carbohydrates: 66g | Fiber: 5g | Sugar: 23g | Protein: 22g

Mini Crumb Cake Bites

Prep Time: 30 minutes | Cook Time: 15 minutes | Serves: 4 to 6

Ingredients:

¾ cup granulated sugar
⅓ cup vegetable oil
1 egg
1 teaspoon vanilla
½ cup milk
2 teaspoons baking powder
½ teaspoon plus a pinch of salt
1½ cups plus 2 tablespoons all-purpose flour
2 tablespoons butter, melted
2 teaspoons ground cinnamon
½ cup packed brown sugar

Preparation:

1. Insert a wire rack in oven on Level 3. Select the BAKE function, 350°F/175°C, for 10 minutes. Prepare oven-safe mini muffin pans with non-stick cooking spray. 2. In a large bowl, mix the oil, vanilla, granulated sugar, and egg. Mix well and stir in the milk. 3. Take a medium bowl, and whisk ½ teaspoon of salt, baking powder, and 1½ cups of flour. Stir the dry ingredients into the wet ingredients, slowly. Fill each muffin cup with 1 tablespoon of the batter. 4. Mix the cinnamon, flour, brown sugar, and a pinch of salt. Top each muffin with ½ to ¾ teaspoon of this crumb topping. 5. When the unit beeps to signify it has preheated, open the oven and place the muffin cups on wire rack. 6. Bake the muffins for about 9 to 10 minutes. Let them cool for a while before taking them out of the pans.

Serving Suggestion: Sprinkle with some sugar and serve with jam.
Variation Tip: You can also add chopped pecans or walnuts to the crumble.
Nutritional Information Per Serving: Calories: 74 | Fat: 3g | Sodium: 42mg | Carbs: 12g | Fiber: 1g | Sugar: 7g | Protein: 1g

Air Fryer Churros

Prep Time: 5 minutes | Cook Time: 20 minutes | Serves: 6

Ingredients:

¼ cup butter
½ cup milk
1 pinch salt
½ cup all-purpose flour
2 eggs
¼ cup white sugar
½ teaspoon ground cinnamon

Preparation:

1. Select the AIR FRY function, 340°F/170°C, for 5 minutes. Select 2 LEVEL. While the oven preheats, prepare the ingredients. 2. Take a saucepan and melt the butter over medium-high heat. Pour in the milk and add the salt. Turn the heat down to medium and bring the mixture to a boil, stirring constantly. 3. Add all the flour at once and keep stirring until the dough comes together. 4. Turn off the heat and let the mixture cool for 5 to 7 minutes. Add the eggs and mix with a wooden spoon. Spoon the dough into a plastic bag with a large star tip. With the help of the star tip, pipe the dough directly into the air fry basket and sheet pan evenly. 5. When the unit beeps to signify it has preheated, open the oven and insert the air fry basket into rail of Level 3 and the sheet pan into rail of Level 1. 6. Cook the churros for about 5 minutes. 7. Meanwhile, in a small bowl, combine the cinnamon and sugar. Put it on a shallow plate. 8. Once the churros are done, roll them in the cinnamon-sugar mixture and serve.

Serving Suggestion: Drizzle with a little honey before serving.
Variation Tip: You can try nutmeg instead of cinnamon.
Nutritional Information Per Serving: Calories: 172k | Fat: 9.8g | Sodium: 112mg | Carbs: 17.5g | Fiber: 0.4g | Sugar: 9.4 | Protein: 3.7g

Apple Chips

Prep Time: 15 minutes | Cook Time: 10 minutes | Serves: 6

Ingredients:

2 golden apples, cored
2 teaspoons white sugar
1 teaspoon ground cinnamon

Preparation:

1. Select the AIR FRY function, 300°F/150°C, for 10 minutes. While the oven preheats, prepare the apples. 2. Thinly slice the apples using a mandolin or a sharp knife. 3. Lay the apple slices in the air fry basket (sprayed with non-stick cooking spray). 4. In a bowl, mix the cinnamon and sugar. Sprinkle the mixture over the apple slices. 5. When the unit beeps to signify it has preheated, open the oven and slide the air fry basket into rail of Level 3. 6. Bake the slices for 10 minutes, flipping them halfway through the cooking time. When done, transfer the chips to a wire rack and let them cool down.
Serving Suggestion: Serve as a delicious, healthy snack any time of day.
Variation Tip: Allspice can be a great substitute for cinnamon.
Nutritional Information Per Serving: Calories: 24 | Fat: 0g | Sodium: 0.9mg | Carbs: 7g | Fiber: 1g | Sugar: 5.9g | Protein: 0.1g

Air Fryer Fried Oreos

Prep Time: 10 minutes | Cook Time: 8 minutes | Serves: 3 to 4

Ingredients:

9 Oreo cookies
1 Crescent Dough Sheet

Preparation:

1. Select the AIR FRY function, 350°F/175°C, for 8 minutes. While the oven preheats, prepare the ingredients. 2. Spread the sheet out. Line and cut it into 9 even squares with a knife. 3. Take the 9 cookies and wrap one in each square. Press the dough to seal. Spray each with some cooking oil. 4. Lay the parcels in the air fry basket on Level 3 in the preheated oven, cook them for 5 minutes, turn them over, spray with more oil, and cook for 3 more minutes or until golden brown.
Serving Suggestion: Sprinkle with powdered sugar or cinnamon before serving.
Variation Tip: Try drizzling with a bit of honey.
Nutritional Information Per Serving: Calories: 67 | Fat: 3g | Sodium: 80mg | Carbs: 10g | Fiber: 1g | Sugar: 5g | Protein: 1g

Fudgy Brownies

Prep Time: 15 minutes | Cook Time: 25 minutes | Serves: 9

Ingredients:

8 ounces semi-sweet chocolate
12 tablespoons butter, melted
1¼ cups sugar
2 eggs
2 teaspoons vanilla extract
¾ cup all-purpose flour
¼ cup cocoa powder
1 teaspoon salt

Preparation:

1. Insert a wire rack in oven on Level 3. Select to the BAKE function, 350°F/175°C, for 25 minutes. Line the sheet pan with parchment paper. 2. While the oven is preheating, chop the chocolate into chunks and melt half of the chocolate in the microwave. 3. Take a large bowl, and mix the sugar and butter using an electric hand mixer. Then, beat in the egg and vanilla until the mixture becomes fluffy, about 2 minutes. 4. Now, whisk in the melted chocolate and stir in the cocoa powder, flour, and salt. Fold gently to mix with the dry ingredients. 5. Fold in the remaining chocolate chunks and transfer to the prepared sheet pan. 6. When the unit beeps to signify it has preheated, open the oven and place the prepared sheet pan on wire rack. 7. Close the oven and bake the brownies for about 20 to 25 minutes.
Serving Suggestion: Drizzle with a little honey or top with melted chocolate and serve with milk.
Variation Tip: Carob powder can be a great substitute for cocoa powder.
Nutritional Information Per Serving: Calories: 404 | Fat: 27g | Sodium: 0g | Carbs: 39g | Fiber: 2g | Sugar: 25g | Protein: 5g

Conclusion

With its revolutionary appearance and extensive functionality, the Ninja Foodi XL Pro Air Oven is the most user-friendly of all the toaster ovens we examined. If you're searching for an oven that can serve you at every meal, despite taking up quite a bit of countertop space in your kitchen (17 x 20 x 13 inches), this one is definitely worth the investment. It performs every task flawlessly, including toasting bread, reheating frozen pizza, baking, and roasting. Additionally, it has the ability to air fry, giving you the capability of multiple appliances in a single unit.

Yes, if you're searching for a countertop convection oven with a variety of cooking options, I'd highly recommend the Ninja Foodi Smart XL Pro Air Oven. It's superior to a full-sized convection oven, in my opinion.

Appendix 1 Measurement Conversion Chart

VOLUME EQUIVALENTS (DRY)

US STANDARD	METRIC (APPROXIMATE)
⅛ teaspoon	0.5 mL
¼ teaspoon	1 mL
½ teaspoon	2 mL
¾ teaspoon	4 mL
1 teaspoon	5 mL
1 tablespoon	15 mL
¼ cup	59 mL
½ cup	118 mL
¾ cup	177 mL
1 cup	235 mL
2 cups	475 mL
3 cups	700 mL
4 cups	1 L

VOLUME EQUIVALENTS (LIQUID)

US STANDARD	US STANDARD (OUNCES)	METRIC (APPROXIMATE)
2 tablespoons	1 fl.oz	30 mL
¼ cup	2 fl.oz	60 mL
½ cup	4 fl.oz	120 mL
1 cup	8 fl.oz	240 mL
1½ cup	12 fl.oz	355 mL
2 cups or 1 pint	16 fl.oz	475 mL
4 cups or 1 quart	32 fl.oz	1 L
1 gallon	128 fl.oz	4 L

WEIGHT EQUIVALENTS

US STANDARD	METRIC (APPROXINATE)
1 ounce	28 g
2 ounces	57 g
5 ounces	142 g
10 ounces	284 g
15 ounces	425 g
16 ounces (1 pound)	455 g
1.5 pounds	680 g
2 pounds	907 g

TEMPERATURES EQUIVALENTS

FAHRENHEIT(F)	CELSIUS(C) (APPROXIMATE)
225 °F	107 °C
250 °F	120 °C
275 °F	135 °C
300 °F	150 °C
325 °F	160 °C
350 °F	180 °C
375 °F	190 °C
400 °F	205 °C
425 °F	220 °C
450 °F	235 °C
475 °F	245 °C
500 °F	260 °C

Appendix 2 Recipes Index

A

Air Fried Churros 115
Air Fried Doughnuts 116
Air Fried Fish Cakes 95
Air Fried Fish Sticks 94
Air Fryer Beef Taquitos 77
Air Fryer Blueberry Bread 37
Air Fryer Chicken Taco Pockets 58
Air Fryer Churros 126
Air Fryer Fried Oreos 127
Air Fryer Low-Carb Taco Casserole 78
Air Fryer Pop-Tarts 38
Air Fryer Ravioli 37
Air Fryer Sweet and Roasted Carrots 113
Air Fryer Sweet Potato Tots 38
Air Fryer Tuna Patties 97
American Roast Beefn 70
Apple Chips 127
Apple Pastries 123
Asparagus with Garlic and Parmesan 109
Avocado Fries 31

B

Bacon, Spinach & Egg Cups 19
Bacon-Wrapped Chicken Breasts 46
Bacon-Wrapped Filled Jalapeno 36
Bacon-Wrapped Pork Tenderloin 66
Baked Beef Stew 76
Baked Duck 48
Baked Honey Mustard Chicken 57
Baked Mozzarella Sticks 34
Baked Pork Chops 74
Baked Potato 109
Baked Potatoes 32
Baked Sardines with Garlic and Oregano 92
Baked Sole with Mint and Ginger 97
Baked Tilapia with Buttery Crumb Topping 89
Balsamic Beef Top Roast 72
Banana & Walnut Bread 17
Banana Bread 20
Banana Pancakes Dippers 126
BBQ Pork Chops 69
Beans & Veggie Burgers 107
Beef Short Ribs 63
Beef Taquitos 29
Beef Zucchini Shashliks 65
Beer-Battered Fish 86
Beet Chips 26
Benefits of Using It 3
Blackened Chicken Bake 42
Blue Cheese Soufflés 101
Blueberry Cobbler 124
Blueberry Hand Pies 119
Blueberry Muffins 120
Breaded Air Fryer Pork Chops 78
Breaded Chicken Tenderloins 53
Breaded Pork Chops 68
Breaded Shrimp 94
Breakfast Bake 14
Breakfast Casserole 20
Breakfast Pizzas with Muffins 23
Brine-Soaked Turkey 44
Broccoli Casserole 105
Broccoli Cheese Casserole 112
Broccoli with Cauliflower 102
Broiled Broccoli 110
Brown Sugar and Garlic Air Fryer Salmon 96
Brownie Bars 117
Brownie Muffins 118
Brussels Sprouts Gratin 106
Butter Cake 124
Buttered Crab Shells 82
Buttered Strip Steak 71
Buttered Trout 83
Buttermilk Biscuits 32
Buttermilk Whole Chicken 52

C

Cajun Salmon 84
Cajun Spiced Whole Chicken 50
Cannoli 116
Caramel Apple Pie 118
Caramelized Baby Carrots 100
Carrot & Raisin Bread 16
Carrot Chips 28
Carrot Mug Cake 122
Cauliflower in Buffalo Sauce 103
Cauliflower Poppers 39
Cheddar & Cream Omelet 12
Cheesy Broccoli Bites 28
Cheesy Chicken Cutlets 52
Cheesy Green Bean Casserole 107
Cheesy Kale 106
Cherry Clafoutis 119
Cherry Jam tarts 118
Chicken Alfredo Bake 56
Chicken and Rice Casserole 45
Chicken Casserole 57
Chicken Kabobs 41
Chicken Potato Bake 45
Chinese Chicken Drumsticks 42
Chocolate Bites 119
Chocolate Chip Cookie 123
Chocolate Soufflé 121
Cinnamon Donut Muffins 24
Cinnamon Rolls 125
Cinnamon Sugar Donuts 21
Citrus Pork Chops 68
Cloud Eggs 12
Cod Burgers 90
Cod Nuggets 27
Cod Parcel 83
Cod with Sauce 92

Cookie Cake 125
Corn on the Cob 38
Crab Cakes 84
Cranberry-Apple Pie 117
Creamy Chicken Casserole 46
Creamy Roast Mushrooms 112
Crispy Air Fryer Fish Tacos 96
Crispy Avocado Fries 27
Crispy Catfish 91
Crispy Chicken Cutlets 49
Crispy Chicken Drumsticks 50
Crispy Chicken Thighs 50
Crispy Cod 87
Crispy Flounder 86
Crispy Prawns 26
Crispy Roasted Chicken 53
Crispy Sirloin Steaks 72
Czech Roast Pork 75

D
Date Bread 17
Deviled Chicken 41
Duck a la Orange 48

E
Eggplant Fries 32
Eggs, Tofu & Mushroom Omelet 12

F
Fajitas 101
Feta Turkey Burgers 44
Fiesta Chicken Fingers 27
Fish in Yogurt Marinade 88
Fish Newburg with Haddock 87
French Toast Bites 37
French Toast 22
Fried Oreo 121
Fried Pickles 31
Fried Tortellini 99
Fudge Brownies 116
Fudgy Brownies 127

G
Garlic Braised Ribs 63
Garlic Butter Salmon Bites 93
Garlic Parmesan Roasted Asparagus 112
Garlic Parmesan Roasted Potatoes 111
Garlic Shrimp with Lemon 92
Garlicky Lamb Chops 62
Garlicky Lamb Steaks 61
German Pancake 24
Gingered Chicken Drumsticks 55
Glazed Beef Short Ribs 71
Glazed Chicken Wings 33
Glazed Pork Tenderloin 79
Glazed Pork Tenderloin 79
Greek Baked Bonito with Herbs and Potatoes 95
Greek lamb Farfalle 64
Green Tomatoes 110
Ground Beef Casserole 76

H
Ham & Egg Cups 18
Ham and Cheese Scones 13
Hard Boiled Eggs 23
Hash Browns 22
Herb-Crumbed Rack of Lamb 62
Herbed Bell Peppers 104
Herbed Chicken Thighs 47
Herbed Chuck Roast 70
Herbed Duck Breast 51
Herbed Lamb Loin Chops 74
Herbed Leg of Lamb 73
Herbed Shrimp 81
Herbed Turkey Legs 44
Herbed Whole Chicken 52
Herby Pork Bake 74
Honeyed Banana 123
Honey-Glazed Chicken Drumsticks 55

I
Italian Baked Meatballs 76

L
Lamb Burgers 71
Lamb Chops with Carrots 73
Lamb Chops with Rosemary Sauce 63
Lamb Chops 77
Lamb Chops 77
Lamb Kebabs 61
Lamb Rack with Lemon Crust 64
Lasagna Stuffed Chicken 59
Lemon Pepper Shrimp 96
Lemony Chicken Thighs 51
Lemony Salmon 81
Lemony Whole Chicken 49
Lobster Tail Casserole 86
Lobster Tails with Lemon-Garlic Butter 95

M
Maple Bacon Salmon 91
Marinated Ranch Broiled Chicken 56
Marinated Spicy Chicken Legs 49
Minced Lamb Casserole 65
Mini Crumb Cake Bites 126
Mini Hot Dogs 33
Mint Lamb with Toasted Hazelnuts 64
Molasses Glazed Duck Breast 53
Mushroom Frittata 21
Mushroom, Broccoli, and Cheese Stuffed Chicken 58
Mushrooms Frittata 15
Mustard Lamb Loin Chops 73

N
Nutella Banana Muffins 120
Nutella Banana Pastries 115
Nuts Crusted Salmon 82

O
Oat Crusted Chicken Breasts 51
Onion Rings 26
Oven-Baked Peri-Peri Chicken 59

P
Pancetta & Spinach Frittata 19
Parmesan Broccoli 105
Parmesan Carrot 111
Parmesan Chicken Meatballs 43
Parmesan Chicken Tenders 54
Parmesan Crusted Chicken Breasts 47
Parmesan Eggs in Avocado Cups 20
Parmesan Flounder 89
Pasta Chips 29
Peanut Brittle Bars 115

Peanut Butter Banana Baked Oatmeal   23
Persimmon Chips   35
Pesto Salmon   85
Pita Bread Pizza   108
Pork Chops with Cashew Sauce   65
Pork Stuffed Bell Peppers   69
Potato & Corned Beef Casserole   21
Potato Bread Rolls   35
Potato Chips   30
Potato Croquettes   30
Prawns in Butter Sauce   88
Primavera Chicken   41
Puff Pastry Danishes   17
Puffed Egg Tarts   14
Pumpkin Fries   28
Pumpkin Muffins   13

Q
Quinoa Burgers   102

R
Raisin Bread Pudding   124
Ranch Kale Chips   31
Ricotta Toasts with Salmon   18
Risotto Bites   29
Roast Beef and Yorkshire Pudding   75
Roast Cauliflower and Broccoli   99
Roast Sirloin of Beef and Port Gravy   77
Roast Sirloin of Beef and Port Gravy   77
Roasted Cashews   30
Roasted Duck   42
Roasted Goose   46
Roasted Green Beans   111
Roasted Peanuts   33
Roasted Vegetables   105
Rosemary Lamb Chops   67
Rum-Glazed Shrimp   85

S
Salmon & Asparagus Parcel   85
Salmon Burgers   87
Salmon with Broccoli   89
Salmon with Prawns   90
Salt and Vinegar Cucumber Chips   39
Sauce Glazed Meatloaf   62
Sausage Patties   22
Savory French Toast   16
Savory Parsley Soufflé   14
Savory Pork Roast   75
Savory Pork Roast   75
Savory Sausage & Beans Muffins   15
Scallops with Capers Sauce   83
Scallops with Chanterelles   97
Scallops with Spinach   84
Seafood Casserole   82
Seafood Medley Mix   93
Seasoned Sirloin Steak   68
Sheet Pan Breakfast Pizza with Sausage & Potatoes   13
Shortbread Fingers   122
Shrimp Fajitas   94
Simple Beef Tenderloin   70
Simple Bread   15
Simple New York Strip Steak   69
Simple Pork Chops   72
Simple Turkey Wings   43
Soy Sauce Green Beans   103
Spanish Chicken Bake   43
Spiced Chicken Breasts   47
Spiced Pork Shoulder   66
Spiced Roasted Chicken   55
Spiced Shrimp   91
Spicy Bay Scallops   81
Spicy Carrot Fries   35
Spicy Chicken Legs   56
Spicy Potato   108
Spicy Salmon   88
Spicy Spinach Chips   36
Steak with Bell Peppers   61
Strawberry Cupcakes   122
Stuffed Eggplants   100
Stuffed Peppers   110
Stuffed Pork Tenderloin   78
Stuffed Pork Tenderloin   78
Stuffed Zucchini   109
Sweet & Spiced Toasts   16
Sweet & Spicy Parsnips   99
Sweet and Sour Chicken Thighs   54
Sweet and Spicy Chicken Drumsticks   54
Sweet Potato Casserole   104
Sweet Potato Rosti   19

T
Tangy Sea Bass   90
Tarragon Beef Shanks   67
Tender Italian Baked Chicken   57
Tilapia with Herbs and Garlic   93
Tofu in Sweet & Sour Sauce   107
Tofu Nuggets   36
Tofu with Broccoli   102
Tortilla Chips   34
Twice Baked Potatoes with Bacon   58

V
Vanilla Soufflé   120
Vegan Cakes   100
Vegan Dehydrated Cookies   39
Vegetable Casserole   106
Veggie Rice   103
Veggies Stuffed Bell Peppers   108
Vinegar Green Beans   104

W
Walnut Brownies   121
Wine Braised Mushrooms   101

Z
Za'atar Chops   66
Zucchini Beef Meatloaf   67
Zucchini Fries   34
Zucchini Fritters   18

Printed in Great Britain
by Amazon

22088330R00079